The Mind of

To our families

The Mind of a Savant

Language Learning and Modularity

Neil Smith and Ianthi-Maria Tsimpli

BLACKWELL
Publishers

First published 1995
Reprinted 1996

Blackwell Publishers Ltd
108 Cowley Road
Oxford OX4 1JF, UK

Blackwell Publishers Inc.
238 Main Street
Cambridge, Massachusetts 02142
USA

British Library Cataloguing in Publication Data

A CIP catalogue record for this book is available from the British Library.

Library of Congress Cataloging-in-Publication Data

Smith, N. V. (Neilson Voyne)
  The mind of a savant: language learning and modularity / Neil Smith and
Ianthi-Maria Tsimpli
    p.   cm.
  Includes bibliographical references and index.
  ISBN 0–631–19016–3 (alk. paper) – ISBN 0–631–19017–1
  (pbk.: alk. paper)
    1. Psycholinguistics.   2. Second language acquisition – Case studies.
  3. Language and languages – Study and teaching – Case studies. 4. Savants
  (Savant syndrome) – Case studies.   5. Modularity (Psychology)
  I. Tsimpli, Ianthi.   II. Title.
  BF455.S544   1995
  401'9 – dc20   94-28662
                                                                     CIP

Typeset in 10/12 Plantin by Photoprint, Torquay, Devon.
Printed in Great Britain by Hartnolls Ltd., Bodmin, Cornwall.
This book is printed on acid-free paper.

Contents

Figures

Foreword
The Generality of the Unique

The study of human psychology often manifests a tension that is not found in the simpler domains of physical science. The tension concerns the respective emphases placed upon the universal and the specific. In terms of theory, one wants an account of what *type* of creature these humans are; and yet it is the rich diversity of *individuals* that is so appealing to all save the most totalitarian mind. Franz-Joseph Gall (1758–1828) was the first neuroscientist to recognize explicitly that these two approaches to human cognition – the investigation of how we differ qualitatively from all other species and of how we differ in talent each from the other – were *not* compatible.

It was Gall's studies of the domain-specificity of 'genius' and 'idiocy' (Lesky, 1979) that drove him inexorably to the conclusion that the human mind/brain was *modular* in character. Exceptional ability in one area did not invariably generalize to other domains of cognition; exceptional impairment in one domain does not inevitably imply a comparable lack of talent in all. The sphere of the skull enclosed not merely two cerebral hemispheres but many more or less independent republics of the mind.

Once the phrenologists' sole major mistake had been disavowed (the shape of the skull is not, in general, a reliable guide to intellectual abilities), Gall's research programme served as a good model for the emerging disciplines of neuropsychology and neuropsychiatry. On the evidence of the effects of discrete brain lesions sustained in adulthood, Paul Broca (1824–80) and John Hughlings Jackson (1835–1911) conjectured correctly that the left hemisphere of the human brain was the seat of the language faculty, while the right hemisphere assumed primary responsibility for visuo-spatial cognition. Echoing Gall's own technique of psychological enquiry, Emil Kraepelin (1856–1926) erected the first modern taxonomy of psychiatric disorders on the basis of what he called the 'method of extreme cases'.

There can be few individuals whose pattern of cognitive competencies is more extreme than that of Christopher – the subject of this book. In brief, Christopher has a range of *in*competencies that are sufficiently severe to necessitate his continued living in a sheltered community despite his being in his thirties. He is grossly impaired on a wide variety of visuo-spatial tasks and cannot reliably find his way around. He fails to conserve number (a task well within the ability of most five-year-olds) and his poor eye–hand co-ordination turns everyday life into an Olympic obstacle race. An unlikely candidate, then, for the accolade of 'savant'? And yet Christopher's skill in English, his native language, *and* up to a score of other languages must make him the envy of poor parochials like us who, on a day trip to Boulogne, cannot remember the French word for bread, much less construct a coherently inflected sentence in that language. As George Orwell might have written: all people are unique, but some are more unique than others.

Although Smith and Tsimpli effectively convey their fascination with the individual person, their monograph is mainly concerned with the detailed implications that Christopher's case holds for general theories of cognition. The fact that highly superior skill in music, the visual arts, mathematics or language (Cossu and Marshall, 1990) can co-exist with average (or significantly below average) ability in other domains is, of course, now widely recognized. The problem was that, with respect to language savants, the level of linguistic sophistication shown by the examiners was often only marginally better than embarrassing. By contrast, Smith and Tsimpli have deployed the full resources of the Principles and Parameters approach to language (Chomsky, 1993) in order to test Christopher's competence to the limits. They have accordingly investigated a sufficient range of structural principles (and their interactions) to be confident that Christopher's knowledge of English grammar is entirely normal.

The theory of Principles and Parameters also provides a solution to the problem of accounting for linguistic diversity within strict universal constraints. The principles of Universal Grammar (UG) include a small number of parameters which become set by exposure to the distinctive syntactic properties of particular languages; the interaction of truly universal principles and language-specific parameters then determines how Italian, say, comes to be very different from English, while both languages still fall within the general theory of what a natural language can be. An important question in the psychobiology of second- (and third- and . . .) language learning thus concerns whether parameters set initially for the native language can be reset for the acquisition of languages learned subsequently.

The languages in which Christopher has considerable facility are drawn from distinct typological families: it is hence possible to ask whether Christopher's command of these languages is bounded by absolute principles of UG, or whether it further extends to new parameter-settings triggered by exposure to languages with a very different surface typology. The tentative conclusion is that absolute syntactic properties of UG under-lie all of Christopher's language learning, but that parameter-resetting has not taken place; although Christopher can translate well between many languages, his competence in production and judgement tests shows considerable direct 'transfer' of specific structural principles from English. This finding confirms other evidence that Christopher's multi-lingualism is based primarily upon a superb ability to acquire lexical entries and their morphological characteristics. My only regret here is that Smith and Tsimpli were never able to study the eminent linguist Roman Jakobson, of whom it was always said that he spoke Russian in fifty languages.

Having established the nature and extent of Christopher's competence with language(s) *qua* formal system(s), it becomes possible for Smith and Tsimpli to enquire how well Christopher can deploy that knowledge in the service of efficient communication. Much previous observational work on 'pragmatics' has been something of a ragbag, but Smith and Tsimpli have succeeded impressively in fractionating the mosaic of Christopher's impaired and intact discourse skills. They provide evidence that he copes well with formal inference determined by logical connectives (*if–then*, *not*, *or*) and quasi-logical vocabulary (*so, after all, moreover*), but is none the less quite unable to understand such metalinguistic constructs as irony and metaphor.

This pattern of dissociation is consistent with earlier evidence (see Code, 1987) that lesions of the right hemisphere impair a range of extralinguistic aspects of language. Christopher's inability to appreciate jokes has been selectively observed in adults with right posterior damage, and a right hemisphere deficit is compatible with the large discrepancy between his verbal and non-verbal IQ. Smith and Tsimpli observe that Christopher 'seems to be incapable of lying', and however desirable this trait may be, it does make him somewhat less than (or more than?) fully human. One might wish that some of our politicians were similarly 'impaired', yet (broadly conceived) the ability to lie is but 'a special case of the ability to entertain counterfactual conditionals' (Marshall, 1971, p.44). This latter potentiality must surely underlie much of our capacity to formulate scientific theories; that enterprise is driven by conjectures and refutations (Popper, 1963).

One final area where Smith and Tsimpli themselves advance some exceedingly bold conjectures concerns the so-called 'central' system. Modern study of the modular mind (Marshall, 1980) did not initially show much interest in the co-ordination and interplay of modules. This lacuna left the investigation of 'thinking', planning and practical reasoning in limbo, a situation that was not exactly helped by Fodor's confident assertion that 'what put it all together' (the Central System) was *in principle* not open to rigorous investigation (Fodor, 1985).

Happily, this scepticism seems unfounded, and Smith and Tsimpli can provide at least a preliminary fractionation of the Central System that throws considerable light on how Christopher manages, as it were, his cognition. The interaction of knowledge and language, and executive control thereof, are illuminated by careful studies of Christopher's (dis-)abilities in forming and manipulating meta-representations in the language of thought. His performance on so-called 'theory of mind' tasks (could he know what you and I know?) is crucial here. Different versions of such tasks yield very different outcomes with Christopher; this result leads Smith and Tsimpli to place the 'theory of mind' module *within* the central system, and to formulate some serious conjectures about the interaction of competence and performance-constraints in successful 'mind-reading'.

In short, *The Mind of a Savant* is an exemplary case-study in cognitive science. One might have hoped that it would also be possible to link Christopher's cognition with his neurological status, but although Christopher does show evidence (from neuroimaging) of cerebral damage, the brain sciences are not yet sufficiently developed (Crick and Jones, 1993) to support *intelligible* correlations between higher mental functions and their physical substrate. As the twenty-first century approaches, Lashley's observation still holds: 'Psychology today is a more fundamental science than neurophysiology. By this I mean the latter offers few principles from which we may predict or define the normal organization of behaviour, whereas the study of psychological processes furnishes a mass of factual material to which the laws of neural action in behaviour must conform' (Lashley, 1930, p.24). Advances in parallel computing and in brain scanning have not (yet) falsified Lashley's claim.

Without even string and sealing-wax, Neil Smith and Ianthi-Maria Tsimpli have employed little more than paper and pencil to conduct their pioneering empirical investigations. That little, however, is much: it is called 'thinking'.

John C. Marshall
Neuropsychology Unit
The Radcliffe Infirmary
Oxford

References

Chomsky, N. (1993) *Language and Thought*. Wakefield, Rhode Island: Moyer Bell

Code, C. (1987) *Language, Aphasia, and the Right Hemisphere*. New York: John Wiley

Cossu, G. and Marshall, J.C. (1990) Are cognitive skills a prerequisite for learning to read and write? *Cognitive Neuropsychology*, 7, 21–40

Crick, F. and Jones, E. (1993) Backwardness of human neuroanatomy. *Nature* 361, 109–10

Fodor, J.A. (1985) Précis of *The Modularity of Mind*. *The Behavioral and Brain Sciences*, 8, 1–42

Lashley, K.S. (1930) Basic neural mechanisms in behavior. *Psychological Review*, 37, 1–24

Lesky, E. (1979) *Franz Joseph Gall: Naturforscher und Anthropologe*. Bern: Huber Verlag

Marshall, J.C. (1971) Can humans talk? In J. Morton (ed.), *Biological and Social Factors in Psycholinguistics*. London: Logos Press

Marshall, J.C. (1980) The new organology. *The Behavioral and Brain Sciences*, 3, 23–5

Popper, K.R. (1963) *Conjectures and Refutations*. London: Routledge and Kegan Paul

Preface

A mighty maze! but not without a plan.
Pope, *Essay on Man*

It has become a cliché to describe the human mind as at once the most complex and the most intriguing entity in the universe. We have written this book in an attempt to gain some understanding of the mind by looking in great detail at one unique individual. We take it for granted that all humans are in essence the same and that insight gained from the study of one will be relevant to the species. It is equally obvious, however, that this essential underlying unity is overlain by a dazzling external diversity. People differ in terms of sex, race, culture, gender, ability, interest, taste, intelligence, language and indefinitely many other properties. Some of these dimensions of differentiation are both well understood and uncontroversially autonomous. No one doubts that the senses are independent of each other and of other attributes such as intelligence. One can be blind without being deaf, mute without being blind or paralysed. Such simple dissociations enable us to see how humans are put together. If being blind always entailed losing one's sense of smell, our theories of the brain and of our senses would be rather different from what they are. Dissociation of a less obvious, and hence more interesting, kind occurs occasionally in the case of 'savants': people who are intellectually and often physically impaired, but who have one dazzling talent. By demonstrating the independence of faculties that normally go together, such individuals allow us to investigate the working of different parts of the mind in a way that would otherwise be impossible. The dissociation of abilities enables us to work on problems which, while dauntingly complex, like Pope's 'mighty maze', are relatively tractable, precisely because their isolation reveals their 'plan'. Savants with mathematical, artistic or musical ability are not common, but they are reasonably well documented. Cases like that of Christopher whom we describe here are, however, vanishingly rare. As far as we know, Christopher is unprecedented in having language and languages as his domain of genius. Despite being unable to look after himself because he has difficulty with everyday tasks that we don't even think about, he can read, write, translate and communicate in some fifteen to twenty languages.

We met Christopher in March 1990 with Dr Neil O'Connor, who had first suggested that we study him, and have seen him every few weeks ever since. Our aim has been to establish the precise nature of Christopher's extraordinary prowess: to see if his knowledge of his native language, English, is the same as that of normal speakers; to establish the range of languages at his command and the depth of his knowledge in each; and to find out how far his linguistic knowledge is integrated into his general cognitive abilities. We anticipated that the research would help us to answer, or at least to frame, a number of questions central to the study of language and mind, and while we are only too conscious of the limitations of any project of this kind, we are confident that we have made progress in several areas. In particular, we have evidence bearing on many issues: on modularity, on the nature of intelligence, on the properties of Universal Grammar, on language learning and the question of parameter (re-)setting, and on the structure of the language faculty and its relation to the rest of the mind more generally.

The book is structured as follows: after introducing Christopher – personally, medically, psychologically and linguistically – we outline the range of theoretical assumptions we wish to presuppose, and set Christopher in context (chapter 1). We then give a detailed account of his performance in his native language, concluding that his competence in English is essentially flawless, and that apparent exceptions to this generalization can be accounted for by reference to extra-grammatical considerations (chapter 2). The third chapter documents the results of a battery of tests on a sub-set of Christopher's 'second' languages, paying particular attention to Modern Greek and the Romance languages French, Spanish and Italian. The next chapter discusses our attempts to teach Christopher languages with which he was previously unfamiliar, so that we could study his learning process while we controlled the input to him. The languages chosen were Berber, spoken in North Africa, and Epun, a language we invented to enable us to test Christopher's reaction to structures which, by hypothesis, could not occur in the world's real languages (chapter 4). The final chapter takes a closer look at Christopher's translational expertise – the talent that first brought him to attention, and then attempts to provide a general account of the full range of his mental abilities. By blending insights from cognitive psychology, the philosophy of mind and theoretical linguistics, we produce a revised model of the mind in terms of which we can describe, and in part explain, both Christopher's exceptional, albeit flawed, talent, and by implication the abilities of normal people (chapter 5).

Throughout the project and the present book we have used batteries of standard psychological and linguistic tests, and also a considerable number of tests of our own devising. As further, if still partial, evidence for our conclusions, we provide documentation of these tests and of supplementary data in the appendices.

It is intended that the bulk of the book be accessible to as wide an audience as possible: not only linguists, psychologists and philosophers, but also the proverbial general reader. In order to justify our conclusions, however, it has sometimes been necessary to provide technical analyses that can be evaluated only by those who have some familiarity with linguistic theory and psychology. Such familiarity can be gleaned from a reading of Smith (1989) but those prepared to believe us can skim the technicalities; we hope the sceptical are persuaded by our arguments.

In the four years that this project has (so far) lasted, we have received a huge amount of help from innumerable people. Our first debt is to Neil O'Connor and Ati Hermelin, who first introduced us to Christopher and who have given us the benefit of their advice ever since. More immediately, we are profoundly grateful to Christopher's family for their constant help and encouragement. We would especially like to thank his sister, Ann Fairclough, who has been a constant source of information and wisdom, and who continued to support us at times of crisis. Of equal importance have been the constructive help and inspirational example of John Carlile and his family. They have been unfailingly co-operative and unfailingly patient, even when our interactions with Christopher have interrupted their routine and disrupted their lives.

In earlier articles about Christopher we have listed the large number of colleagues who have given us the benefit of their knowledge either about matters of theory or about many of the awesome number of languages that Christopher knows. We would like to repeat our thanks to all of them here, while singling out the following, who have been of constant or special help: Alexia Antjaka, Misi Brody, Noel Burton-Roberts, Robyn Carston, Annabel Cormack, Karen Corrigan, Rita Manzini, Jamal Ouhalla, Anna Roussou, Amahl Smith, Ivan Smith, Hans van de Koot and Deirdre Wilson. We are likewise indebted to the Leverhulme Trust whose generous support, under grant number F.134AS, made this research possible.

All the preceding people have played an invaluable role in the research we are reporting on, but it should be obvious that the star of the show and the person to whom we owe the most is Christopher himself. His unfailing co-operativeness and enthusiasm for languages have made our task a personal as well as an academic pleasure. Knowing Christopher has enriched our lives.

Finally, our debt to our families, named and nameless, is boundless: to them we dedicate this book, with love and gratitude.

1
Language and Intelligence

Introducing Christopher

Personal history and family background[1]

Christopher is unique. He is institutionalized because he is unable to look after himself; he has difficulty in finding his way around; he has poor hand–eye co-ordination, turning many everyday tasks such as shaving or doing up buttons into a burdensome chore; but he can read, write and communicate in any of fifteen to twenty languages.

Born in January 1962, he was diagnosed as brain-damaged at the age of six weeks. Although he was late in walking and talking, his main interest from about three years was books: never fairy stories, but books providing factual information, such as the telephone directory, dictionaries, and Ladybird books about flags or foreign currencies. At the same age his interest in the advertisements in the local newspapers provided his family with the first clear evidence that he could read; and read not only the usual way, but upside down or sideways on. At about six or seven he took an interest in technical papers written in foreign languages that his sister brought home from work, beginning an obsession with languages that was reinforced by watching the Mexico Olympics on television, and that has lasted all his life. Even his play-time (at school and at home) was frequently devoted to games in which he pretended to be from a foreign country, speaking a foreign language: for instance, he used a towel as a turban or as a bullfighter's cape, and pretended to be an Arab or a Spaniard. He had a precocious talent, but he was also afflicted with a minor speech defect, poor eyesight and a degree of clumsiness that seemed to confirm the diagnosis of mental handicap.

Most of his childhood was spent in 'special' (ESN) schools,[2] though as a result of his mother's efforts on his behalf he was later transferred to a school for the physically handicapped, where he could receive greater individual attention. At school he was quiet and solitary; he showed no interest in the children's material on display, but rather read books on history and geography that the teacher had borrowed from the local library for herself. His future preoccupations were already visible in the fact that he could spell any word he was ever asked to; that he had a passion for identifying political figures; and that while other children did sorting and matching exercises for their mathematics, an enlightened teacher allowed Christopher to check share prices in *The Financial Times* and compare prices in different currencies.

At school as at home, his greatest love was reserved for foreign languages, for which he showed a surprising proficiency. On one occasion his teacher showed him a piece of card with printing on it in a language she did not recognize. Christopher immediately identified it as Polish and explained that it gave instructions that the garment to which it was attached should at all times be dry-cleaned and not washed. When asked who had taught him Polish, he replied: 'Nobody', and when questioned further about how he knew what it said, answered that he 'just did'. In fact his sister's husband speaks Polish, and it is clear that interacting with him was the source of Christopher's ability in this language. His apparent obliviousness to this fact is not untypical, even though his long-term memory is usually good.

For the last few years he has lived in a sheltered community (one of the Camphill Communities),[3] where he can lead a reasonably normal life, working in the garden, carding wool, watching television and endlessly studying languages. He receives consistent love, affection and support from his family, whom he visits regularly and who periodically take him on holidays abroad with them. Since we met him he has visited Canada, Turkey, Greece and Mallorca – where he acted as enthusiastic and much appreciated interpreter between German and Spanish for his fellow tourists – and he has visited Holland with us.

Double dissociation

There have been many cases of savants[4] documented in the literature:[5] calendrical calculators who can tell you on which day of the week any date in the last or next century falls; artists like Nadia (Selfe, 1977) or Stephen Wiltshire (Wiltshire, 1987; O'Connor and Hermelin, 1987; Hermelin and O'Connor, 1990) whose drawings are of professional standard, but who are otherwise incapable of leading a normal life and are virtually speechless; musicians who can play complex passages after a single hearing but cannot look after themselves. Such savants are frequently autistic, and usually linguistically handicapped, with minimal command of any language or other communication skills. Treffert (1989: 66) writes that savants' skills, 'however many they have, do not include the acquisition of language'; and when they are occasionally described as having the 'gift of tongues' (for example, Howe, 1989: 10; Treffert, 1989: 9, 71–2), the context makes it clear that such people are merely good mimics who can repeat passages from various languages 'parrot-fashion' with minimal, if any, understanding.

Yet Christopher's talent is precisely in the area where the typical savant is defective: in the acquisition and use of language. Although no one else has been reported as displaying the multi-lingual prowess that Christopher does, these cases illustrate the same dissociation between linguistic and general cognitive abilities as is exhibited by such individuals as Laura (Yamada, 1990; see also Smith, 1991), by Williams Syndrome children (see, e.g., Bellugi et al., 1993), by 'chatterbox' children (see, e.g., Cromer, 1991), and by hyperlexics (see, e.g., Cossu and Marshall, 1986), all of whom have great linguistic ability in the presence of severe cognitive deficits. Examples in the opposite direction – cases of people with impaired language in the presence of normal intellectual ability – are provided by some deaf people, some aphasics, and by those suffering from SLI (Specific Language Impairment), where brain damage (in some cases genetically caused) occasions a language deficit independently of the rest of the cognitive profile (see, e.g., Gopnik, in press; Gopnik and Crago, 1991; for further discussion, see pp. 40–2 below).

The existence of these varied conditions provides a classical example of *double dissociation*:[6] language can be impaired in someone of otherwise normal intelligence, and – more surprisingly – someone with intelligence impaired by brain damage may none the less have normal, or even enhanced, linguistic ability. It is worth emphasizing that this latter possibility constitutes a refutation of any position that insists on 'cognitive prerequisites' for the development of language (e.g., Slobin, 1973; Piaget, 1970; cf. Cromer, 1991; Karmiloff-Smith, 1992a; Smith 1994).

Medical and psychological profile

In this section we provide a summary of Christopher's medical background, including an outline of his performance on a battery of psychological tests.

His medical history is somewhat opaque. Christopher, who is right-handed, was born when his mother was forty-five years old. Early in pregnancy she had contracted German measles, but was assured by doctors that it was beyond the period when the baby could be harmed. Towards the end of pregnancy she had a bad fall, and towards the end of a long labour the nurses sent for oxygen, presumably because of foetal distress, though the record is not clear. During the first few weeks of life Christopher was difficult to feed and was always throwing his head around. At approximately six weeks he was admitted to hospital where, as O'Connor and Hermelin (1991: 674) report 'his mother was told that he was brain-damaged at birth', though no reason for such a diagnosis was given. Later institutional records suggest hydrocephaly, and an EEG carried out at the age of thirteen 'revealed some oddities including slow waves in the frontal lobes' (O'Connor and Hermelin, 1991: 674). A year later 'his intra-cranial pressure showed no abnormality but in 1982, at age twenty, he was diagnosed as "possibly having hydrocephalic brain damage and severe neurological impairment of his motor co-ordination, amounting to apraxia" ' (ibid.: 675). It seems reasonably clear that there is brain damage of some kind, but there is insufficient evidence to allow any causal correlation with his psychological profile. In August, 1993 he had an MRI scan, which revealed 'moderate cerebral atrophy with wide sulci over both hemispheres. The cisterna magna was slightly larger than usual and the cerebellar vermis was hypoplastic' (O'Connor et al., 1994). Such a configuration is not untypical of high-functioning autism (see Courchesne et al., 1988), but there is no obvious connection between cerebellar hypoplasia and the unusual pattern of cognitive abilities shown by Christopher. While it is gradually becoming possible to account for certain pathologies in neuro-anatomical terms, we are still far from being able to explain Christopher's (or any other subject's) enhanced performance in such a way.

Psychologically the picture is complex, but perhaps somewhat clearer. The most salient feature is a striking mismatch between his verbal and non-verbal abilities, supported by test results over a prolonged period and with recent documentation across a wide range of different tests. The basic generalization is that he combines a relatively low performance IQ with an average or above average verbal IQ.[7]

The standard 'performance' IQ test, which is supposed to involve no or minimal verbal ability, is *Raven's Matrices*,[8] on which Christopher has on different occasions scored 75 or 76 (where the average is 100), and the Wechsler Scale test *WISC-R, UK* on the performance part of which he has scored at different times 42, 67 and 52 (again, the average is 100). This is in striking contrast with the verbal part of the same test, on which he scored respectively 89, 102 and 98. On the *Columbia Greystone Mental Maturity Scale*, administered at age 29.2, he scored 68, indicating a mental age of 9.2 and an IQ of 56.

A further test which is supposedly independent of verbal ability is the

Embedded Figures Test (see Witkin, 1969), in which the subject has to match geometric shapes presented on a flash card with concealed representations of those same figures embedded in more complex designs by tracing out the relevant pattern on the latter. Christopher's responses seemed to be random, and it was reasonably clear that he had no idea what was going on. He scored one out of twelve, and even this was of dubious validity, as his tracing of the figures was too clumsy to be convincing.

Similarly non-verbal is the Goodenough *Draw a Man Test* on which Christopher scored 40 (at age 14) and 63 (some years later). Some indication of his artistic ability is given by his drawing of the authors given overleaf (p. 6).

Although number is sometimes thought to be parasitic on language (see, e.g., Chomsky 1991b: 50), Christopher fails on *Conservation of Number* tasks. We administered a simple number conservation task which involved Christopher in judging whether two wires contained the same number of beads, when these were (a) aligned so that the beads on the two wires were identically positioned, and (b) arranged so that the beads on one wire were spread out to form a longer line than those on the other. Christopher was consistent in claiming that whichever line the beads were spread out on contained more items than the other. Children normally conserve number by the age of five (see Karmiloff-Smith, 1992a, for recent discussion), and it was striking that Christopher maintained his view in the face of contrary judgements on the same task by a number-conserving five-year-old child.

Despite this failure to conserve number, Christopher experiences no difficulty in counting arrays of items displayed either in a straight line or in a circle (see Karmiloff-Smith, 1992a) and he is able to carry out simple arithmetic calculations involving addition, subtraction and multiplication. The type and limit of his ability in this domain are illustrated in the following examples, where Christopher's contribution is shown in inverted commas:

1 (a) $\begin{array}{r} £6.12 \\ 2.23 \\ \hline \text{'8.35'} \end{array}+$ (b) $\begin{array}{r} £14.99 \\ 1.66 \\ \hline \text{'£16.55'} \end{array}+$

(c) $\begin{array}{r} £5.50 \\ 2.25 \\ \hline \text{'3.25'} \end{array}-$ (d) $\begin{array}{r} £3.05 \\ 1.99 \\ \hline \text{'£1.16'} \end{array}-$

(e) $\begin{array}{r} 17 \\ 5 \\ \hline \text{'85'} \end{array}\times$ (f) $\begin{array}{r} 33 \\ 6 \\ \hline \text{'198'} \end{array}\times$

Although Christopher has not been diagnosed as autistic[9] we discovered

Figure 1.1 *Drawing of Ianthi and Neil*

with some surprise that he has difficulty with some tasks classically associated with autism. Specifically, on a simple version of the '*Sally-Anne*' *Test* (see Frith, 1989; Perner, 1991; Baron-Cohen et al., 1985; Leslie, 1987; Leslie and Frith, 1987) it appeared that Christopher consistently failed to impute appropriate beliefs to others. We tested him as follows. We 'hid' a child's toy in full view of Christopher and a five-year-old child, Alexia,[10] ensured that both knew where it was, and then sent the child out of the room. In her absence, but still with Christopher watching, we moved the toy to a new hiding place. At this stage we asked Christopher where Alexia would look for it, and he indicated the *new* hiding-place. On subsequent trials we also checked that Christopher could remember where the item had originally been hidden, and that he was aware that the child had not been present when the object was moved. The results were the same and his behaviour was consistent on a repetition of the task with a different object and different hiding-places. When asked how the child could know where the object now was, Christopher responded either 'I dunno' or 'Because you put it there'.

Perhaps surprisingly in view of this result, Christopher performed entirely appropriately on the 'Smarties' test (see Perner et al., 1987; Karmiloff-Smith, 1992a), and a variant of the 'appearance/reality' test (see Flavell et al., 1986; Fodor, 1992). In the first of these tests a child is shown a Smarties container and asked what it contains. Typically, he or she responds 'Smarties', and is then shown that the container actually contains something different (in Christopher's case some plastic balls). The subject is next asked what a friend, who has not seen inside the container, will respond when asked what is in it. Three-year-old children and autistic subjects typically respond that the friend will say there are balls (or whatever) in the container; older children – and Christopher – answer correctly that the friend will assume there are Smarties in it. For the second of these tests, we presented Christopher with a plastic imitation of a chocolate biscuit. As expected, he identified it 'correctly' and even attempted to bite it. When he had realized that it was made of plastic, we asked him both what it was and what it looked like. He answered appropriately that it was plastic and looked like a chocolate biscuit, whereas three-year-old children typically reply that it looks like what it is: namely, a piece of plastic or whatever. As is evident from these results his performance is complex. However, his behaviour on further tests designed to establish his ability to impute (false) beliefs to others (the *Shapes Test* and the *Opaque Box Test*) was consistent with his performance on 'Sally-Anne'. We describe these tests and discuss their implications in chapter 5.

On many of these tests, Christopher performed at an impaired, sometimes at a severely impaired, level. This is in marked contrast with his performance on verbal tests. We have already noted his performance on the verbal part of the WISC scale test, and this behaviour is corroborated by his performance on, for example, the *Gapadol Reading Comprehension Test*. On this test Christopher scored at the maximum level, indicating a reading comprehension age of 16 years 10 months; a result consistent with his performance on the *Peabody Picture Vocabulary Test*. O'Connor and Hermelin (1991) devised a multi-lingual version of this test on which Christopher scored as shown in (2):

2   English   121
     German   114
     French   110
     Spanish   89

That is, his performance is consistently above the average of 100, not only in his native language, English, but in French and German as well. Even on Spanish he performs within normal limits and, intuitively, his Spanish is as good as his German, though not nearly as good as his French or Modern Greek, for instance.

This mismatch between verbal and non-verbal tests was borne out by his performance on the *Gollin Figures*. In this test the subject has to identify either objects or words from partial representations of them, the aim being to effect the identification with the minimal amount of information. (Each item is cued in three stages: a minimal partial outline; a fuller but still incomplete representation; and a complete representation.) Impression-istically, Christopher did markedly better on words than on objects, identifying objects on average at exposure 2.4 and words on average at exposure 1.7, prompting us to explore this aspect of his abilities further with our own test.

Building on the interesting discrepancy in the Gollin test between Christopher's identification of words and objects, we devised a further experiment to see if his superior performance on words was consistent.[11] We presented him with successive approximations to three different kinds of representation: words of English; (symbols of) objects; and words of Greek. The stimuli were presented in the form of computer print-out in approximately twenty successive stages. The first stage contained minimal information (roughly 6 per cent), so that the item represented was essentially unrecognizable. Succeeding stimuli increased the amount of information monotonically, until at the final stage the representation was complete. Three stages of each of the three kinds of stimuli can be seen in figures 1.2–1.4. Figure 1.2 shows the *earliest* representation on which either Christopher or one of the controls correctly identified the items concerned; figure 1.3 shows the *average* stage at which Christopher and the controls correctly identified the representation; and figure 1.4 shows the *latest* stage at which Christopher or any of the controls correctly identified the relevant item.[12]

The test consisted of some twenty-five items (see Appendix I for details), and subjects were told that the stimuli could be either words or objects, and

Figure 1.2   *The earliest stage at which the word/object was identified*

if words, in either English or Greek.[13] It is striking that Christopher was (by far) the worst on object recognition, but second best on word recognition. This is particularly noteworthy given that the controls included several undergraduate and postgraduate linguistics students, who can be assumed to have considerable familiarity with the written word.

It is also worth noting that the only putatively English 'word' that took

Figure 1.3 *The average stage at which the word/object was identified*

more than eight stages for Christopher to recognize was '1962' (his birth year). In fact he recognized it as a number at stage five yet still tried to sound out putative letters. (For these reasons we have excluded '1962' from the calculations.) The difficulty occasioned by this example is in contrast

Figure 1.4 *The latest stage at which the word/object was identified*

with the expected ease with which he recognized his own name 'chris'. We do not think this advantage distorts the results in any way (especially as one of the controls, also named 'Chris', seemed to receive no benefit). Even when he had correctly recognized that some stimulus represented an object rather than a word, Christopher frequently tried to sound out the phonetic value of putative letters that might be formed by the sub-parts of the object. On the other hand he never guessed at names of objects after recognizing something as a word. He often asked for clues (which were never given) such as 'what do you use it for?', when attempting to identify objects. At stage four of the aeroplane he asked, 'Do you use it in the home or in an aeroplane?', yet he was still unable to identify the representation as an aeroplane for another four stages.

Linguistic prowess and non-linguistic disability

In this section we give an initial overview of the range and nature of Christopher's exceptional linguistic talent. He first came to scholarly attention because of his remarkable ability to translate from and communicate in any of a large number of languages. He has some knowledge (ranging from fluency to the bare elements) of: Danish, Dutch, Finnish, French, German, Modern Greek, Hindi, Italian, Norwegian, Polish, Portuguese, Russian, Spanish, Swedish, Turkish and Welsh. The passages listed here (taken from Smith and Tsimpli, 1991: 318–22) give a fair indication of the breadth and depth of his expertise:

(a) *Danish*
Men Jeg havde hverken onkler eller tenter i København, så jeg kom først dertil, da jeg var så stor, at jeg gik i skole og vidste, at det var Danmarks hovedstad og den største og vigtigste by i landet.

But I had neither uncles nor aunts in Copenhagen, so I didn't get to go there until I was old enough to be at school and learnt that Copenhagen was the Capital of Denmark and the biggest and most important city in the country.

'But I had neither uncles nor niece – nor aunts – in Copenhagen, so I came first there as I was a very big man, when I went to school and knew that it was Denmark's capital and the biggest and importantest – and the most important town in the whole country'.

(b) *Dutch*
'In elk geval,' zegt ze 'ik zal de ketel opzetten voor een kopje thee.' 'Ja graag, en dan moet ik eens opstappen. Ze zal niet weten waar ik blijf.'

'Anyway,' she says, 'I will put on the kettle for a cup of tea.' 'Yes thanks; and then it will be time for me to go. She'll be wondering when I'm coming.'

' "In any case," he – she says, "I will put the kettle on for a cup of tea." "Yes please, then I must stop. You know, you you you should not – she shall not know where I am." '

(c) *Finnish*

Mikon veli, kolmetoistavuotias Yrjö, tulee kirjakaupasta kirja kädessään, otsa rypyssä. Muuan herrasmies astuu tiellä häntä kohti. Poika ottaa lakin päästään: 'Hyvää päivää, tohtori!' 'Päivää, päivää, Yrjö . . . mikä tuo kirja on?'

Mikko's brother, the thirteen-year-old George, comes from the bookshop with a book in his hand, frowning. A gentleman is walking towards him on the road. The boy takes his cap off. 'Good morning, Doctor!' 'Good morning, George . . . What is that book?'

'On the thirty, the thirty-second year of George, the . . . a bookshop . . . Miss – what's a gentleman. "Good morning, Doctor!" "Morning, morning, George. How are you?" '

(d) *French*

Nous faisions pique-nique au bord de la route nationale qui s'étendait devant nous, toute droite et bordée d'arbres.

We were having a picnic beside the main road which stretched away in front of us, dead straight and lined with trees.

'We had a picnic at the route, at the board of the road, which ran behind us, straight and full of trees.'

(e) *German*

Wolfgang und seine Schwester machen einen Ausflug mit dem Zug. Sie wohnen in einem Dorf. Heute fahren sie in die Stadt. Sie gehen in ein

Warenhaus. Wolfgang kauft ein Radio, Sigrid braucht eine Lampe für ihren Schreibtisch.

Wolfgang and his sister are going on an excursion by train. They live in a village. Today they are going to the city. They go into a shop. Wolfgang buys a radio, Sigrid needs a lamp for her desk.

'Wolfgang and his sister are on a . . . with the train. They live in a village. Today they go and visit a city. They go in a shop. Wolfgang buys a radio. Sigrid buys a lamp for her writing-table.'

(f) *Greek*
Otan perase t'amaksi, epsakse ja tis pantufles tis, ala ena paljopedho ihe pari ti mja ki efevje jelontas.

When the car passed, she looked for her slippers, but a naughty child had taken one and was leaving laughing.

'When she passed the car . . . when the car passed, she was looking for her slippers but an old child had taken one away and left . . . and was laughing.'

(g) *Hindi*
Ek nadi: ke kina:re, ek baṛe se peṛ par, ek bandar rahta: tha: . . . Ek din ek magar tairta: hua: kina:re par a:ya:.

On the side of a river, on a large tree, lived a monkey . . . One day a crocodile came swimming along to the side.

'On the side of a road, a big something, a man fell down <NS – do you know what *bandar* is? C – 'monkey'> . . . One day, *but* one day <NS – OK *magar* is 'crocodile'>, the crocodile came to edge . . .'

(h) *Italian*
Per caso in quella stessa mattina un'amica era venuta a trovare la signora ed era rimasta a farle compagnia mentre finiva di vestirsi. L'amica aveva notato i cassetti aperti.

By chance, that very morning a woman friend had come to visit the lady and had stayed to keep her company while she finished dressing. Her friend noticed the open drawers.

'In case, just in case in this morning a friend came to find the lady and she was stayed while she was dressing. Her friend had noticed the open cassettes.'

(i) *Norwegian*

'Når kommer Per hjem?' 'Vanligvis til middag, litt over to. Å Hjørdis – du blir vel en stund? Du kan jo bli til middag hvis du vil. Tenk om du hadde ringt på forhånd – ja for telefon har vi da, på grunn av alle bestillingene.'

'When does Peter come home?' 'Usually for dinner, just after two. Oh Hjørdis – you will stay for a while I hope? You can stay for dinner if you like. What if you had phoned beforehand – yes because we do have a phone, because of all the orders.'

' "When is Peter coming home?" "Usually at midday, a little over two. Ah Hjørdis, you are well – an hour. You can stay till midday if you want to. Think that your phone [inaudible] beforehand. Yes on the telephone we have, on the ground of all orders." '

(j) *Polish*

Musiałem go wrzucić do wozu siłą. Położył się na podłodze i zamknął oczy, nie chcąc widzieć, co go jeszcze czeka.

I had to throw him into the car with force. He lay down on the floor and closed his eyes, not wishing to see what awaited him.

'I had to take him out of the car strongly and put – he put himself on the floor and opened his eyes – and shut his eyes, not wishing to see what was waiting for him.'

(k) *Portuguese*

O cão estava imóvel no passeio, olhando fixamente a luz vermelha. De súbito luz verde, automóveis a travar – e o cão atravessou para o lado de lá.

The dog was standing still on the pavement, staring at the red light. Suddenly a green light, cars braking – and the dog crossed to the other side.

'The dog was immovable in the passage, looking the light, of the green light. <IT: What does this [*fixamente*] mean? >Fixed – the green, the red light. All of a sudden a green light, motor-cars crossed, and the dog crossed by by that side.'

(l) *Russian*
Oktyabr byl na redkost' xolodnyi, nenastnyi. Tesovye kryshi pochernely.

October was unusually cold and wet. The wooden roofs grew black.

'October was as careless cold and unhappy. The winter days were black.'

(m) *Spanish*
Hablaban todos al tiempo y sus voces se confundían con la del televisor sobre una banqueta minúscula, en el rincón que formaba la pared con la puerta de acceso al vestíbulo.

They were all talking at the same time and their voices merged with that from the television on a small stool in the corner between the wall and the door to the hall.

'They spoked they spoke once all at a time and their voices were confused with that of the television beneath a blanket, a small blanket, in a corner which won the wall – the wall with the with the access door to the hall.'

(n) *Swedish*
Mia sitter uppkruppen i kökssoffan med knäna uppdragna och fötterna instoppade i den randiga nattskjortan. Katten spinner i hennes knä.

Mia is curled up on the kitchen sofa with her knees drawn up and her feet tucked into her stripey nightie. The cat is purring on her lap.

'Mia is sitting, crouched down in the kitchen sofa with her knees bent and her feet tied up in the lovely night-shirt. The cat spins in her knee.'

(o) *Turkish*
Tatilde, herkes görmediği yerleri gezmeğe gider. Hem bilgilerini geliştirirler, hem eğlenirler ve hem de yeni yeni yerler görürler.

On holiday everyone goes to visit places they haven't seen. Either they are strengthening their knowledge, or they are enjoying themselves, or they are looking at totally new places.

'On holiday when I was staying in different places I saw different places. The people were were scientists and some are students and some are new [inaudible] new places.'

(p) *Welsh*

Hylo, Tom. Sut mae? Ga i ddod i mewn? Cei, wrth gwrs. Dere i eistedd ar y fainc 'ma.

Hello Tom. How are you? May I come in? Yes (you may), of course. Come and sit on the bench here.

'Hello Tom. How are you? Can I come in? Of course you can. Come and sit on the bench here.'

Though he has a smattering of a few other languages as well, his knowledge of them is probably inadequate to make detailed exemplification worthwhile or even feasible. For instance, he claimed to know Hungarian, but was unable to translate a fairly elementary passage from that language; he knows a few words of Arabic, but can neither read it nor sustain a conversation for more than a moment or two; he began to learn Hebrew (see O'Connor and Hermelin, 1991: 676), but when tested was unable to do more than pick out the odd word in an O-level passage; and he can exchange greetings in Japanese, Thai and sundry other languages from around the world, but professes no greater expertise than that.

It is important to note that the languages concerned come from a wide range both genetically and typologically. Although the majority of them are Indo-European, Finnish and Turkish are genetically unrelated, being respectively a member of the Finno-Ugric group of the Uralic language family, and a member of the Turkic sub-family of the Altaic languages. Similarly, although most of them are spoken in Western Europe, this does not apply to Hindi, Polish or Russian, and while most of them are typologically SVO languages (that is, the canonical word-order is one in which the subject precedes the verb which in turn precedes the object), Welsh is VSO, Hindi and Turkish are SOV and the word-order of others is superficially mixed to a greater or lesser degree (for example, German and Modern Greek). Although Christopher professed to find the 'exotic' languages more difficult than the familiar ones spoken closer to home, it is also noteworthy that he coped remarkably well when confronted with Berber, which is typologically and genetically unlike most of the languages he already knew (see chapter 4 below for detailed discussion).

Furthermore, the languages he knows are written in different scripts: Greek, Cyrillic (for Russian) and Devanagari (for Hindi). Christopher's reading and writing of Greek is fluent, and he has no trouble with Cyrillic (although, as will be seen below, his knowledge of Russian is somewhat problematic). When we first met him, his knowledge of Hindi was largely restricted to the spoken form of the language, but after being given a Hindi grammar (McGregor, 1972) he made rapid progress in learning the script and can now read the language as well, albeit without much fluency. Like most professional linguists Christopher can also identify languages from their written form without being able to speak or translate them, so he immediately, and correctly, identified Bengali, Chinese, Czech, Gujarati, Icelandic and so on, when presented with examples of them, and when given a postcard with 'thank you' written in a hundred languages on it, he identified twenty-nine of them.[14]

It is also striking that Christopher is not entirely reliable with regard to the breadth and depth of his own linguistic abilities. As we reported earlier (Smith and Tsimpli, 1991: 318), his knowledge of Russian is moot. Despite denying knowledge of the language, because of his failure to identify an elementary greeting correctly, he was none the less able to give a translation (albeit somewhat inaccurate) of a Russian short story written in Cyrillic script. It may well be that his frequent claims to 'know a language' are more an assertion of his ability to identify the language concerned, for example, on the basis of its distinctive writing system, than a claim for verbal fluency.

Another point to note in this overview of Christopher's expertise is the speed and facility with which he picks up[15] languages. Apart from the obvious fact that anyone who knows as many languages as Christopher does must acquire them fairly fast, we have both anecdotal and systematic evidence for his ability. In March, 1992 shortly before he was due to appear on Dutch television, it was suggested that he might spend a couple of days improving his rather rudimentary Dutch with the aid of a grammar and dictionary. He did so to such good effect that he was able to converse in Dutch – with facility if not total fluency – both before and during the programme. More impressively, when he began learning Berber (see Smith et al., 1993, and chapter 4 below) he took to the language enthusiastically, seeming 'thoroughly to enjoy teasing out the details of the subject agreement system; and after a few minutes he was able to suggest the correct verb form to accompany a masculine as opposed to a feminine subject (converting "teswa" to "yeswa") despite there having been only two relevant examples' (Smith et al., 1993: 286). Moreover, on the occasion of his second lesson (three weeks after the first), he was able to translate simple sentences on demand, despite having spent only an hour or so on revision in the intervening period.

In addition to his polyglot ability, Christopher shows considerable skill in playing sundry word games in various languages. Examples are provided by 'word-making'. In this game/exercise the subject is given a word and asked to construct as many words from it as he or she can in a given time.

Given the head-words in (3) in English, German, Greek and Dutch, Christopher produced the examples beneath them in a few seconds:

3(a) *DISASTER*
   STAR, SISTER, DARE, TEA, ASTER, SID, RIDE, READ, TEAS, TEAR

 (b) *REGENSCHIRM*
   SCHIRM, ICH, MEIN, SCHNEE, REGEN

 (c) *ΚΑΤΑΣΤΡΟφΗ*
   ΣΤΡΟφΗ, ΡΟΗ, ΤΡΟφΗ, ΑΣΤΡΑ, [ΚΑΤΑΤΡΟφΗ], ΣΟΡΑ, ΣΟΡΟ, [ΟφΗΣ], ΚΟΡΗ, ΤΑΡΑΣ, ΤΑφΗ, [ΚΟΣ], [φΟΤΑ], ΚΑΤΑ[16]

 (d) *BARMAN*
   BAR, MAN, MAAR, RAAM, NAAM, NAM, MAAN, MA

Given this ability, it is not surprising that Christopher is good at anagrams and crosswords. He was presented with the task in (4) (from a children's puzzle book) and completed it with enthusiasm and considerable ease (Christopher's answers are given on the right).

4 BIRD ANAGRAMS
   Unjumble the letters and find 10 common seabirds
   (a) FUPNIF   PUFFIN
   (b) NANGET   GANNET
   (c) TREN   TERN
   (d) BOLLRAZIR   RAZORBILL
   (e) WELRUC   CURLEW
   (f) CARMORTON   CORMORANT
   (g) KAWITEKIT   KITTIWAKE
   (h) DIREE CUDK   EIDER DUCK
   (i) REHRING LULG   HERRING GULL
   (j) YESCHOTCARERT   OYSTERCATCHER

It took him 2 minutes 30 seconds to complete this task, but this time included his being prompted with the first letter for 'gannet', together with a discussion of their greedy habits, remarks on the fact that the Chinese used cormorants to catch fish for them (which Christopher knew), on the fact that eider ducks provide feathers for eiderdowns, questions about the Greek word for 'puffin', and so on. He was likewise able to complete a crossword, whose clues are exemplified in (5). Christopher's answers are given in parentheses.

5   Where the Great Barrier Reef is found (9)   (Australia)
    A fish made in heaven (9)   (Angelfish)
    What the Great Barrier Reef is made of (5)   (Coral)
    The Great White and Basking are types of (5)   (Shark)

This proficiency, matched by his ability to write backwards and locate words in hidden squares, is in marked contrast with his inability to master games such as word-ladders. Thus presented with several examples of how to get from 'HEAT' to 'FIRE' or from 'LOVE' to 'HATE' as illustrated in (6):

6   HEAT – HEAD – HERD – HERE – HIRE – FIRE
    LOVE – HOVE – HAVE – HATE

he seemed never to understand the task. Similarly, we found it impossible to get him to give judgements about what was a possible word of English (or other languages). Given the list in (7) and asked to mark which words might be possible words of English, even though he might not know them, he simply crossed out everything, except 'TSIMPLI':

7   STORKIN   KLUWER   MUDMUD   OVALO
    GNUT   TSIMPLI   SNOOVE   PLISS
    BNICK   SKAGLISH   LSIP   FNUG
    SPHENIC   GREFT   SPACK   BLICK
    UNGLE   WOOOM   NTENT   MAWK
    TSICK   PSACK   RPIG   GRUNBLE
    KMOW   BPOAT   VROKE

That he really has slightly better knowledge of possibility than this is attested to by the test given in (8):

8   The Unilever company has invented a new form of soap and wants a good name for it. Put the following suggested names in order of preference and add a new name of your own:

    (a)   Uni-sope
    (b)   Psoon
    (c)   Snoaf
    (d)   Kill-grime

(e)   Thirteen (unlucky for dirt)

(f)   ?

If the soap was to be marketed in Greece, which order would you put the names in?

Although Christopher neither ordered the names nor suggested new possibilities, it is perhaps not insignificant that for English he ticked 'Uni-sope' and 'Kill-grime', whereas for Greek he ticked 'Psoon' and 'Thekatria'[17] while crossing out 'Uni-sope' and 'Snoaf'.

Finally, we should mention that Christopher has never been able to devise a winning (or non-losing) strategy for noughts and crosses (tic-tac-toe) or draughts (checkers), although he is quite happy to play them. Indeed, he is usually unable even to draw a grid for noughts and crosses and frequently tries to put in several marks at a time. A typical example of his attempts in this direction is given in (9):

9

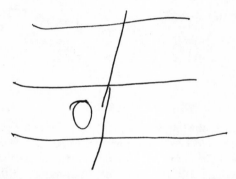

However, if his opponent deliberately contrives to lose – by putting her crosses in inappropriate squares of the grid, so that Christopher's only option is to 'win' – he recognizes that he has won, and shows some pleasure in the fact.

Not the least remarkable aspect of Christopher's talent is that it has flourished in an institutional setting, prompting the question of how he has learnt his various languages. In many cases, for example the Scandinavian languages, he has simply devoured introductory books of the *Teach Yourself X* or *Y in Three Months* variety, and for these languages his pronunciation is fairly bad. Other languages he has picked up by interacting with native speakers: he gains great pleasure from using such people as linguistic informants. In these cases, such as Hindi, his pronunciation is somewhat better, though even here native speakers may find it initially almost impossible to decode what he says. Finally, for some languages, for example, French, German and Spanish, he has received explicit instruction and even has formal qualifications (specifically GCE 'Ordinary' level). While still noticeably 'schoolboyish', his accent in these languages, as in Modern Greek for which he has had most practice over the last four years, is distinctly better than the others. It should go without saying that his slight speech defect, allied with a tendency when excited to speak faster than is advisable, can make his language hard to follow: particularly if, for instance, he is translating between languages one barely knows oneself.

Theoretical Background

To make possible an understanding of Christopher's case from both a psychological and a linguistic perspective we introduce certain fundamental notions of current linguistic theory, and embed them within a more general framework of a theory of cognition. We outline the innateness hypothesis[18] as it relates to language, and Fodor's (1983) modularity hypothesis, as reformulated in the light of Anderson's (1992a) cognitive theory of intelligence and Sperber and Wilson's (1986) theory of relevance.

Innateness

That some aspects of our linguistic knowledge are innate (more accurately, 'genetically determined') follows from a number of considerations. The most compelling of these are on the one hand, the existence of universal properties of language and, on the other, the poverty of the stimulus: the fact that as speakers of a language we know more than it is possible for us to have learned on the basis of the input we are exposed to.[19] In the present context, postulating the innateness of a body of information specific to language accounts for a variety of psycholinguistic phenomena: first, the uniformity of the mature state of linguistic competence attributed to all native speakers of a language; second, the existence of common developmental patterns in the process of first language acquisition; third, the occurrence of cases of neurological breakdown resulting in selective impairment to the linguistic component of our mental architecture. (cf. p. 3).

Principles and parameters The part of our linguistic knowledge that is innate, that is, available by biological necessity, is known as Universal

Grammar (UG). UG consists of a set of principles, some of which are absolute and some of which are parameterized. Absolute principles, such as the principle of structure dependence, define the design characteristics of language. Parameterized principles, such as the null subject parameter, provide a set of alternative options according to which languages may differ; in this case for instance, whether they allow null-subjects. In other words, principles of UG are responsible for the underlying similarities across languages, while parameters are responsible for cross-linguistic variation (see Chomsky, 1986a). All languages constrained by UG are, by definition, 'possible' languages, and the standard assumption for first language acquisition is that linguistic development is constrained by principles of UG in the sense that all intermediate stages of development observe the restrictions imposed by UG.

Closely associated with the assumptions of the innateness hypothesis is the notion of 'critical period'. The idea is that biological systems, of which one is language, are particularly sensitive to incoming perceptual stimuli during a specific stage of development. If for any reason language fails to develop during this period, then normal linguistic competence may never be attained. The best-known example of such a case is Genie (Curtiss, 1977), whose isolation and severe deprivation over a period of twelve years resulted in her being permanently linguistically impaired.

The acquisition of one's first language takes place during this critical period, when the innately available body of information which constitutes UG interacts with linguistic experience to set parameters to their target value; that is, the value for the language being acquired. At this level of abstraction, there is general consensus among researchers working within this framework, but differences of opinion appear when details of the actual course of linguistic development are taken into consideration. Current debate is divided between two incompatible and competing theories of first language acquisition: the maturation and the continuity approaches.

Continuity vs. maturation   A major issue in first language acquisition is identifying and explaining the child's transition from one stage of development to another. In a continuity framework (e.g. Pinker, 1984; Hyams, 1987), this development is viewed as a process in which the child matches parametric values with the appropriate syntactic categories when he or she is presented with relevant linguistic input. This presupposes the existence of a pre-existing structure with some parametric values associated with, for example, inflectional categories, underspecified (Weissenborn, 1990; Pierce, 1989; Hyams, 1987; Wexler, 1993). Child grammars are constrained by principles of UG and, in some versions of the theory, by initial parameter settings with a 'default' or 'unmarked' status (Hyams,

1986). When triggering data, that is, linguistic data that serve as triggers for parameter-setting, become available, the grammar gradually changes, signalling a transition from one stage of acquisition to the next. When this process is complete the mental representation of the grammar is said to have reached the mature or steady state.

By contrast, a maturational account necessarily presupposes that certain constructs of the innately available linguistic information are subject to a predetermined order of emergence. This implies that transitional stages in linguistic development result not only from mapping triggering input onto a given body of information, but also from intrinsic changes caused by a biological programme affecting the language module exclusively.

Depending on the syntactic theory assumed, different versions of this approach attribute maturational restrictions to different elements of the grammar. According to one school of thought, maturational constraints affect particular principles of UG (Felix, 1984; Borer and Wexler, 1987, 1988). An alternative view restricts maturation to the set of functional categories. This approach differs from the preceding one in that principles of UG are taken to be available throughout the process of language acquisition, whereas the set of functional categories (such as inflection, complementizers, determiners, case) is not available at the early stages of development (Guilfoyle and Noonan, 1988; Radford, 1990; Tsimpli, 1992). According to this approach, language acquisition does not consist in assigning appropriate features to an underspecified, albeit fully fledged structure; rather, it consists in a process of structure-building which correlates with the emergence of functional categories in the language module.

We will maintain that the set of functional categories constitutes a sub-module of UG, namely the UG lexicon. Each functional category is associated with an entry specified for relevant functional features (Tsimpli and Ouhalla, 1990). Parameterization is then defined in terms of a finite set of alternative values that a functional category can be associated with. Cross-linguistic variation is thus restricted to differences in the parametric values of functional categories (Chomsky, 1991c; Ouhalla, 1991; Pollock, 1989). These assumptions, in conjunction with a maturational approach to language acquisition, have certain implications: first, the inaccessibility of the functional module at the early stage of acquisition; and second, the lack of cross-linguistic (i.e. parameterized) differences in early grammars. Moreover, if we assume that the critical period hypothesis is correct, maturational constraints on the functional module can be interpreted as entailing its complete inaccessibility after the end of this period. The importance of this suggestion in the current context is that it has clear implications for adult second language learning: UG may still be available but parameter-resetting can not be. We come back to this issue later in this chapter.

Although a detailed discussion of issues in first language acquisition is beyond the scope of this monograph (see Atkinson, 1992; Roeper and Williams, 1987; A. Smith, 1988; Tsimpli, 1992), we will briefly present some of the ideas relevant to our discussion of Christopher's performance in his first and other languages. In particular, the role of morphology and its status in the organization of the grammar is an issue that will be shown to raise interesting questions about Christopher's exceptional language learning abilities.

The morphological component as an interface level

According to some researchers, the claim that functional categories mature is supported by morphological evidence (see, e.g., Radford, 1990). The idea is that there is a systematic correlation in early grammars between the absence of functional categories in the syntax and the absence of their morphological realization. Early data from some languages, for example English, seem to support this correlation to a certain extent. Thus the absence of the functional category DET correlates with the fact that early noun phrases include no determiners; and inflectional morphology seems to be missing from the verbal form, mirroring the absence of the syntactic category INFL. Pushed to its logical conclusion, this correlation suggests that syntactic properties associated with functional elements can only be shown to be part of the child's grammar if these functional elements are morphologically realized in a consistent way.

However, data from languages which have a rich morphological system of case and inflection seem to counter-exemplify this strong generalization (see Tsimpli, 1992). Early data from Greek and Spanish, for example (Pina, 1984), show that agreement morphology is available from the earliest appearance of verbal forms. Similarly, aspectual distinctions in Greek, Spanish, Irish, German and English appear to be morphologically marked in a way similar to the corresponding adult grammars. From this, however, it does not follow that the corresponding syntactic categories have matured in the sense that they are able to project the relevant X-bar structure. Thus, unless one attempts to define morphological constraints as independent of syntactic ones it seems that the differences mentioned above require an independent explanation. In other words, if morphological realization corresponds to syntactic availability the question that needs to be answered is why the same functional category emerges or matures in one language earlier than in another. This problem is particularly evident in a maturational approach where the effect of triggering data is not the only way of accounting for changes in emerging grammars. That is, if structure-building is the result of an in-built programme, morphological triggering alone cannot be a satisfactory explanation of the course of language acquisition. Nevertheless, if the availability of triggering data is a partial answer to this problem, what needs to be explained is the extent to which rich morphology is a 'stronger' trigger than impoverished morphology. Is it a universal rule that rich morphology has particular syntactic consequences or is it the case that variation in syntactic terms is not necessarily reflected in morphological properties? For example, although it is true that most null-subject languages exhibit rich subject–verb agreement morphology, languages like Chinese and Japanese are null-subject languages with no such morphological realization. Accordingly, Jaeggli and Hyams (1988) suggested the Morphological Uniformity Hypothesis, according to which languages could be pro-drop if they were morphologically consistent, either by having distinct forms for all members of the paradigm or by having the same form for all members of the paradigm. If the null subject of finite clauses is syntactically realized as pro in all null-subject languages, should we expect a difference in the acquisition process of these languages depending on the presence or absence of a morphological trigger? Further, should we expect languages like English, with almost non-existent agree-ment morphology, to exhibit patterns of acquisition parallel to those of morphologically similar but syntactically distinct languages? It is well known that linguistic elements with different syntactic feature specification may be homophonous: 'that' in relatives and embedded declaratives, for instance (see Rizzi, 1990). Presumably the 'acquisition' of these homo-phonous elements can be said to have occurred if the distinct features are acquired and associated (in this case) with the C head in the respective constructions. In the absence of definitive positive answers to such questions, it seems that morphological properties alone are inadequate to characterize the notions of 'strong' and 'weak' triggers in an account of language acquisition.

On the other hand, there do seem to be constraints defined exclusively on the basis of morphological properties. For example, the affixal nature of a functional morpheme is relevant in defining the obligatory movement of this element to an appropriate host category at the level where morpho-logical constraints apply (Lasnik's Filter or the Stray Affix Principle: see Pesetsky, 1989). Moreover, in derivational morphology, morphological rules are standardly assumed to apply independently of the syntax; and much of inflectional morphology has been argued to be the result of verb-raising to inflectional heads in the structure of the clause (Baker, 1988; Pollock, 1989; Ouhalla, 1991; Chomsky, 1991c). Within a minimalist approach, however, verbal forms are inserted as morphologically complex units and head-movement is motivated by syntactic (feature-checking) considerations (Chomsky, 1993a). We can thus conclude that syntax and morphology are to be kept distinct, with any possible interaction theoretically formulated in a specified way.

If this conclusion is correct, the alleged correlation between syntax and morphology in early grammars cannot be taken at face value. If functional categories, on one hand, and their morphological realization, on the other, belong to independent components of the grammar, the emergence of morphology and syntax could be argued to exhibit differences in virtue of the differences in the constraints that regulate each of the two components.

In an attempt to generalize beyond issues of first language acquisition, we suggest an extension of the traditional distinction between syntax and morphology. Specifically, we assume that the morphological component constitutes an interface level between the grammar and the conceptual/mental lexicon (see Tsimpli, 1992). Unlike the functional module, the mental lexicon is assumed to form part of the central cognitive system. One reason for distinguishing between a conceptual lexicon and a linguistic lexicon is that the former corresponds to the vocabulary used in the language of thought, in logical inferencing and indirectly in real (truth-conditional) semantics. Assuming that this vocabulary reflects mental properties which are not purely linguistic, and further that it does not need to refer to language-specific differences in the syntax proper, we suggest that mental entities featuring in this interface level of representation are not contained within the language module. The mapping of concepts and conceptual structure onto words and argument structure in a given language is carried out in the interface module, that is, the morphological component, the level that contains the morphological realization of both functional and substantive categories. The morphological component constitutes an *interface* in that it is accessible to both grammatical categories – functional categories and substantives – each set belonging to an independent component of the mental system.

The nature of the interface level that we have characterized as the morphological component can be further specified in the light of certain assumptions about concepts within a relevance-theoretic account of cognition.

Relevance and modularity

Relevance Intuitively, an utterance or other stimulus is relevant if it tells you something you didn't know, or weren't consciously aware of before.

Such information is context dependent, in that an utterance is relevant in a context if you can use it, together with that context, to deduce something which was apparent from neither of them taken alone: whether this is new information, the strengthening of a previously held assumption, or the contradiction of such an assumption. Every utterance has a variety of possible interpretations, not all of which are equally accessible to the hearer on a given occasion. Hearers are equipped with a single, general criterion for evaluating such interpretations as they occur to them; a criterion, moreover, which is sufficiently powerful to exclude all but a single interpretation. This 'criterion of consistency with the principle of relevance' starts from the general claim that human cognition is relevance-orientated. Relevance itself, as indicated informally above, is defined as a joint function of the achievement of contextual effects and the amount of effort needed to achieve them. The 'principle of relevance' states that communicated information creates an expectation of relevance: engaging someone's attention by speaking to them guarantees that (you think) what you are saying is worth their attention. (You may of course be wrong.) An utterance is 'optimally relevant' if it achieves enough effects to be worth the hearer's attention and does so without causing undue processing problems. An utterance is then consistent with the principle of relevance 'if and only if the speaker might rationally have expected it to be optimally relevant to the hearer on [a given] interpretation'. (Smith and Wilson, 1992: 6).

Relevance theory makes specific assumptions about the nature of what we refer to as the mental lexicon, postulating that each concept is characterized in terms of three entries: logical, encyclopaedic and lexical (Sperber and Wilson, 1986: 86). The logical entry can be best exemplified by reference to natural language connectives, such as *and*, *or*, *if*, which have been argued to be semantically equivalent to the corresponding truth-functional connectives (Grice, 1967; Carston, 1993; Smith, 1983a; Smith and Smith, 1988). The encyclopaedic entry refers to idiosyncratic knowledge associated with a certain concept; for example, the entry for 'cat' may include information about its domestic nature and that it is furry, as well as cultural or superstitious beliefs associated with it. The lexical entry includes phonological, morphological and semantic information as well as categorial features. In this respect, the lexical entry is used in the standard sense (Chomsky, 1965; see also Andrews, 1988).

Notice that not all conceptual addresses have entries of all three types. For example, the logical entry of a concept like 'cat' is unspecified, as it has no function corresponding to an element in formal logic. Similarly, natural language connectives have a logical entry and a lexical entry, including morphophonological properties, but probably lack an encyclopaedic entry.

Encyclopaedic entries differ widely from person to person, as they contain idiosyncratic information which, by definition, may vary across individuals. The logical entries and lexical entries, however, being associated with formal systems, logic and language respectively, vary minimally, if at all, across speakers of the same language.

Crucially, note that entries associated with the same concept do not necessarily belong to the same mental system. Lexical entries, for example, contain linguistic information and so belong to the language module, whilst encyclopaedic entries contain remembered information and so belong to the central system. If we define entries in terms of their functional properties, then logical entries belong to the level or levels at which (valid) inferencing and truth-conditions are relevant. If this level is post-LF but prior to at least some aspects of pragmatic analysis we can assume that it is not fully contained in the language component (Wilson and Sperber, 1986, 1993; Clark, 1991). Similarly, encyclopaedic entries refer to extra-grammatical information and are relevant to central processes, such as inferencing and pragmatic interpretation. Therefore, neither the logical nor the encyclopaedic entry fall within the language module properly speaking.

Let us now concentrate on the lexical entry. Following the discussion on pp. 25–7, it seems that the morphological component we characterized as the 'interface level' is a plausible candidate for the location of the lexical entries of concepts. Recall that the morphological properties of both substantive and functional categories are assumed to be realized at the interface. If this is correct, then what is standardly referred to as the lexicon is being interpreted in our terms as the morphological component. However, there are certain differences between the information contained at the interface level and that contained in what is standardly referred to as the lexicon. In particular, whereas the latter is understood to be the basis from which syntactic representations are formed, the former is not characterized as such. While interaction between them is possible, the two components are dissociated and parallel. In other words, morphological properties do not constrain syntax and thus need not necessarily reflect syntactic properties. The assumption that the lexical/morphological component is not the input to the syntactic structural level implies that the well-formedness of the syntax-morphology mapping must be checked independently, by means of an algorithm, most plausibly SPELLOUT in the sense of Chomsky (1993a). Moreover, the interface nature of the lexical component discussed here means that it is not necessarily the only level at which information related to the lexical elements is contained. If functional categories are part of the UG lexicon and substantive categories are part of the mental lexicon, the morphological representation of each member of the two sets is uniquely available at the interface, even though their sources differ.

As will be seen later in this chapter, assumptions about the nature of the interface level, the language module, the central (cognitive) systems, and possible interactions between them, are directly related to our analysis of Christopher's exceptional language *vis-à-vis* his other cognitive abilities. In this respect, the above account of the interface level as including lexical information can be viewed as an example of interaction between different sub-systems of the mental organ. In terms of the Modularity thesis suggested by Fodor (1983), the mapping process suggested above can be understood as characteristic exclusively of interface levels, as the nature of modules, in particular their property of informational encapsulation, prohibits any other kind of interaction. Fodor's view of mental architecture makes explicit claims about perceptual systems, including language, while claims about central cognitive systems are relatively vague.[20] Christopher's case presents a challenge to us to reconsider and elaborate on Fodor's views in connection with the nature of the central systems.

Modularity According to the modularity hypothesis, the human mind is not an unstructured entity but consists of components which can be distinguished by their functional properties. The basic distinction relevant to cognitive architecture is that between perceptual and cognitive systems, where the former pertains to the sensorium plus language, while the latter refers to 'central' systems responsible for the fixation of belief, for thought and for storing knowledge.

Perception is carried out by *modular systems* which are domain-specific, fast, mandatory, subserved by specific neural architecture – hence subject to idiosyncratic pathological breakdown – and most importantly are *informationally encapsulated*. This notion refers to the impossibility of total interaction between intra-modular operations and the central system(s). More precisely, the claim is that operations within modules are inaccessible to central control; the flow of information is only bottom-up. A clear example is provided by the existence of optical illusions such as the Müller–Lyer illusion (in which a line with inward-pointing arrowheads is seen as longer than a line of the same length with outward-pointing arrowheads) which are still seen as illusions even when one knows the facts. In the case of the language module, informational encapsulation implies that certain levels of representation, for example syntactic and phonological representations that are completely internal to the language module, are inaccessible to central operations. Pragmatic interpretation in contrast is an interactive process involving the output representation of the language module and central systems, where general or encyclopaedic knowledge is stored.[21]

Modules also differ from central systems in being equipped with a body of genetically determined information specific to the module in question which, in the case of language, is UG. This information, in conjunction with algorithms necessary to account for language learning, constitute the basis for claims of innateness. Thus, modularity and innateness within Fodor's theory are intertwined notions.

Moreover, as indicated by Fodor's 'First Law' (see note 20), the central systems are assumed to be resistant to scientific theorizing, precisely because of their putative lack of modular characteristics. We shall argue later that some parts of the central system are quasi-modular in structure, but it is clear that central processes such as inferencing are qualitatively different from processes found in modules. That is, central processes are not domain specific and involve information drawn from the sensorium as well as knowledge couched in propositional form in the memory store. It follows that we cannot always generalize from what we know about modular operations to central ones.

Anderson's theory of intelligence

Despite this widespread pessimism about the tractability of non-modular systems to investigation, Anderson's (1992a, 1992b) theory of intelligence is an attempt to formalize properties of central systems within a (modular) theory of mind. Anderson's model (see figure 1.5) is explicitly designed to be compatible with the Fodorian distinction between modular input systems and putatively non-modular central systems (but see the discussion of central modules in chapter 5). Accordingly, the knowledge store or encyclopaedic memory which is at the heart of the model is built up on the basis of input from (Fodorian) modules and from the Basic Processing Mechanism (BPM). Modules are essentially identical across the species, and hence contribute minimally to individual differences in intelligence. On the other hand the BPM, which implements thinking, is held to be 'responsible for the phenomenon of psychometric g, because it varies in its speed among individuals in the population' (Anderson, 1992a: 58). That is, he postulates a knowledge-free processing parameter which, precisely because of its role in 'implementing thinking', correlates with and indeed underlies knowledge-rich performance. Anderson further claims that his BPM is 'central' in Fodor's sense (p. 66), and in the absence of any discussion of an 'executive' *homunculus* or meta-component (cf. Sternberg, 1988, and Shallice, 1988, for relevant discussion), it is tempting to associate such an executive with it.[22]

As modules are, by hypothesis, informationally encapsulated, their

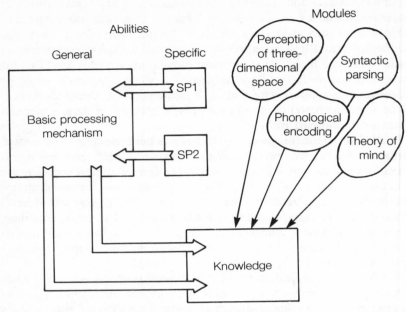

Figure 1.5 *Anderson's model*
Source: *Anderson (1992a)*

outputs must be evaluated by considerations of *relevance* before they can constitute appropriate input to the Knowledge Base. Although Anderson is somewhat reticent on the subject, we assume that this *evaluation mechanism* is mediated by the third main component of the model consisting of 'specific processors' (SP), of which Anderson postulates at a minimum two. While these both (all) have Turing machine power (see Anderson, 1992a: 96), they differ in terms of the operations they carry out and/or in terms of the representations they range over. Thus, they are analogous to computer languages where, for instance, the declarative PROLOG is good for semantics, C is ideal for number crunching, and COBOL is best suited for business purposes, even though each one of them can do anything either of the others can.

The two specific processors that Anderson proposes are the traditional 'visuo-spatial' and 'verbal-propositional' ones. The 'verbal' SP is pre-eminently devoted to *successive* processing, which 'takes place in a temporal sequence' (Anderson, 1992a: 83), and is held to underlie proficiency in serial recall, digit span, and so on. The 'visual' SP is pre-eminently devoted to *simultaneous* processing, which 'involves the synthesis of elements into groups and entails holistic, spatial representations' (ibid.), and is taken to underlie proficiency in memory for designs, tests of visualization and perhaps tests such as Raven's Matrices. As the operation of the SPs is mediated by the BPM (see figure 1.5), their efficacy is dependent on the latter's inherent speed. That is, whatever the efficiency of the SPs, this may be obscured if the BPM is unable to cope adequately with the representations it receives from them. It follows that significant differences in the operating power of the SPs will only be manifest in the presence of a relatively unimpaired BPM.

In addition to the foregoing, Anderson's model is completed by a set of further (non-Fodorian) 'modules Mark II' responsible for 'fetch-and-carry' operations and for over-learnt routines.[23] The former of these are not really 'modular' in any usual sense of the term but allow, for instance, for information to be retrieved from memory. The latter, over-learnt, processes may be closer to (encapsulated) modularity. They are putatively involved in any of a range of activities from tying one's shoelaces to calendrical calculation, though as Anderson has little to say about the place of skills in his model, it is hard to be more specific.

While we agree with Anderson on many aspects of the overall structure of his model, there are areas of disagreement as well. An important case in point is provided by his assumptions about the theory of mind and its location in the system. For Anderson it is a (Fodorian) module, whereas we consider it to be part of the internal structure of the central system. (See Smith and Tsimpli, 1993, where we suggest the model in figure 1.6 to replace Anderson's in figure 1.5, and especially chapter 5 for justification and further modification.)

A crucial characteristic of the theory of mind is that it involves the formation of second-order representations, enabling subjects *inter alia* to project other people's thoughts. We would like to argue that such projection is carried out by embedding one proposition under another which, by means of a modal predicate, attributes the statement to a referent distinct from the subject.

We shall come back in chapter 5 to a detailed discussion of this issue in relation to Christopher's performance in psychological and linguistic tests involving second-order representations. For the moment, it suffices to say that a common claim in the literature on autism is that a general characteristic of autistic people is their inability to form second-order representations (for discussion, see a number of the contributions in Baron-Cohen et al., 1993). In terms of a theory of the central systems this could be viewed either as a malfunction of the subcomponent referred to as theory of mind or as the reflex of a more general deficit (see Smith and Tsimpli, 1993: 428).

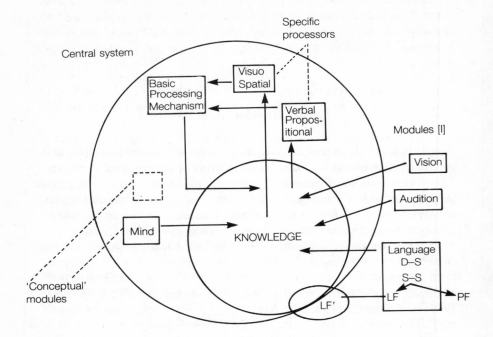

Figure 1.6 *Anderson's model revised*
Source: *Smith and Tsimpli (1993)*

If pathological disorders involve selective impairment of parts of the central system, we can use them to gain insight into its structure. More importantly, such evidence would indicate that Fodor's assumptions about some of the characteristics of the mind-brain need to be reformulated in order to accommodate mental components which satisfy only some of the defining criteria of modules. In any case, the property of informational encapsulation appears to characterize modular rather than quasi-modular central systems, even if the existence of the latter casts doubt on the assumption that the properties of central systems resist scientific theorizing.

In this context we need to reconsider the assumption that the lexical entry of concepts is contained within the morphological component. Such an assumption is consistent with the claim that central systems have limited access to modules only if the morphological component constitutes an interface between the language module and the mental lexicon. This position is at variance with standard assumptions about the lexicon according to which it constitutes the base from which syntactic structures are projected. If 'lower' levels are less accessible to cognition, it would follow that lexical information is similar, in terms of encapsulation, to syntactic information. We will argue, however, that whereas syntax seems to be impenetrable by central systems, i.e. it is strictly modular, lexical information is not.

Second language acquisition

Recent research in second language acquisition within the principles and parameters framework has addressed a number of controversial questions. The most important of these are the respective roles of UG and of the first language in the process of second language acquisition. Different possible answers to each of these questions have considerable theoretical consequences and make powerful predictions with regard to the L2 data.

There are certain radical differences in an individual's acquisition of his or her first and subsequent languages. First, while negative evidence in the form of explicit instruction and correction is implausible (for both empirical and theoretical reasons – but see Bowerman, 1987, and Braine, 1963) in first language acquisition, it is not totally excluded in second language learning. Second, the fact that, pathological cases aside, adult second language learning is at least temporally related to cognitive maturity distinguishes it from first language acquisition, where cognitive development is still under way. This relates to the first point because, if negative evidence does play a role in second language learning, this can be attributed to the fact that the availability of a hypothesis-formation and confirmation procedure which is sensitive to all types of evidence (including negative evidence) presupposes a certain cognitive maturity. The third and most crucial difference between first and second language acquisition concerns the question of ultimate attainment (Birdsong, 1992). The usual failure to achieve native-like competence in a second language contrasts sharply with one of the basic characteristics of the first language: namely, the uniform attainment of a mature steady state in a deterministic fashion.

One well-known approach (Clahsen and Muysken, 1986; Bley-Vroman, 1989) suggests that the acquisition of a second language is qualitatively different from that of a first language. The core idea is that for first language acquisition the language module, i.e. UG and parameter-setting, can provide an adequate description of the process involved, whereas learning a second language crucially involves general learning mechanisms. That is, inductive learning strategies are crucially operative in the processing of L2 input data, and the construction of the L2 grammar is mediated by mental mechanisms which lie outside the language module.

However, this hypothesis has been challenged by recent experimental studies which suggest that principles of UG constrain L2 grammars much as they constrain L1 acquisition (White, 1989; Schwartz, 1993; Schwartz and Sprouse, 1993; Eubank, 1993). This alternative view holds that second language acquisition is similar to first language acquisition in all the theoretically important respects: namely, in the role of principles of UG and in the availability of parametric choices. More precisely, the assumption is made that parameter-resetting does take place, albeit in a comparatively delayed fashion, as the parametric values of the first language have already been set. 'Transfer errors' are then accommodated within this approach as reflecting transitional stages in the development of the second language.[24] Crucially, however, knowledge of the first language does not prevent L2 learning from operating under the same principles that L1 acquisition does.

Assuming our earlier claims about the maturation of functional categories in first language acquisition are correct, they have specific implications for any language learning process which occurs after the critical period. If the functional module is subject to maturational constraints and the possibility of parameterization depends on the accessibility of the functional module, it follows that adult second language learning cannot involve parameter (re)setting (see Tsimpli and Roussou, 1991; Tsimpli and Smith, 1991).

If maturational constraints are operative, the idea is that the linguistic sub-module affected becomes inaccessible after the relevant period. Accordingly, as principles of UG constitute a universal template on which any human language is based, they always constrain language acquisition, be it L1, L2 or Ln. In the event that a learner's L2 grammar appears to approximate to that of a native speaker, the theory assumes that it none the less does not have the same status. Rather, where the first language differs from the second language, native-like performance is taken to be a function of an alternative choice regulated by UG and adopted by the L2 grammar (cf. Sorace, 1992). Needless to say, this assumption can be justified only if the second language learner's performance diverges from that of the native speaker in some relevant respect. In sum, while this approach to second language acquisition is theoretically not implausible, its validity depends crucially on the issue of ultimate attainment. Thus, although investigations of the developmental process of second language acquisition can be fruitful with regard to the two basic issues in the field, namely the role of UG and of the first language, it seems that questions concerning the absence of parameter resetting can be answered only in the light of what constitutes a possible final state in second language learning.

Hypotheses

Keeping in mind the above discussion of modularity and linguistic theory we can now view Christopher's case in perspective. The relevant questions are the extent to which Christopher's linguistic and other behaviour can be described within the bounds set by Fodor's theory of mental architecture; and whether any reformulations of the theory are necessary for an adequate descriptive account of this unique case.

As regards linguistic theory, in particular as it involves second language learning, the issues are equally if not more complex. Can Christopher's linguistic performance in his non-native languages be described independently of his general cognitive abilities or is there some parasitic relation between the two? Further, is this interdependent relationship evident at all stages of his 'second' language learning or does it become relevant only in the later stages? How can such suggestions be accommodated in a general theory of second language acquisition?

Modularity

Assuming that the basic thesis concerning the modular status of the language faculty is correct (but see chapter 5 for some modifications and reservations), Christopher's case is important for obvious reasons. The sharp contrast between his verbal and non-verbal performance in a range of psychological tests gives clear *prima facie* support to the claim. In particular, his average or above-average performance in tasks involving language shows that whatever his impairment may be it has not affected those mental operations that crucially or exclusively involve language.

Assuming further that the biological development of modular, perceptual systems is independent of the development and level of attainment of the central systems, Christopher's native language competence is of vital importance. If it can be demonstrated that his knowledge of his first language is comparable to that of any other native speaker of the language, we can conclude that the underlying language-specific mechanisms are basically intact. This, however, represents just a first and fairly naive approach to the problem. As we are dealing with linguistic performance, there are certain phenomena, of sentence processing for example, that cannot be explained on an exclusively linguistic basis. Recall that constructing higher levels of representation on the basis of contextually determined pragmatic inferencing involves an interactive process between language, the central knowledge store and real semantics. Given that the nature of the interface levels and of central operations is to a large extent unclear, a performance deficit involving pragmatic or logical structures in relation to a linguistic input may muddy an otherwise clear picture. Specifically, performance limitations may in Christopher's case obscure the initial distinction mentioned above between 'language' and 'central cognitive abilities'.

In an attempt to dissociate core linguistic, i.e. modular, from interactive, i.e. non-modular levels of representation, our aim was to test Christopher on syntactic phenomena in English which have received a plausible account within the framework of current syntactic theory. If his performance is comparable to that of other native speakers we can claim that an account of his linguistic knowledge requires no stipulatory assumptions added solely to accommodate his exceptional case. In order to clarify the areas in which Christopher's linguistic performance may deviate from that of a normal speaker, we have therefore carried out further investigations of his linguistic behaviour. In some cases, for example metalinguistic negation, we argue that this crucially involves extra-linguistic knowledge. If we conclude that there is indeed such divergence from the norm, this need not necessarily impugn the initial claim that his competence is intact. More precisely, the modularity thesis can still be supported even if in certain respects Christopher's linguistic behaviour appears to be abnormal, provided that the relevant respects are not strictly internal to the language module. The question of clarifying the nature of the deficit concerned remains, of course.

With respect to operations carried out by the central systems, the issues are much more complex. Christopher's translating abilities, although remarkable in terms of speed, are unusually flawed in terms of sensitivity to contextual information and linguistic constraints. If such linguistic constraints are observed in other tasks involving his knowledge of other languages, we have to assume that the particular task of translation makes only restricted use of linguistic information. We therefore face the question of how to identify the areas that are actively involved in translation and, to the extent that the output is deviant in Christopher's case, of how to describe the deficit in relation to other areas of his performance which exhibit similar shortcomings. We will discuss Christopher's translations in more detail in chapter 5.

Psychological tests standardly associated with the investigation of autism (see pp. 5–7) raise interesting questions about the quasi-modular nature of the central systems, for instance, the theory of mind. Christopher's performance in such tasks, especially when compared to his ability in, for instance, pragmatic inferencing, is indicative of the distinct status of the underlying mechanisms involved in carrying out central operations. Such results from Christopher's performance are crucial in specifying what constitutes a deficit in his non-linguistic cognitive abilities. One of the puzzles that any case of the savant syndrome presents is the contrast between a specific, enhanced mental talent and an otherwise subnormal mind. The picture in Christopher's case would be particularly elegant if the language module was normal, some processing mechanism associated with linguistic decoding was enhanced, and the rest of his cognitive abilities were severely damaged. However, any evidence that some central operations may be more or less affected than others complicates the picture and requires a more elaborate theory of the central systems to accommodate Christopher's case. For instance, in addition to his quasi-autistic performance on some tasks such as the 'Sally-Anne' test, Christopher fails to conserve number (see p. 5), and it is tempting to attribute this too to a deficit in some dedicated sub-part of the central system.

Second language learning

Christopher's linguistic talent is characterized as exceptional for various reasons. First, the speed with which he learns a new language and his ability, after minimal exposure to the new data, to construct sentences observing morphological and syntactic requirements is remarkable[25] (see chapter 3). Second, his knowledge of vocabulary in the languages he knows (which naturally varies depending on the time he has spent on each) and his ability to access this knowledge instantly are unusual when compared to standard cases of second language learners.

To formulate testable hypotheses about Christopher's second language learning we need first to find similarities, if any, between his production data and well-formedness judgements, on the one hand, and those of average second language learners, on the other. If it transpires that the status of Christopher's 'second' languages is comparable to that of other learners we can assume that any theory of second language acquisition that accounts for them would also account for him. However, as is well-known, there are distinct stages in the process of second language learning, each of them characterized by such considerations as the occurrence of 'transfer errors', the degree of deviance from the target second language, and the nature of that deviance, that is, whether it corresponds to an option made available by UG, albeit not that of the target grammar, and so on (see White, 1989, among others). As already discussed (see pp. 35–6), one of the most crucial questions on which much of the issue of the nature of second language learning, as opposed to first language acquisition, depends is the notion of ultimate attainment. Assuming that in the standard case second language learners may achieve considerable fluency or even near-native-like competence,[26] Christopher's case raises the question of whether it is plausible to characterize his knowledge of French and Greek, the languages he is most fluent in, as near-native-like or not? If not, as our results so far show, then he is not comparable to other second language learners in that he exhibits a cut-off point beyond which any further restructuring of his L2 grammar becomes impossible. Our hypothesis on this issue involves characterizing the difference between Christopher and others in terms of the nature of the underlying mechanisms responsible for this contrast. Thus we need to determine whether his limitations are properly linguistic, revolving around the inaccessibility of parameter-resetting, or whether they are the result of an interactive process. In the latter case this might involve a deficit in some processing or evaluation mechanism responsible for filtering out unanalysable data and reassessing them on the basis of options which are made available by UG and which may or may not be instantiated in the first language. This is perhaps a normal result of constructing interlanguage grammars, and Christopher's peculiarity is in part that his progress is subject to premature 'completion'.

Christopher in context

There are now several well-documented cases of dramatic dissociations between linguistic and general cognitive abilities which serve as an instructive comparison with Christopher's case. These include cases of fluent language in the presence of severe cognitive deficit, and seriously impaired language in the presence of high non-verbal intelligence. The former include Williams Syndrome children (see, e.g., Bellugi et al., 1993; Thal et al., 1989), 'chatterbox' children (see, e.g., Cromer, 1991); hyperlexics (see, e.g., Cossu and Marshall, 1986), and the case of Laura (Yamada, 1990). The latter include some aphasics, who may be 'severely impaired in aspects of their language, but can often perform normally on other cognitive tasks' (Karmiloff-Smith, 1992a: 169, citing Shallice, 1988), many autistic people, who may combine impoverished language with otherwise normal intelligence (see, e.g., Fay, 1993; Frith, 1991), and SLI children (van der Lely, 1994; van der Lely and Stollwerck, in prep. a, in prep. b), who are in some sense the mirror image of Christopher in that they exploit central processes to get around their linguistic deficit.[27] The most striking example, however, is the case of the family, half of whose members have (over a period of some three generations) been documented as suffering from a morphological deficit (Gopnik, 1990 and in press; Gopnik and Crago, 1991; Hurst et al., 1990). Gopnik and her colleagues hypothesize that 'one particular level of grammar that represents abstract morphological features[28] is impaired' (Gopnik and Crago, 1991: 34), and that 'apparent competence exhibited by the adults appears to be a result of a lexical learning strategy rather than the construction of rules' (ibid.: p. 47), as 'grammatical rule-processing and lexical memorization are two psychologically, linguistically and neurologically distinct processes, one of which can be impaired relative to the other' (Gopnik, in press: 40). As will be seen in chapter 5, we suggest a model of the mind and the language faculty which includes a 'functional lexicon' of syntactic categories and an interface between the language module and the central system. Gopnik and her colleagues suggest that the family's deficit resides precisely in that morphological domain in which Christopher excels, suggesting strongly that it is indeed an autonomous component that can be selectively impaired or spared. For Gopnik's subjects it seems to be the case that the deficit in the morphological component stems from the lack (or unavailability) of the primitives of the morphological system. That is, the rules which specify lexical representations and derivations from these representations (for example, by defining their boundaries in the sense of Kiparsky, 1982, and Gordon, 1989) are inaccessible. This shows trivially that the acquisition of morphological entities, as suggested here, does not consist in memorizing level 1 units separated off by # boundaries.

Despite the dissociational similarities among these cases, Christopher is distinct in at least two, related, respects. First, his ability in English is normal and as his intellectual deficit is nowhere near as severe as that of some Williams Syndrome subjects, for instance, the remarkable aspect of his talent resides entirely in its multi-lingual nature. Second, his English *is* normal, whereas that of the other categories mentioned is remarkable only in contrast with the subjects' other deficits. That is, although Williams Syndrome children have remarkable linguistic ability, their knowledge of English is none the less inferior to that of normal subjects (see Bellugi et al., 1993). Similarly, Laura's ability in English is impressive in comparison with that of other subjects of a comparably low IQ, but is very far from normal (see Smith, 1991, for discussion); and the remarkable linguistic abilities of hyperlexics are again remarkable only in contrast with their other (dis)abilities.

Two further points need to be stressed. First, in contrast to the SLI cases, there is no evidence that Christopher's disability is in any way genetically determined. Second, the linguistic complementarity between Christopher and the other cases cited is not perfect. Although SLI children appear to have a deficit in that (morphological) domain where Christopher's ability is perfect, there are significant mismatches. None the less, it is of interest that a comparable range of structures and functions in the morphological system seems to be affected in cases of genetic as of traumatic impairment, suggesting that the basic outline of our account is accurate.

2

The First Language

Introduction

We have suggested that a key area of our investigation is Fodor's (1983) modularity hypothesis, in particular as it pertains to the relation of the language module to central systems. If the steady state of a native speaker's linguistic knowledge is correctly characterized as being modular, we need to look at Christopher's unique talent in the context of his knowledge of his first language, English. That is, we need to establish whether encapsulated cognitive processes, in this case those of a formal linguistic kind, are affected in any way by whatever deficit is responsible for Christopher's relatively poor performance on non-verbal tasks. This in turn, however, presupposes that we have a reliable basis for judging Christopher's linguistic knowledge, an assumption that is not unproblematic.

The most difficult problem that we confront in addressing this issue is that so-called grammaticality judgements inevitably reflect not only linguistic knowledge *per se*, but also the effect of processing strategies and of performance limitations. As we are heavily dependent on such judgements for our analysis of Christopher's knowledge, our interpretation of his responses needs to be both sensitive and subtle, especially when these responses relate to garden-path constructions and to marked or discourse-biased structures. Failure to disentangle the conflicting roles of these different elements could lead us to underestimate or otherwise misrepresent Christopher's knowledge of his first language. However, after looking at several thousands of judgements over a period of four years, we think that Christopher's consistency justifies us in claiming that his knowledge of his first language is essentially perfect.

Syntax

Normal judgements

In establishing that Christopher's knowledge of his first language is, in general, entirely comparable to that of normal native speakers, we used a variety of tests. These included straightforward judgements of well-formedness, in which he had simply to indicate whether a stimulus sentence was 'good' or 'bad'; an elaboration of this in which he had also to provide better versions of sentences which he found in any way unacceptable; forced choice tests, in which he had to select his preferred form of two or more alternative sentences; correction of 'translations' from other languages, in which we asked him to mark homework exercises by Ianthi's mythical sister; and so on. Occasionally we also used translation exercises to determine which reading of ambiguous sentences he preferred, and for some judgemental tests we asked him to indicate how certain he was of his judgements. In fact he virtually always professed himself completely certain of his judgements, so we omitted this request after a few sessions.

The claim that Christopher's linguistic competence falls within normal limits is based on his performance on a variety of structures including declaratives, passives, negatives, interrogatives, relatives, clefts, pseudo-clefts, and others and involving variations in agreement, word-order, the use of polarity items, and so on. Initially we plied him with relatively simple examples, and gradually increased the complexity of the stimuli throughout the project. At the beginning, the data presented to Christopher consisted mainly of simple declaratives and interrogatives, where the appropriate linguistic judgement required the correct choice of preposition, word-order, and selectional requirements of the predicate and so on, as illustrated by the examples below. (A representative selection of Christopher's judgements over the whole project is given in Appendix II).[1]

1   My shoes is dirty   [R]
1'   'My shoes are dirty'

2   Remember Susan to feed the dog   [R]
2'   'Tell Susan to feed the dog'

3   He put the car to the garage   [R]
3'   'He put the car in the garage'

| 4 | A book was given John by Peter | [R] |
| 4' | 'A book was given to John by Peter' | |

| 5 | Which you thought was an interesting idea? | [R] |
| 5' | 'Which have you thought was an interesting idea?' | |

| 6(a) | John wants no apples | [OK] |
| (b) | John wants not apples | [R] |

| 7 | I wonder that Mary was so upset | [R] |
| 7' | 'I wonder why Mary was so upset' | |

| 8(a) | It is easy to make John laugh | [OK] |
| (b) | John is easy to make Peter laugh | [R] |

| 9 | John and Susan often write to each other | [OK] |

| 10 | I'm sure that Peter will remember what to say in the interview | [OK] |

| 11 | The weather today is beautiful, is it? | [R] |
| 11' | 'The weather today is beautiful, isn't it?' | |

| 12 | Himself believes John to be happy | [R] |
| 12' | 'He believes John to be happy' | |

| 13 | Never before have I seen such a scene | [OK] |

| 14 | Landing planes are very dangerous | [OK] |

| 15 | John gave a gift Susan | [R] |
| 15' | 'John gave a gift to Susan' | |

| 16(a) | Anybody can go in this room | [OK] |
| (b) | Anybody can't go in this room | [R] |

| 17 | What he bought was a new car | [R] |
| 17' | 'What he had bought was a new car' | |

| 18 | Who did you say Mary met at John's party? | [R] |
| 18' | 'Whom did you say Mary met at John's party?' | |

19   Mary thinks high of himself   [R]
19'   'Mary thinks high of herself'

20   It is reading newspapers that I like most   [R]
20'   'It is reading newspapers that I like the most'

As can be seen from examples 1–16, Christopher's judgements are normal
and his suggested corrections appropriate. Examples 17–20 are slightly less
clear-cut, but do not, we think, vitiate the judgement that his linguistic
knowledge falls within normal limits. Examples 17 and 20 are well-formed
with and without Christopher's changes, and we suspect that his
suggestions are a function of his desire to do something positive, even if it is
strictly unnecessary. He gave no evidence on other occasions of finding
such stimuli sentences unacceptable. Example 18 was characteristic of a
number of Christopher's changes, which are presumably due to school-
based prescriptivism, but which he implemented inconsistently. He in fact
said that 18 was all right, but 'better' if the wh-phrase was changed to
'whom'. Example 19 was correctly amended as far as the choice of reflexive
pronoun is concerned, but Christopher failed to correct 'high' to the
expected 'highly'. As he once corrected 'highly' to 'high' on a similar
example, we assume that this is a reflection of a dialect difference: for many
speakers of (non-standard) English 'high' would be correct in such
sentences.
    There were only two examples from the first sets of data whose
corrections were in fact inappropriate:

21   What you think is this new book about?   [R]
21'   'What do you think is this new book about?'

22   How come you goed home so early?   [R]
22'   'How come did you go home so early?'

and as such 'corrections' were not repeated in subsequent exercises,
we deem them to be unsystematic errors due to tiredness or lack of
attention.
    Subsequent sessions with data including complex embedded and adjunct
clauses which demanded the tapping of intuitions about ungrammatical
structures involving preposition stranding, pied-piping, island-effects, the
presence of resumptive pronouns in relative clauses, and so on, elicited
comparably sophisticated responses, as can be seen in examples 23–36:

23   The lady, I saw, who bought a present for Bill   [R]
23' 'The lady I saw bought a present for Bill'

24   This is the girl that I saw her with John at the cinema   [R]
24' 'This is the girl that I saw with John at the cinema'

25   The girl who that you saw this morning is John's sister [R]
25' 'The girl that you saw this morning was John's sister'

26   John tried Peter to escape from prison but he didn't succeed [R]
26   'John tried with Peter to escape from the prison but he didn't succeed'

27   What did Susan buy clothes and?   [R]
27' 'What clothes did Susan buy?'

28   Who does John wonder whether Mary knows?   [R]
28' 'What does John wonder if Mary knows?'

29   Mary believes the claim which John is a very intelligent man [R]
29' 'Mary believes the claim that John is a very intelligent man'

30   What did Peter ask who left behind?   [R]
30' 'What did Peter ask who was left behind?'

31   Scarcely had Bill arrived when he burst into tears   [OK]

32   Which student do you think that could solve the problem? [R]
32' 'Which student do you think could solve the problem?'

33   What time is the shop open until?   [OK]

34   This is the doll which the silly clown danced last night [R]
34' 'This is the doll which the silly clown danced with last night'

35   Which buildings are the tourists looking at now?   [OK]

36   At which pictures were the children laughing this morning? [OK]

Although his corrections of some ungrammatical sentences are themselves ungrammatical (e.g. 28', 30'), probably because it is not self-evident

what the well-formed congeners of these examples should be, Christopher's
judgements were consistently accurate and 'normal'. The overall picture
regarding his first language seems entirely consistent and regular.
However, there is a small set of constructions which seem to render this
conclusion problematic. These constructions are what are referred to in the
literature as *dislocation, topicalization* and (a sub-set of) *extraposition*
structures. A basic property shared by all these structures is that they
manifest a coreference relation between a pronoun (or an empty category)
in an argument position and a constituent occupying an A'-, non-operator
position. In the next section we discuss these problematic structures and
compare Christopher's performance on them with his performance on
structures standardly assumed to involve operator-movement.

Coreference relations in the syntax

Topicalization and dislocation   In English, constructions involving coreference between nominal expressions, one of which occupies an A'-position,
include wh-interrogatives, clefts, relatives, parasitic gaps, *easy-to-please*
structures, dislocation and topicalization.[2] The last two are assumed to be
distinct from the former in a number of ways, as can be seen by contrasting
example 37, a wh-interrogative with 38, a left dislocation structure:

37   Who$_i$ did you see t$_i$?

38   John$_i$, I saw him$_i$.

For reasons to do with the LF-properties of wh-phrases (Chomsky, 1981a,
1986a, 1986b; Browning, 1987) , the wh-phrase in 37 is assumed to be an
operator. The dislocated element 'John' in 38, on the other hand, does
not have operator-like properties. As suggested in Chomsky (1982), the
representation of dislocation constructions involves a relation of predication
between the dislocated element and the rest of the clause. He argues that
this representation is relevant not at LF but at a different level, which he
calls LF', where the predication relation is expressed. The relationship
between the dislocated constituent and the rest of the sentence in a left
dislocation structure is similar to that in relative clauses and clefts, where
the relationship between the head of the relative and the relative clause is
likewise that of predication. The difference between 37 and 38 resides in
the different structural positions that the wh-phrase and the dislocated

constituent occupy, namely an operator and an A'-(non-operator) position respectively. These differences are represented structurally here:

39 [$_{CP}$ who$_i$ [$_{C'}$did [$_{IP}$you see t_i]]]

40 [$_{CP}$ [$_{TOP}$ John$_i$ [$_{CP}$ [$_{IP}$ I saw him$_i$]]]]

In those languages which have syntactic focus: Greek, Hungarian, Korean and Berber, among many others, another form of operator-movement is also postulated. Unlike English, these languages manifest a process of focusing which bears certain similarities to wh-movement, and is therefore assumed also to involve the formation of an A'-chain, with the focused element an operator (see, e.g., Choe, 1987; Brody, 1990; Tsimpli, 1994). Consider 41 in this respect, where capitals indicate heavy stress:

41 To YANI$_i$ idha t$_i$
    the Yani-acc saw-1s
    It is Yanis that I saw

Christopher's performance on focus structures in Greek and Berber will be discussed in chapters 3 and 4 respectively. What is relevant to the current discussion is that the function of (identificational) focusing in English is usually borne by a cleft construction. Contrastive focus, on the other hand, is normally conveyed by topicalization, as in 42:[3]

42 John$_i$, I saw t$_i$.

Topicalization in English contrasts with dislocation in that the latter involves the presence of an overt pronoun in the base-generated position, while the former involves a gap (compare 38 and 42). Although there are certain technical complications, which we discuss briefly below, the differences between topicalization and dislocation can arguably be reduced to the availability of the resumptive pronoun strategy for dislocation structures and of a distinct adjunction position for topicalization (but see note 4).

Chomsky (1977) has shown that topicalization, like wh-movement but unlike dislocation, gives rise to island phenomena as illustrated in 43:

43 *the boy to whom the books John gave away
    *to whom the books did John give away?

Following Lasnik and Saito (1984), Culicover (1991) argues that topicalization involves adjunction to IP rather than substitution to a Spec position, and he suggests an account of topic-islands which presupposes Cinque's (1991) assumption that a maximal projection which is not c-selected is a barrier to extraction. In the case of topicalization, the higher IP node is c-selected by C while the lower one is not, thus creating a barrier in the sense of Chomsky (1986b).

Although these facts suggest that topicalization and wh-movement share certain properties, we would like, for the purposes of the current discussion, to concentrate on their differences: namely, that in topicalization there is no substitution movement of the topicalised constituent to an A'-, operator position, and that the adjunction movement involved does not correlate with I-to-C movement. Left dislocation constructions share the properties just outlined, in that the dislocated element is not in an operator position, and left dislocation does not trigger subject–auxiliary inversion. It is this aspect of dislocation and topicalisation constructions, together with their interpretational possibilities, that we focus on.

Given a configurational definition of operators (Chomsky, 1981a; Browning, 1987), it is clear that the adjunction structure involved in dislocation and topicalization constructions cannot involve operator-like elements.[4] The simplest alternative is to treat dislocation and topicalization constructions as instances of coreference rather than of binding relations. Specifically, in dislocation constructions the relationship between the dislocated element and the clause containing the resumptive pronoun is that of predication. Similarly, following Cinque (1991), it could be argued that in topicalization constructions, the empty category is a pro which is coreferential with the topicalized element, again giving rise to a predication relation between the topicalized constituent and the clause containing the pronoun. Assuming that the topic element is not an operator, the relationship between it and the pro in the argument position cannot be that manifest by an operator-variable structure; that is, it is not exclusively a binding relation.[5] In this respect, dislocation and topicalization have at least one coreferentiality property in common. What is crucial is that topicalization, as exemplified in 42, contrasts with wh-movement both as regards the properties of their respective preposed elements and as regards the relationship between this element and the one in the thematic position.

As far as their interpretational possibilities are concerned, the similarity between topicalization and dislocation constructions is clear: in both there is a relation between a topic and the rest of the clause, that is, a topic–comment structure. Further, there is in both constructions an intonational break between the preposed element and the rest of the sentence, that is, a property standardly attributed to topic–comment structures but one which is not shared by constructions involving operator-movement. It can

accordingly be argued that a predication relation is involved in both
topicalization and dislocation constructions.

To summarize, the distinction between topicalization and dislocation on
the one hand, and constructions involving operator-movement on the
other, can be drawn in the following way. All constructions involve
coreference, that is, representations which include two coindexed links,
but in operator-movement constructions binding of the variable by the
operator in SpecCP is also involved. Moreover, operator-movement, as
exemplified by the structure in 39, is generally assumed also to occur in
restrictive relative clauses, embedded interrogatives, *easy-to-please* constructions, parasitic-gap constructions and clefts.

With the above discussion as background, let us now turn to Christopher's
judgements of such constructions, representative examples of which are
provided in 44–50 and in a number of the earlier examples cited:

44   This is the bench on which the girls sat yesterday afternoon [OK]

45   Which insurance did the old man worry last weekend?   [R]
45'   'Which insurance did the old man worry about last weekend?'

46   What did John believe the claim that Mary said?   [R]
46'   'What did John claim Mary said?'

47   It is Mary that has passed these exams   [R]
47'   'It was Mary that has passed these exams'

48   John is easy to please him   [R]
48'   'John is easy to please'

49   This is the girl that I saw her with Bill at the cinema   [R]
49'   'This is the girl that I saw with Bill at the cinema'

50   What did John seem to have forgotten to remind Mary
       to bring?   [OK]

As these examples show, Christopher's acceptability judgements are
similar in relevant respects[6] to those expected of any native speaker of
English. However, his performance is not always equally straightforward,
as is evident from the examples in 51–61:

51   Susan, I met her yesterday   [R]
51'   'I met Susan yesterday'

52   Me, I don't like football   [R]
52'   'I don't like football'

53   Steven, they saw during the break   [R]
53'   'They saw Steven during the break'

54   The Greek ones, Mary got   [R]
54'   'Mary got the Greek ones'

55   I met her yesterday, Mary   [R]
55'   'Yesterday, I met Mary'

56   John, I like very much   [R]
56'   'I like John very much'

57   Mary, I met her at the cinema   [R]
57'   'I met Mary at the cinema'

58   Susan, I left her at home   [R]
58'   'I left Susan at home'

59   I sent it to Mary, that book about the Greek islands   [R]
59'   'I sent that book about the Greek islands to Mary'

60   Mary, she returned to Greece yesterday   [R]
60'   'Mary returned to Greece yesterday'

61   He stayed at Mary's house, Steven   [R]
61'   'Steven stayed at Mary's house'

Christopher's reaction to these sentences is interesting, and puzzling, for two reasons. First, his judgements on these dislocation and topicalization constructions contrast with his judgements on the vast majority of other constructions (e.g. 44–50) which involve movement and/or coreference between two positions in clause structure. Second, it seems unlikely that the contrast in his judgements could derive from his purely syntactic knowledge, as this would suggest the peculiar situation in which the syntax of his first language is non-native-like only as far as topicalization and dislocation constructions are concerned.

It might be objected that, because he is mostly presented with written input, sentences such as those in 51–61 are not favoured by discourse considerations, as they would be if the input was oral. However, 52, 53 and

54 were included within longer passages that were presented to him for correction. In other words, there was sufficient contextual information to motivate the topicalization or dislocation, yet the *only* sentences he corrected in these passages were precisely the ones in 52–54.[7] The passages are given in 62–64:

62 John, Steven and Peter decided to go to the theatre last Thursday. They were supposed to meet in front of the tube station which was very close to the street where the theatre was. The performance started at 7 o'clock so they agreed to meet at 6.30. John and Peter were on time but Steven wasn't. John and Peter waited for 15 minutes and then they started walking towards the theatre. They had a drink and then they went inside to find their seats. Steven, they saw during the break. He was late because his car had broken down.

63 Peter and Mary collect stamps. One day they were given 10 very old stamps both English and Greek. Peter took the English stamps and added them to his collection. The Greek ones, Mary got. She spent a long time trying to understand what was written on them.

64 Steven invited Peter to his place to watch the match together. Steven asked his neighbour, Bill, to come around too. He didn't know that his neighbour didn't like football at all so Steven was very surprised when Bill told him very angrily: 'Me, I don't like football.'

It appears then that the possibility that Christopher rejected these constructions because they exhibit a marked word-order which is infelicitous in the absence of contextual or discourse information is dubious. Moreover, he freely accepts cleft constructions, even when they are presented completely dissociated from discourse or context, despite the fact that these too are 'marked' in having a focus interpretation.[8] Thus, he did not correct sentences such as those in 47[9] or 65–67:

65 It is reading newspapers that I like the most   [OK]

66 It is for this reason that only Mary believes Peter was angry   [OK]

67 It is only John that I like   [OK]

The objection that Christopher's flawed performance on dislocation and topicalization structures is due to the fact that they were presented to him in written form is untenable for a more direct reason. In a later session he was presented with sequences like 68 orally, and was strikingly consistent in rejecting all examples involving dislocation or topicalization, even though they were presented to him suitably contextualized and with the appropriate intonation contour (a fall–rise on 'keys' and a high fall on 'car'):

68   I parked the car and went indoors. My keys I left in the car   [R]
68'   'I left my keys in the car'

It is important to emphasize that the validity of the above discussion and of the tentative account that follows rests on the assumption, generally accepted in the GB literature, that dislocation and topicalization structures *are* indeed fully grammatical. It should be mentioned, however, that native speakers differ in their judgement of the acceptability of such examples. Indeed, judgements differ not only in such a way that some speakers find them totally unacceptable, others marginal and others perfect, but some speakers have different intuitions about the relative well-formedness of the two construction types. If these judgements reflect a difference at the level of formal grammar, it would be possible to maintain that Christopher's rejection of such sentences is not a matter of defective performance. That is, he may, as a matter of dialectal difference, belong to the set of native speakers who find such constructions odd and unacceptable. On the other hand, if the interpretation of such sentences by native speakers who find them marginally acceptable relies heavily on the construction of an appropriate discourse context, Christopher's performance may be the result of inadequacy in this domain. That is, if he fails to exploit contextual information appropriately in general, this would imply that even the presentation of the relevant data in context would not affect his reaction. Keeping these reservations in mind, we none the less assume that such constructions are part of the grammar of English and that their status is fully grammatical. For the reasons outlined here, however, our account of Christopher's performance must remain tentative.

Extraposition   Let us now turn to the extraposition structures that are also characteristic of Christopher's non-native-like performance. As shown by the examples in 69–75 below, only a sub-set of the cases in which there is coreference between an 'it' in object position and a clause are unacceptable according to Christopher's judgements, as in 69–70. He accepts coreference between a pronoun and a CP if that pronoun is in subject position as in 71–73, or in object position followed by an adjective as in 74 and 75. Only if these last two conditions fail to obtain is the sentence rejected.

69   I resent it that you eat biscuits   [R]
69'   'I resent that you eat biscuits'

70   I didn't suspect it for a moment that you would fall   [R]
70' 'I didn't suspect for a moment that you would fall'

71   It bothers me that you could do such a thing   [OK]

72   It seems unnecessary that he should come   [OK]

73   It should be emphasised that not only is this crazy it
     is insane as well   [OK]

74   I find it strange that he failed the exams   [OK]

75   I consider it immoral that you lie to him   [OK]

The question is whether Christopher's performance on these structures should be related to his rejection of dislocation and topicalization structures.

Let us begin with a closer look at the 'extraposition' structures. In sentences where the pronoun precedes an adjective, the structure involves the verb sub-categorizing for a small clause. In other words, the pronoun is in a subject position, specifically the subject of the predicate AP. The relevant well-formedness condition in such cases is the Principle of Full Interpretation (or the Extended Projection Principle) specifying that predicates be licensed by a c-commanding subject. In sentences where the pronoun occurs in subject position, it is either raised there from the subject position of the small clause inside VP or, given Belletti and Rizzi's (1986) analysis of psych-verbs, from the VP complement position of the psych-verb, where raising is required for Case reasons. Given that the subject position in these cases is not a theta-position, raising of the pronoun is possible. Crucially the pronoun in such cases is not an expletive element and, as before, either the Principle of Full Interpretation or the Extended Projection Principle accounts for the syntactic properties of the pronoun. It is thus clear that both in constructions with the pronoun in subject position and in small clause structures, the pronoun is *independently* required; that is, its properties are not merely those of extraposition where it serves as a copy of the real, CP, antecedent. In examples like 69 and 70, on the other hand, which are clear cases of extraposition, the pronoun occupies the object position and is not required for any independent syntactic reasons.

The pronoun in object position cannot be an expletive, as it occupies a theta-position and, as it is understood as coindexed with the proposition, it bears no semantic features. Pesetsky (1991) argues that the representation of sentences such as 76, which contain a non-expletive 'it', involves a rule of '*if*-copying' at a post-LF level, and looks like 77:

76 I would hate it if John left

77 I would hate [that John left] if he left

It is fruitful to extend this line of reasoning to dislocation examples in general. In these constructions the pronominal element is a copy of the referential NP, and assuming that they always involve a predication relation between the antecedent and the copy (whether null or overt), their representation could be instantiated at a post-LF level in that the process of replacement and the well-formedness of the post-LF representation itself depend on the predication relation holding syntactically.

We can now understand the post-LF level as operating *beyond* the syntactic levels of representation, in particular, after LF. Operator–Variable structures in binding relations and quantification are represented at LF; coreference relations, which may or may not also involve Operator–Variable structures, are represented at post-LF.

With this discussion in mind, let us reconsider Christopher's performance on the relevant constructions. Assuming that his syntax is flawless, the fact that he does not correct operator–Variable structures such as wh-movement is straightforward. Syntactically, dislocation, topicalization and extraposition structures should also be allowed, but these involve a further, distinct level, which is also relevant to the representation of coreference relations. Assuming further that the nature of post-LF is such that it plays no role in deriving the meaning of sentences, their correct interpretation remains unaffected.

Relative clauses and cleft constructions also manifest coreference relations which do not involve binding in the LF sense and, as we have mentioned before, Christopher has no difficulty accepting such constructions. Why is this the case? Relative clauses involve predication but not copying: more specifically, the head of a relative clause is theta-marked and case-marked independently of its role as the head of the relative, as in 78 and 79:

78 I saw the man$_i$ Op$_i$ that t$_i$ gave the books to John

79 The person$_i$ Op$_i$ that Mary loved t$_i$ deserted her

Similarly, in cleft-constructions, the position of the clefted element is that of the predicate of a small clause so, all else being equal, they pattern with relatives and with structures where 'it' appears in the subject position of a small clause with an adjectival predicate.

In Tsimpli and Smith (1993) we suggested that Christopher's rejection of the English constructions discussed in this section could be attributed to a deficit associated with the unavailability of a level of representation beyond the syntax proper. Although the exact nature of this level was not specified, the crucial point is that we can maintain the claim that Christopher's syntax is identical to that of any other native speaker. Moreover, given that his problematic performance does not seem to affect interpretation – that is, he appears to understand the sentences involved – we can assume that his corrections of these structures indicate that they cause him unnecessary extra processing. This burden can then be reduced by deleting one of the two coreferential elements, leaving the other in its canonical position. Two points immediately arise: first, the need to provide independent evidence to support the idea that Christopher's linguistic performance deteriorates when the processing load is increased; second, the nature of the processing strategy. We supply independent evidence from Christopher's reactions both to nth order approximations to English (see pp. 73–4) and to garden-path constructions (see pp. 58–60). As regards the second issue, it could be that the problem is caused by the fact that, at a superficial level, the dislocated, topicalised or extraposed constituent does not appear in its canonical position. This would imply that Christopher should have similar problems with constructions that involve word-orders other than subject–verb–object (SVO), assuming that this is the basic sequence. Given that English exhibits fairly rigid word-order, this claim cannot be easily tested on his first language but, as will be seen in chapter 3, Christopher corrects clitic-left dislocation sentences in other languages, even though in most cases he assigns them the appropriate interpretation, just as he does with the English examples discussed in this section. Moreover, he seems to reject non-SVO structures in languages where this word-order is possible and even relatively unmarked. The problem remains, however, that because we are dealing with non-native languages in these cases, it is difficult to answer with certainty whether the problem is due to processing, exclusively to the syntax, or to an interaction between the two.

Garden-path and centre-embedding constructions

That processing problems may be the cause of Christopher's atypical reaction to dislocation and topicalization examples comes from the other major area where his judgements of well-formedness deviated from what one would expect simply on the basis of grammaticality: garden-path

sentences and centre-embedding constructions. Such examples have
figured prominently in the psycholinguistics literature (for a useful
summary, see Gorrell, 1995), and it is well-known that they cause
serious processing difficulties to normal subjects. Christopher is normally
happy to give judgements of well-formedness in both his native and other
languages, and when he was first confronted with these examples he
showed his normal readiness to co-operate. However, after a few minutes of
being confronted with ever more examples of a type which are clearly
problematic for him, he began to show signs of distress. Whereas normal
subjects are initially puzzled by such examples and then backtrack in order
to arrive at a coherent interpretation of them, Christopher appeared to be
completely bewildered. If Gorrell (1995: 65) is right in claiming
that 'if the correct resolution of an ambiguity cannot be accomplished
within the constraints of determinism, then conscious problem-solving is
required', and if we are right in suggesting that Christopher's judgements
stem from a central rather than a modular deficit, then this response is not
unexpected.

We began by confronting Christopher with simple examples of centre-
embedding of the kind given in 80–81, where he was asked to indicate his
preference for the various sentences:[10]

80(a)	He put down the child	[OK]
80(a)'	'il a mis l'enfant' [*sic*]	
80(b)	He put the child down	[R]

81(a)	He put down the child that had sat down	[OK]
81(b)	He put the child that had sat down down	[R]

Christopher's reactions indicated that he preferred the order
'verb + particle + NP' (see 80), implying that his rejection of 81(b) may
be the result of this rather than a processing difficulty with centre-
embedding as such. We then moved on to standard garden-path sentences
of the type illustrated in 82–87:[11]

82	While Mary was mending the sock fell on the floor	[R]

83	The horse raced past the barn fell	[R]

84	They told the girl that Ian liked the story	[OK]
84'	'Ipan sti kopela oti o Ian agapise tin istoria'	
	They told the girl [that Ian loved the story]	

85   Fred told the man that he hired a story   [OK]
85'   'O Friderikos ipe ston anthropo oti proselave mia istoria'
      Fred told the man [that he hired a story]

86   Susan convinced her friends were unreliable   [?]
86'   'I Susana pistike oti i fili tis itan anaksiopisti'
      Susan was convinced that her friends were unreliable

Christopher's judgments of sentences 84–86 are interesting in virtue of the Greek translations he provided. There is ambiguity in 84 between a reading where the CP is a complement of the verb and a reading where it is a relative clause modifying the object, 'the girl'. Christopher accepted this sentence and his translation shows that he assigned it the preferred interpretation where the CP is a complement.[12] The same strategy is implemented in 85, where the difference from 84 is that one reading of the structurally ambiguous sentence is bizarre. Yet Christopher both read it and translated it unambiguously as '[Fred told the man [that he hired a story]]'. In other words, he chose the CP complement structure despite the semantic anomaly of the resulting interpretation.

His reaction to 86 was puzzling. It was the only one of more than fifty examples that he failed to mark as either good or bad, and his Greek translation indicates that he had accessed the ungrammatical garden-path reading of the English. This translation is well-formed: the verb has been changed into the passive form and the complementiser *oti* has been inserted to introduce the clause *her friends were unreliable*. Although he failed to access the correct interpretation of the English sentence,[13] Christopher could obviously project a well-formed structure that made the input transparent for processing purposes. The same analysis was in fact transferred (perhaps by perseveration) to the next, unproblematic, example in 87, which Christopher changed from a grammatical 'garden-path' construction into an ungrammatical form that avoided the garden-path, although here his Greek translation shows that he had some difficulty with this interpretation.

87   John persuaded him friends were unreliable   [R]
87'   'John persuaded his friends were unreliable'
87"   'O Yanis ton – tu epise oti i fili itan anaksiopisti'

On balance it seems clear that processing sentences of this degree of complexity was beyond Christopher's ability, and hence lends support to our claim that the root of his anomalous responses lies in performance limitations rather than in a deficiency of his language module itself.

Semantics

Negative sentences

Christopher was tested on a range of negative sentences with the aim of investigating both his syntactic and his semantic and pragmatic abilities in this domain. His performance on simple negative constructions, with the negative element appearing in either the matrix or the embedded clause, was perfect – even when the sentences included negative polarity items or involved negative inversion (see pp. 45–7 and Appendix II for represent-ative examples). However, some aspects of negation – both syntactic and interpretational – caused him difficulty. The former involve examples where negation exhibits blocking effects in constructions involving adjunct or argument extraction (Rizzi, 1990; Laka, 1990), Tsimpli and Roussou, 1993). The latter centre on the interpretation of negative sentences that involve 'metalinguistic negation', a phenomenon that results from the interaction of semantic and pragmatic principles (Burton-Roberts, 1989, 1993; Carston, 1994; Chapman, 1993; Horn, 1989).

The first set of problematic examples was included in a test which consisted of negative and positive sentences where a preposed adjunct, either wh-moved or clefted, could be construed as modifying either the matrix or the embedded predicate. The motivation for this choice of material was that in positive sentences the adjunct can be associated with either the matrix or the embedded predicate, but in negative sentences the embedded reading is blocked. The sentences were presented to Christopher either in isolation or in the form of paired questions referring to a test sentence which was part of some longer passage. Examples of sentences which allow both construals are given in 88–89, together with Christopher's judgements:

88   When did Susan ask Bill to buy the book?
     A   She asked him yesterday
     B   She asked him to buy the book before he takes his exams
     Christopher: Both appropriate.

89   Why do you think Peter was angry?

A   Because Mary hasn't written to him for a long time
B   Because he slammed the door when he was leaving the class
Christopher: Both appropriate

Examples of negative sentences which allow only one construal elicited a parallel reaction from Christopher, as shown in 90 and 91:

90 It was yesterday that Mary didn't ask Bill to take her to the cinema
    A.   She didn't ask him yesterday but she asked him some other day
    B.   She didn't want to go to the cinema yesterday
    Christopher: Both appropriate

91 When the results of the history exams were announced every student was very surprised by the fact that Mary got the highest marks. It is well known that she is not a hard-working person and in all the other subjects she got very low marks. Mary said that she was very well-prepared for her history exams but once before she was caught copying from her book during the examination, so she does not seem to be a very honest person either.
    A.   It is for this reason that no one believes that Mary was telling the truth
         Does (A) mean:
          (i) This is the reason that nobody believes so?
         (ii) This is the reason for Mary not telling the truth?
         or can it mean both (i) and (ii)?
    Christopher: Both appropriate

As shown by Christopher's undifferentiated judgements, he fails to observe the blocking effect of adjunct extraction across a negative. Although his performance is at variance with that of normal speakers, such examples are notoriously difficult to process, for various reasons. Partly, identifying the syntactic effect of negation necessitates projecting an interpretation in which a plausible answer is associated exclusively with one clause or the other. This problem should, in principle, have been solved for Christopher by our presenting him with both the relevant alternatives, but he none the less failed to respond appropriately. It is not the case that such examples involve simply a judgement of the grammaticality of a single string; rather they necessitate the subject performing in addition an inferential operation on that string to determine whether or not the interpretation arrived at is coherent. Such examples provide difficulties of two kinds: on the one hand, they are syntactically complex and presumably hard to parse; on the other, they raise the processing problem we have just alluded to. Given

Christopher's putatively intact syntax and the problems he experiences in
other areas of processing, we assume that his judgements in this case are not
a function of the former domain.

The situation is clearer when we turn to examples of the type illustrated
in 92–96, which involve metalinguistic negation:

92   Goliath wasn't tall, he was a giant   [R]

93   I don't just like Alexia, I love her   [R]

94   Fred didn't contract a disease, he fell ill   [R]

95   John didn't try to translate the book into Armenian, he
      succeeded in translating it   [R]

96   I couldn't not see him   [R]
96'   'I could not see him'

Burton-Roberts (1989: 229) has suggested that many such sentences give
rise to a semantic contradiction (but see Carston, 1994, for discussion).
Despite this, they are universally acceptable because they are characteristically used to deny the validity of the preceding utterance, either in virtue
of lexical choice or phonological form. The successful interpretation of
such examples by normal speakers involves them in first identifying the
contradiction and then constructing a second-order representation in
which the scope of the negation, at some conceptual level, is restricted to a
sub-part of the proposition expressed. Christopher's rejection of such
examples is systematic and extends to languages other than English, as with
the Greek examples 97 and 98:

97   Dhen prospathisa na dhiavaso afto to vivlio, to dhiavasa
      xoris kamia dhiskolia   [R]
      'I didn't try to read this book, I read it without any difficulty'

98   O Yanis dhen ine xontros, ine varelas   [R]
      'Yanis is not fat, he is a barrel'

The only relevant examples which he accepts and understands
appropriately, despite their deviation from the orthographic norm, are of
the kind in 99:

99   He can't say tomahto, he says tomayto   [OK]

Presumably, the absence of contradiction in these cases and Christopher's familiarity with dialectal variation are jointly sufficient for him to find them unexceptionable. It is, moreover, striking that Christopher's rejection of examples involving metalinguistic negation extended even to those such as 100–101 where there was overt indication of the function of negation: namely, to qualify the degree to which the property negated held:

100   Goliath wasn't just tall, he was a giant   [R]

101   Goliath wasn't only tall, he was a giant   [R]

It is important to note that the contradiction in these examples is conceptually derived, that is, it does not fall within the grammar proper. For example, the deduction that a 'giant' is 'tall' involves accessing encyclopaedic information (or at least a meaning postulate) associated with the concept 'giant' and using this entailment as a stage in the interpretation process. Thus we can maintain our view that Christopher's anomalous reactions are independent of his purely linguistic knowledge. The implication is that he arrives at a contradiction at the first post-linguistic level, is unable to proceed any further and gives his judgement accordingly. If, as was said above, the subsequent stages of interpretation involve the construction of second-order representations, it follows that Christopher's judgements here are of a piece with his reaction to theory of mind tasks (see pp. 74–8 and chapter 5 for further discussion).

Rhetorical questions

The semantic and pragmatic limitations manifest in Christopher's difficulty in finding appropriate interpretations for certain negative sentences is further reflected in his reaction to rhetorical questions. Presented with examples of the kind in 102 and 103, where a rhetorical intention is either the only or the overwhelmingly preferred possibility, Christopher systematically offered an inappropriate, literal, interpretation:

102   Maria: 'It is my birthday today and nobody has wished me "Happy
        Birthday" yet.'
        Steven: 'Poor Maria! Well, who has ever remembered your birthday?'

103   Susan: 'I read today in the newspaper that someone killed a three-
         year-old child. I couldn't believe it. Who would kill a child?'
      Maria: 'I read it too. It's incredible.'

When asked what he thought would be a suitable response to the question
in 102, Christopher made various literal suggestions, and for 103 replied:
'A murderer'.

   Again, this reaction was consistent across languages, indicating that it
reflects a general conceptual deficit rather than some idiosyncratic
linguistic defect. Moreover, whereas all rhetorical questions in English
allow of a literal interpretation, however unnatural it might be in the case of
examples like 102 and 103, in Greek there are sentences which can only be
interpreted rhetorically because of their linguistic form.[14] For instance, the
example in 104 excludes a literal interpretation because of the presence of
the polarity item *pote* (= 'ever'):

104   I Maria ine poli paraponiara. Oli tin ora tin akus na lei:
      'Maria is always complaining. All the time you can hear her say:
      "Pjos me voithise pote na vro dhulia, na mazepso lefta, na aghoraso
         spiti?"
      "Who has ever helped me find a job, get money, (or) buy a house?" '

Christopher apparently found the question entirely normal, and answered
without hesitation: 'Her mother'.

   We assume that, as far as linguistic semantics is concerned, the
interpretation of wh-questions or focus-constructions necessarily involves
the representation of the clause excluding the presupposed wh- or focused
element (Tsimpli and Roussou, 1993). In the case of rhetorical questions of
the kind in 104, there is no presupposition involved, as the interpretational
possibilities of polarity items and wh-phrases have conflicting requirements. So, whereas a normal wh-question asks for the value of a variable,
which can range from referential to zero, in rhetorical questions only the
latter is possible.[15]

   Pragmatically, rhetorical questions are necessarily echoic, and hence
necessitate a further inferential process, probably in the form of the
construction of a second-order representation, just as in the case of
metalinguistic negation, the use/mention distinction, and so on, with all of
which Christopher has comparable difficulty (see pp. 74–8, and Smith and
Tsimpli, 1993).

   In sum, it appears that Christopher's (linguistic) semantics is intact and
that here as elsewhere his abnormal responses are attributable to the fact

that his interpretation process stops at a stage prior to enrichment to a full propositional form. Accordingly, constructions that *require* such enrichment are beyond the range of his linguistic talent.

Tense harmony

One last area in which Christopher's judgements deviate from those of normal speakers again straddles the border between the linguistic and the interpretational. It is well known that English displays sequence of tense phenomena, such that the time referred to in the embedded clause of an example like 105 may be present, despite the overt morphological marker of the past. That is, 105 is ambiguous, allowing a reading in which the time of speaking Berber is simultaneous either with the time of thinking or with the time of speech:[16]

105   John thought that Chris spoke Berber

Although such temporal dependence is the norm in English, it is possible to avoid it and use the so-called present tense in the embedded clause, as in 106:

106   John thought that Chris speaks Berber

with the effect that the speaker takes on responsibility for the current relevance of the embedded proposition. Christopher finds such non-harmonic tenses unacceptable. He changed 106 to 106', and corrected 107 in a similar way, as indicated:

106'   'John thought that Chris spoke Berber'

107   Some of us believed that only Hassan knows Arabic   [R]
107'   'Some of us believed that only Hassan knew Arabic'.

He insisted on such changes even when the non-matching version is as likely as the matching one, as illustrated in 108:

108   The defendant denied that he takes hashish   [R]
108'   'The defendant denied that he took hashish'

In fact, his responses to a range of such examples show that it is not only sequence of tense 'violations' that occasion him difficulty, but disharmonic temporal phenomena more generally. For instance, he rejects examples in which the temporal reference of a tense marker and a temporal adverbial clash, as in 109:

109   Fred left tomorrow according to the original plan   [R]
109′   'Fred will leave tomorrow according to the original plan'

and he ignores the idiosyncratic selectional requirements of certain predicates in order to ensure temporal matching, as in 110 and 111:

110   It is time that we left for Newcastle   [R]
110′   'It is time that we leave for Newcastle'

111   It is time that the children go to bed   [OK]

The requirement for time matching between a tense marker and an adverbial is apparently stronger than the requirement for straightforward sequence of tense matching, as Christopher corrected 112 to 112′, despite the fact that they are equally well-formed:

112   Tom heard that his friend was coming tomorrow   [R]
112′   'Tom heard that his friend will be coming tomorrow'

With the exception of the selectional requirement of the predicate 'it is time that', all these examples involve an interpretative stage in which some second-order representation is projected (see pp. 74–8). This representation may be a 'scheduled event', as in 109 and 112, where the scheduling requires an agent other than the speaker; or it may be the assumption of responsibility for the relevance of the embedded proposition by someone other than the subject of the sentence (specifically, the speaker). In either case, the pragmatic requirements conflict with the simplest interpretation of the syntax, resulting in Christopher's deviant judgements. Furthermore, if Hornstein (1990) is right in claiming that sequence of tense phenomena are to be accounted for at a level LF′ beyond LF, it may be the case that we can generalise the use we made of Pesetsky's 'post-LF' in accounting for topicalization and dislocation structures to this area as well. As Pesetsky's and Hornstein's notions of post-LF are not identical, we leave the issue unresolved.

These examples on the borderline between the grammatical and the pragmatic lead us naturally to a discussion of Christopher's pragmatic ability in general.

Pragmatics

One of the central issues that we have addressed is the extent to which Christopher's linguistic expertise is integrated into his general cognitive ability. If we are right in assuming that, to a first approximation, Christopher's condition is correctly characterized in terms of an intact language module co-existing with an impaired central system, then we expect to see the inappropriate or anomalous use of his (essentially perfect) linguistic knowledge that we have just documented. We now look more generally at his interpretation of utterances and his productive use of language both in spontaneous speech and in his reactions to further test material of a non-syntactic nature.

Spontaneous speech

Informal conversation with Christopher can tend to be monosyllabic, as illustrated in the dialogue in 113, recorded at the beginning of our second visit to see him (cited from Smith and Tsimpli, 1991: 326):

113 NS Do you know how this [tape-recorder] works, Christopher?
     C   Yes.
     NS How do you work it?
     C   Dunno.
     NS You don't know either. Have you got one?
     C   Yes.
     NS What do you use it for?
     C   Music.
     NS Music?
     C   Yes.
     NS Do you use it for languages as well?
     C   Spanish.
     NS Spanish?
     C   Yes.
     NS You've got Spanish cassettes?

C   Yes.
NS   And what are they like?
C   They are talking.
NS   What are they talking about?
C   Food, mainly.

Since we have got to know Christopher better, conversations are a little less laconic, but are still not entirely smooth and are frequently sidetracked by issues of language. Some flavour of normal interaction with him is apparent in the transcription in 114, recorded some two and a half years later than that in 113. Christopher had been giving well-formedness judgements on English sentences exemplifying metalinguistic negation, when he suddenly and spontaneously changed the subject. Crucial background knowledge (the exploitation of which by Christopher is itself not without interest) is that Ianthi comes from Chios, that Christopher had just had a holiday in Turkey, and that his sister Ann, who arrives in the middle of the discussion, had come to collect him and take him to her home for the week-end.

114   C   Do they also talk, um, I think that when, if I go to Greece, I might be able to, and pick up a bit of um, um of Chios accent as well.
      IT   Yes, definitely.
      C   Have you got any mon – do you spend any money in – How much Greek money do you have?
      IT   With me? Now?
      C   Yes.
      IT   I don't have any. Actually I have at home. I could bring you . . . eight hundred er drachmas.
      C   How much is that? I have Turkish . . .
      IT   It's not even three pounds. A pound is 350 drachmas.
      NS   How *was* your Turkish trip?
      C   It was OK.
      IT   Ah, you went to Turkey?
      C   Yes.
      IT   And?
      C   I, I spoke Turkish most of the time.
      IT   Really. How do you say 'how are you?' in Turkish?
      C   Nasılsınız
      IT   What?
      C   Nasılsınz [Mispronounced]

                                                          [Ann arrives]

A   Hello, Christopher.
C   Hello. [spoken expressionlessly]
NS   We were just asking Chris about his Turkish trip.
A   Well, I haven't seen you since you came home from Turkey,
     'cos you went with Steve and Adele.
C   Yes.
A   And we were still away, you see, so my elder brother brought
     him back.
C   Yes.
A   I've written him a couple of letters but he hasn't . . .
C   I sent you one. [spoken very forcefully]
A   Oh, he did; there was one waiting for me when I got back, and
     it said I should try belly-dancing as it was very easy.
                [All laugh, including Christopher]
C   Um I haven't packed my case yet, my case. [spoken worriedly]
A   That's all right. You don't need to pack everything . . . All you
     need is your razor.
C   Yes.
NS   And thank you for the card you sent me from Turkey, Chris.
C   Yes.

Christopher's contributions are either extremely brief, or tend to the
inconsequential. However, they are sufficiently germane to make formal
testing of his pragmatic abilities necessary and desirable. It is to this that we
turn next.

Inferencing

At the heart of the pragmatic theory we are using is the notion of relevance,
defined in terms of contextual effects and processing effort (see pp. 27–30).
The effort involved in computing these effects depends on 'three main
factors: the linguistic complexity of the utterance; the accessibility of the
context; and the inferential effort needed to compute the contextual effects
of the utterance in the chosen context' (Smith and Wilson, 1992: 4–5). In
the present case, it seems likely that *linguistic* decoding is the same for
Christopher as for anyone else (but see the discussion on pp. 182–7); and
his preoccupation with languages will always make a context involving
languages more accessible than one not involving them. What needs to be
investigated are the nature of, and any limits to, his inferencing ability.
   To this end we first conducted a number of tests designed to see if he
could use the standard forms of conversational inference typical of normal

users (see Smith and Tsimpli, 1991). Somewhat to our surprise, his performance in such tasks was close to faultless. Christopher is demonstrably able to use all the 'traditional' devices shown in 115(a)–(d), as well as the more theory-dependent processes in 116(a)–(b), and he can do it using encyclopaedic information of the usual kind:

115(a)	Modus ponens	$[P \to Q, P \text{ therefore } Q]$
(b)	Modus tollens	$[P \to Q, -Q \text{ therefore } -P]$
(c)	Modus tollendo ponens	$[P \text{ or } Q, -P \text{ therefore } Q]$
(d)	Modus ponendo tollens	$[P \text{ or } Q, P \text{ therefore } -Q]$

116(a)   Use of implicated assumptions
   (b)   Use of implicated conclusions

Examples of each of these are given in 117(a)–(d) and 118(a)–(b) respectively. In these examples, Christopher was presented with the dialogue in written form and asked to underline the appropriate response. His (correct) response is indicated in each case.

117(a)   Michael said: 'If George comes I shan't be able to play.'
   Fred said: 'George is coming.'
   Do you think Michael will be able to play?
   Yes/*No*/Don't know

   (b)   Anne asked: 'Can you drive a Rolls-Royce?'
   Billy answered: 'I don't drive big cars.'
   Do you think Billy can drive a Rolls-Royce?
   Yes/*No*/Don't know

   (c)   Angela said: 'Either Bill stole the bicycle or he was given it.'
   Mary said: 'Bill never steals.'
   Do you think Bill was given the bicycle?
   Yes/No/Don't know

   (d)   Mary said: 'Would you like to spend your holiday in Morocco or Algeria?'
   Helen replied: 'I'd like to go to Algeria'.
   Do you think Helen would like to go to Morocco?
   Yes/*No*/Don't know

118(a)   Bill said: 'Do you speak Portuguese?'
   Fred answered: 'I speak all the European languages.'

Do you think Fred can speak Portuguese?

Yes/No/Don't know

(b)   John said: 'Would you like some coffee?'
      Mary replied: 'Coffee would keep me awake.'
      Do you think Mary accepted the coffee?

Yes/*No*/Don't know

We also established that his abilities extended to more complex examples of the kind given in 118(c), indicating that he was not simply unthinkingly exploiting internalized 'frames': in this case to the effect that coffee and sleep don't go together, but was calculating effects 'on-line'.

118(c)   Mary said: 'I have to work all night tonight.'
         John said: 'Would you like some coffee?'
         Mary replied: 'Coffee would keep me awake.'
         Do you think Mary accepted the coffee?

Yes/No/Don't know

There were only two examples from this task with which he had difficulty or made mistakes. The first were cases where he failed to notice tricks, in which the relevant names in the dialogues had been switched; giving, for instance the exchange in 119 instead of that in 118(a):

119   Bill said: 'Do you speak Portuguese?'
      Fred answered: 'I speak all the European languages.'
      Do you think Bill can speak Portuguese?

Yes/No/Don't know

This 'mistake' seems both understandable and 'normal': at least to the extent that various of our colleagues gave the same judgement. The second was a case reproduced in 120, which gives rise to a contradiction:

120   Michael said: 'If George comes I shan't be able to play.'
      Fred said: 'If George comes and Nick comes you *will* be able to play.'
      Mary said: 'George is coming and Nick is coming.'
      Do you think Michael will be able to play?

Yes/No/*Don't know*

In these circumstances it is entirely appropriate to respond 'Don't know', even though a positive response, based on just the last two lines before the question, might have been expected.

Discourse structure

Christopher also performed adequately, if not perfectly, in a further test of his pragmatic ability revolving around the use of various discourse connectives. Blakemore (1987) has analysed a number of connectives in terms of their contribution to the processing rather than to the conceptual content of utterances (see also Wilson and Sperber, 1993). Thus, *so* does not contribute to the truth conditions of the sentence containing it, but rather instructs the hearer to process what follows it as a conclusion (usually, but not necessarily, a conclusion which follows from the immediately preceding utterance). *After all*, on the other hand, introduces not a conclusion but a piece of evidence for the proposition immediately preceding it. Accordingly, 121 has two interpretations, as differentially highlighted in 122:

121   The Minister was guilty. He resigned.

122(a)   The Minister was guilty. So he resigned.
   (b)   The Minister was guilty. After all he resigned.

The correct use of these connectives requires a subtle and sophisticated understanding of the discourse structure of whole texts, so we devised some simple examples to test Christopher's mastery of them. The test (see Smith and Tsimpli, 1991: 329–330) took the form of brief stories in which he had to fill a gap with one of the forms *After all/Anyway/Moreover/So/Therefore/You see*, as illustrated in 123:

123(a)   Jill was waiting for her boyfriend in the park. She was very depressed and miserable – she'd just lost the pet dog her boyfriend had given her.

After all

   (b)   Last year I planned to study a new language. Alan said that Norwegian was easy to learn, but Fred said Danish was even easier – I decided to start Danish.

So

We had anticipated *You see* rather than *After all* in 123(a), but Christopher's choice is clearly not inappropriate, and his performance was generally acceptable and displayed ability in procedural as well as conceptual interpretation.

It should not be thought that Christopher's pragmatic ability is without problems. In a number of areas he shows a marked disability *vis-à-vis* normal speakers. An obvious example in a related domain is his poor identification of appropriate referents. Given examples such as those in 124:

124(a) John telephoned Bill. He needed to speak to him.
  (b) John telephoned Bill. He refused to speak to him.

where the pragmatically natural interpretation is for *he* to refer to John in 124(a) but to Bill in 124(b), Christopher consistently interpreted the *he* in both examples as referring to John. That this is not due to a syntactic condition, requiring that the antecedent of a pronoun be a subject, is clear from his ready acceptance of examples like 125:

125(a) John telephoned Mary. She refused to talk to him.
  (b) John telephoned Mary. She wanted to talk to him.

A more striking example of his failure adequately to deal with the structure of discourse is provided by his reaction to *n*th order approximations to English texts, of the kind illustrated in 126.[17] In these passages we have respectively seventh-, fifth-, second- and tenth-order approximations to English. For example, 126(a) was constructed by taking seven words from a passage, omitting the next seven words, taking the next seven, and so on. Christopher noticed nothing wrong with this text and happily translated it into French. With 126(b) he observed that the text was 'jumbled' but still proceeded to translate it unconcernedly into Greek.[18] Only with 126(c), constructed by taking the first two words of successive paragraphs, did he baulk at translating.

126(a) The Pharaohs had enough stone to build enough papyrus, too, so there was nothing as large as floating islands. The papyrus a modest fifth of the Sphinx's length. Of the underworld of mummies and stood it made us realise what giant structures.

  (b) In the year 1786, an at the High Court in discovery. He was Sir William an oriental scholar before reading, three years earlier, he had Sanskrit, the language in which texts of India are written, fourth to the sixth centuries, was no longer spoken but scholarship and literature.

  (c) The lawsuits in 1980 in a previously best but not my real the pope Woody was he was meanwhile she by Annie when Woody Mia found at the in February Valentine with still Mia Woody held the story people argued most courts in the one thing.

(d)   The idea of languages being related to one another was many of the languages of contemporary Europe – for instance Italian, in grammatical structure. Indeed in this case the explanation was was Latin, which of course exists today in written form.

It is unlikely that anyone with normal pragmatic ability would react as unconcernedly as Christopher did to these passages. This accommodation is doubtless due in part to his consistent desire to co-operate in everything demanded of him and to say and do what he believes we want, but it is also we think symptomatic of the mismatch between his linguistic abilities and his rhetorical exploitation of them. We return to the issue in chapter 5.

Meta-representation

In addition to his problems with reference assignment and discourse structure, Christopher had systematic difficulty with a range of other phenomena, all of them involving second-order or meta-representation. By way of providing introductory background, it should perhaps be noted that Christopher is invariably truthful – indeed, he seems to be incapable of lying – and that he has a considerable dislike of fiction in general (and of children's books in particular). Fiction and lying both involve representing states of affairs as other than they are, something apparently alien to him. This behaviour is consistent with a number of other pragmatic idio-syncrasies, some of which we have already discussed earlier in this chapter, and which are listed in 127:

127(a)   His inability to handle irony and metaphor
   (b)   His inability to understand jokes
   (c)   His insensitivity to the use/mention distinction
   (d)   His judgements of metalinguistic negation
   (e)   His judgements of 'scheduling' sentences.

All of these involve what Sperber and Wilson (1986) term 'interpretive use', a form of second-order representation. They write (ibid.: 228–9):

any representation with a propositional form . . . can be used to represent things in two ways. It can represent some state of affairs in virtue of its propositional form being true of that state of affairs; in this case . . . the representation is . . . used *descriptively*. Or it can represent some other representation which also has a propositional form – a thought, for instance – in virtue of a resemblance between the two propositional forms; in this case . . . the first representation is an interpretation of the second one, . . . it is used *interpretively*.

We illustrate each of the categories in 127 in turn. Confronted with examples such as those in 128, where the context or co-text made only an ironic interpretation plausible, Christopher provided a literal interpretation or, in the case of 128(c), simply rejected the sequence as unacceptable:

128(a) He's a fine friend
   (b) John and Mary went to a party, where both of them became very sick, and had to go home early, because John gave Mary too much to eat and drink. John said: 'What a wonderful party!' What do you think Mary said?
   (c) The judge told the traitor that he was 'a credit to his country'. Do you agree?

In Sperber and Wilson's terms, irony and related tropes are examples of echoic 'interpretive use' which involve 'second-degree interpretations of someone else's thought' (ibid.: 238). Such meta-representational ability would appear to be impaired in Christopher (for further discussion see pp. 174–87). His reaction to metaphor is similar. Although he can cope to a limited extent with standardised metaphors – his response to 'Why is Jesus called the Good Shepherd?' was 'He herded people' – his reaction to being asked to explain the meaning of anything more creative, such as the examples in 129:

129(a) No man is an island
   (b) Standing on the shoulders of giants

was a baffled 'I don't know'.

The case of jokes is similar. Whether all jokes are treated as involving interpretive use, as Ferrar (1993) has suggested, or as simply necessitating the accessing of two different interpretations (see, e.g., Jodlowiecz, 1991), they clearly impose considerable cognitive demands on the hearer; demands that appear to be beyond Christopher's abilities. If he hears or reads a joke of an institutionalized form, as in 130:

130 Diner: 'Waiter, what's that fly doing in my soup?'
     Waiter: 'It looks like the breast-stroke, Sir'.

he recognizes it, on the basis of his general knowledge, as a joke, and gives a
stylized 'ha, ha, ha', but neither appreciates it nor is able to explain why one
might find it funny. Similarly, if provided with both question and answer,
he can recognize riddles (as in 131):

131   What animal can you never trust?
      A cheetah.

as such, and can access the two meanings of the phonological sequence
involved, but is more taken with the incorrect spelling of the 'cheat'
interpretation than with any possible wit. That this is not simply a
reflection of sophistication in his sense of humour is seen in his reaction to
examples such as those from Lukes and Galnoor (1987), all of which he
took to be literal, and unfunny, stories, with no apparent inkling that they
might be in any way bizarre, incongruous or humorous. Consider the
examples in 132–134, with Christopher's reaction to them.

132   On the other side of the moon the Russian and American astronauts
      met, and said: 'Endlich können wir unsere Muttersprache sprechen'.

When asked why the astronauts spoke in German, Christopher replied
'because they were on the moon', and ended saying that the story 'doesn't
make sense'.

133   A Russian minister visits a car factory. The manager goes out of his
      way to show him around and at the end of the tour offers the minister
      a free car.
          'Oh no,' says the minister, 'I can't accept it'.
          'In that case I'll sell it to you for five roubles.'
          The minister hands him a ten rouble bill: 'In that case, I'll have
      two.'

After Christopher had insisted on translating this story into Greek, the
conversation in 133' ensued:

133' NS   Why didn't he accept the car?
      C   Because it was only five roubles.
      NS   But he then said he'd want to buy two. So why do you think he
           said that?
      C   Because five roubles times two is ten roubles.

NS   And why do you think that story's there?
C   Pass.
IT   Is this a joke?
C   Yes.
IT   Why?
C   Dhen ksero [I don't know].

134   Castro visits Moscow and is taken on a tour by Brezhnev. First they
go for a drink and Castro praises the beer.
'Yes, it was provided by our good friends from Czechoslovakia.'
Next they go for a ride in a car and Castro admires the car.
'Yes, these cars are provided by our good friends from
Czechoslovakia.'
They drive to an exhibition of beautiful cut glass, which Castro
greatly admires.
'Yes, this glass comes from our good friends in Czechoslovakia.'
'They must be very good friends,' says Castro.
'Yes, they must,' says Brezhnev.

We again interrogated Christopher about this story, and he was able to tell
us without hesitation that Castro was 'the Cuban leader', but probing about
the punch line produced the exchange in 134':

134'   NS   Why do you think he says that?
C   Because they ARE very good friends.
NS   Why are they very good friends?
C   Because they live next door to Brezhnev.
NS   So why does that make them good friends?
C   Because they like each other.
NS   Is this a serious story or a joke?
C   It's a serious story.[19]

A further case involving the representation of a representation is
provided by the *mention* as opposed to the *use* of linguistic terms.
Christopher's interpretation of mention is less clear-cut, appearing to
depend in part on whether appropriate orthographic conventions are
respected or not. Thus he finds 135(a) acceptable, but 135(b) unacceptable:

135(a)   Dogs have four legs
    (b)   Dogs has four letters

but he happily accepted both sentences in 136:

136(a)   Chris is a great linguist
  (b)   'Chris' is a great name

Given his preoccupation with the written word and his sensitivity to
typographical errors and punctuation, it may be that these examples are
liable to alternative explanation.

A slightly different example of second-order representation involving
metalinguistic negation has already been discussed on pp. 60–3, where it
was argued that the speaker is rejecting not the truth of the proposition
expressed, but the linguistic form of the representation by which it is
expressed. Although he once accepted 137:

137   John isn't just tall, he's a giant

he was usually consistent in rejecting all such examples. Indeed, on re-
testing with comparable examples (e.g., 100 and 101 above and their
translation equivalents in Greek), he again consistently rejected them.

A final example of Christopher's difficulty in this meta-representational
domain arises with the interpretation of 'scheduled events', where the
linguistic form represents a plan for a future state of affairs rather than a
description of that state of affairs itself. Such examples typically give rise to
deviations from canonical temporal structure, as in example 112 above and
138 below, both of which Christopher unambiguously rejected:

138   John said that Harry is leaving the next day

The first of these, 112, involves a sub-sequence 'his friend was coming
tomorrow' which is superficially temporally anomalous, and the second is
only interpretable as a historic present, another case of interpretive use (see
Smith, 1990, for discussion). In chapter 5 we argue that all these cases in
which Christopher experiences difficulty with second-order representations fall together with other aspects of his mental make-up.

Conclusion

Although the picture is extremely complex, we think that we have
established that Christopher's linguistic competence in his first language is
as rich and as sophisticated as that of any native speaker. Moreover, despite
his intellectual deficit, this linguistic knowledge is integrated into his

general cognitive functioning sufficiently to allow him to pass some tests of his pragmatic (inferential) ability successfully. None the less, it is clear that some linguistic phenomena lie outside his capabilities. We have argued that these are *not* due to a deficit in his grammar, but rather that they arise from processing difficulties which involve the interaction of his modular, linguistic faculty with central system operations. We return to the details of this interaction in the final chapter, after we have investigated more closely his abilities in his non-native languages.

3

'Second' Languages

Introduction

As we have seen, Christopher's linguistic abilities are exceptional both in the *speed* with which he acquires new languages and in his *fluency* in those languages he already knows but in which his knowledge is clearly not native-like.[1] By 'fluency' in this case we mean the ease with which he switches from one language to another in translation and in metalinguistic tasks, whether these are straightforward or 'forced choice' grammaticality judgements, the correction of sentences in various languages, and so on. Detailed discussion of Christopher's performance in acquiring new languages under conditions of controlled input is provided in the next chapter. In this chapter we concentrate on his linguistic performance in some of his 'second' languages, in particular those in which he is most competent: Modern Greek, French, Spanish and Italian.

The initial focus of our discussion will be to distinguish different aspects of his grammatical knowledge, contrasting his morphological and lexical prowess on the one hand with his less remarkable syntactic ability on the other. We account for this contrast by reference to three variables: the difference between grammatical choices that are parameterized; interference from the first language; and Christopher's resistance to the expected effects of a consistent input. As regards the first of these, we argue for a position which excludes the possibility of parameter resetting, at least in Christopher's case. For the second, we note that interference from English is both overwhelming and abnormally persistent with Christopher. The third, we suspect, should be attributed to the effects of computational complexity; that is, any input that diverges from the patterns of the first language gives rise to processing complexity, that complexity increasing in direct proportion to the degree of divergence.

Background Information

Christopher's real 'second' language is French, which he started learning at about the age of six from his sister's French books. He was taught Spanish for a brief period at a later stage and he has learned Italian from books. When we first met him early in 1990, his spoken Greek was not as fluent as it is at the time of writing, some four years later, but his knowledge of the case, agreement and declension paradigms was strikingly good even then. He claims to have learned the language from Hugo's *Greek in Three Months*, which teaches the spoken ('*demotic*') form of modern Greek. However, Christopher is also aware of certain regular differences between this and 'puristic' ('*katharevousa*') Greek, indicating that his exposure to the language cannot have been restricted to this book. Moreover, his familiarity with the issue of 'diglossia' in Greece (see, e.g., Ferguson, 1959) as well as with differences among Cretan, Cypriot and standard Greek, demonstrates that his encyclopaedic knowledge of languages that we have already documented in chapter 1 includes Greek.

For each of the languages of which he claimed any knowledge, the first task Christopher was presented with was translation. Although his performance left much to be desired both from the point of view of pragmatic coherence and the syntactic well-formedness of the output (see pp. 12–18 and 156–63), his translation has been a fairly accurate source of information about his grasp of vocabulary and about his facility in accessing lexical items and mapping their morphological properties from one language to another. However, subsequent tasks which included translation only as a subsidiary component indicate that his translating abilities underestimate his knowledge of the syntactic and semantic properties of the languages he knows. This leads us to believe that, impressive though it may be, Christopher's performance in translation is not an accurate reflection of his knowledge. In the normal case, translation involves interaction between linguistic, lexical and central processes, jointly deployed to bring about effective communication (see, e.g., Gutt, 1991). In Christopher's case, however, communication seems to be largely irrelevant, with translation being simply a linguistic exercise, largely divorced from central control. It is accordingly not surprising that translation underestimates his real knowledge. We return to this issue on pp. 163–4.

The Lexicon

Before discussing specific syntactic phenomena in Christopher's second languages, we should observe that he manifests an attention bordering on obsession with the orthographic form of words and their morphological make-up. This is particularly evident with languages that have a fairly rich morphological system and with those that do not make use of the Roman alphabet, such as Greek, Hindi and Arabic. At each meeting Christopher shows great interest, even joy, in isolating words from newspapers, writing them on a piece of paper and (depending on their syntactic category), identifying appropriate features of their number, case, gender and agreement systems. He then typically provides, or asks us to provide, other forms of the paradigm in question, often with comments on usage. The exchanges in 1–4 are typical:

1 (Discussing Hindi)[2]
   C   'I will walk' – maī . . .
   NS   'Maī ja:ū:ga:'
   C   Or if it's a woman
   NS   Or 'maī ja:ū:gi:'

   C   And if it's 'we'?
   NS   'Ham ja:ēge'
   C   For both. [*Scilicet* male and female]
   NS   That's right.

2 (Reading a Hindi grammar (McGregor, 1972))
   C   I thought 'book' was 'kita:b', but 'pustak' is another word
   NS   You can use either.
   C   Well as I'm a foreigner, I can use 'kita:b'.
   NS   Yes.
   C   Because 'pustak' would be a bit more formal.

3 (Discussing Berber with Jamal Ouhalla)
   C   Is it 'g' 'h' in all tenses?
   JO   Yes.
   C   For 'you'?
   JO   In all tenses it's 'g' 'h'.
   C   For 'you'?
   JO   For 'you' it's *t* at the beginning and *t* at the end.[3]
   C   Is that the present tense? . . . How does it become the perfect?
        . . . Is it the same for both men and women? . . .

4 (Discussing the conjugation of the verb 'to cover' that he had come across in a Greek newspaper: he spontaneously wrote down the three examples in (a)–(c) in Greek script; 'pp' stands for 'past participle')

(a) 'Imun skepasmenos me vroma'
was-1s covered-pp-masc.sing.nom with filth
(b) 'Imun skepasmeni me supa'
was-1s covered-pp-fem.sing.nom with soup
(c) 'Imaste skepasmenes me omixli'
were-1p covered-pp-fem.plur.nom with fog

It is striking that this behaviour was associated not only with languages such as Greek in which he is quite fluent, but also with languages such as Hindi and Arabic in which his knowledge is relatively limited. In fact, when he was introduced to Berber, a language he didn't know at all previously (see chapter 4), he concentrated his efforts to a considerable extent on identifying morphological distinctions and trying to form paradigms for newly acquired lexical items.

This aspect of Christopher's performance reflects his enhanced ability to register pairings of morphological form and semantic content on minimal exposure. As a result of induction or instruction, this process gives rise to the construction of a rule of derivational or inflectional morphology. Consider in particular overgeneralization, where he produces new forms in a paradigm of which he has not previously encountered all instances. To be able to do this he must exploit a rule he has already acquired and then identify a stem in the stimulus to which the rule can apply. Overgeneralization is particularly evident in cases where Christopher's knowledge of the language is very limited, such as in Berber, Hindi and Arabic, but even in Greek he sometimes produces forms that are not part of the language. For instance, on analogy with regular forms such as those in 5(a) and 5(b), he produced the form in 5(c):

5(a) li-menos ('solved')
 (b) grammenos ('written') (from *graf-menos* by regular assimilation)
 (c) 'Ime vlemmenos' – I am seen
   am seen

where the first person masculine singular participial ending *-menos* has been added to the present stem *vlep-* (with concomitant assimilation), even though this form does not exist.

As has been frequently noted in the literature on first language acquisition, overgeneralisation is a commonly attested phenomenon which constitutes evidence for the rule-based nature of grammars (see Brown and Bellugi, 1964: 150, for a typical early example). Somewhat more problematically it has also figured prominently in discussions of the nature and role of negative evidence in the acquisition of a range of structures exemplified by dative-shift and causativization (Bowerman, 1987; Braine, 1963; Marcus et al., 1992; Pinker, 1989; Randall, 1990). The central issue is that it is unclear how a child can 'retreat' from a grammar which overgeneralizes if positive evidence alone serves as the trigger for the development of its knowledge of lexical and morphological structure.

An evaluation of alternative solutions to this problem is not directly relevant to our discussion, but we wish to emphasize that over-generalization, as manifest in production errors, is mainly associated with information in the lexical component. Such errors include processes of both derivational and inflectional morphology: the affixation of the past tense morpheme -ed to verbs, of the plural morpheme -s to nouns; the formation of *sunny* from *sun*, and so on. By contrast, overgeneralization is *not* associated with phenomena dependent on parameter-setting, where this is understood (along the lines described on pp. 22–5) as the matching of parametric values with appropriate functional heads in the structure of the clause. In this framework, parametrically based aspects of first language acquisition are argued to be deterministic, with the learning mechanism allowing only a minimal number of alternative possibilities to be entertained at any stage of grammatical development (cf. Borer and Wexler, 1987).[4] Morphological and lexical aspects of language acquisition are in large part independent of parameterisation, are non-deterministic and allow of correspondingly different developmental processes.

However familiar or unfamiliar he is with the languages concerned, the most impressive aspect of Christopher's linguistic talent is his learning, accurate or inaccurate, of lexical and morphological information. Assuming that the morphological component is a distinct sub-part of the human mind-brain whose internal structure can be independently characterized, we wish to argue that learning lexical and morphological properties does not entail learning the syntax associated with those properties. In the normal case native speakers give evidence of their linguistic competence by showing mastery of all components of the grammar. However, if we can establish the respective autonomy of the lexical-cum-morphological component on the one hand, and the syntactic component on the other, we expect to find cases of development or impairment in which lexical rather than syntactic entities are affected. In first language acquisition it is generally agreed that the presence or absence of functional morphemes is not necessarily reflected in the syntactic realization of functional features (or heads) in clause structure.[5] For instance, the absence in early acquisition of a morphologically realized determiner system does not entail the absence of a D head and its projection in the structure of the clause (see Wexler, 1993), as such a projection may be independently required for semantic or syntactic reasons, (e.g., for abstract Case-assignment, for characterizing definiteness or the notion of 'argument', and so on). Conversely, the presence of some restricted 'tense' morphemes in the early stages of acquisition does not imply that this morphology is used in the same way as in the target grammar to denote tense distinctions (represented by syntactic features on a T head, for instance).[6]

Christopher acquires morphological rules faster than syntactic ones, and we will try to show in the following sections that not only does morphology have priority over syntax, but that there is a striking contrast between those of his language-learning mechanisms which are sensitive to lexical and morphological properties and those which are operative at the syntactic level. The basis of Christopher's exceptional second language learning ability, then, lies in this 'enhanced' lexical sub-component, which appears to be constantly receptive to new input of the relevant kind: that is, he is sensitive to lexical rather than to sentential properties.[7] In contrast, structural differences between his first and other languages appear difficult for him, in that he fails to integrate them into his linguistic knowledge, even in those languages to which he has had prolonged exposure, including direct and explicit instruction (see pp. 91–120).

Cognates

The contrast between the lexical and the syntactic components implies that their development in second language acquisition need be neither parallel nor equally successful. Research into the L2 lexicon suggests that the representation of lexical items of both native and non-native languages should be included in a single component in which the *entries* of words, and in particular their recognition elements (Marslen-Wilson, 1989) or *addresses,* are linked on the basis of morpho-phonological similarities (Carroll, 1992). 'Cognate-pairs' are then argued to be represented in the lexicon by linked addresses, thus indicating their coexistence in a single cognitive system (see Fromkin, 1987). In 'cognate-pairing' the idea is that lexical recognition involves the activation of an L1 address by an L2 stimulus.

The definition of 'cognate' is a matter of controversy. We follow Carroll (1992) and Cristoffanini et al. (1986) in assuming that similarities in morphological and/or phonological rather than etymological or semantic properties are the defining characteristics of cognates.[8] This assumption is consistent with the idea that morpho-phonological properties are the primary formal features on which lexical accessing operates, as suggested by the Cohort Model (Marslen-Wilson, 1987, 1989; Marslen-Wilson and Tyler, 1980). The underlying assumption is that the lexicon is the 'central link' in language processing and probably in language learning as well. In the psychological model of linguistic and morphological representations adopted here, this assumption is plausible in that the lexical entry is associated with, but still distinct from, the logical and encyclopaedic entries. In lexical retrieval the lexical entry is primarily triggered in the *access* and *selection* stages, which are automatic and non-inferential; the logical and encyclopaedic entries are activated during the *integration* stage, which presumably involves contextual information and inferencing.

According to Carroll (1992), the (flawed) performance of L2 learners in tasks involving cognates suggests that the accessing of lexical items is a modular process in that morpho-phonological information contained in the lexical component is retrieved without resort to other lexical information of a semantic/pragmatic nature. In other words, cognate-pairing is an encapsulated quasi-perceptual phenomenon rather than a central process involving the use of propositional knowledge and inferencing.[9]

Against the background of our earlier suggestion that Christopher's lexical component is in some way enhanced, but that his second language learning is in many ways similar to that of normal subjects, we devised a set of items to test his performance on the translation of French–English cognates. For various reasons our predictions as to his performance in such a test could not be absolutely clear. In particular, although we expected his performance to be average or above average, his unusual talent made it unclear to what extent it would be flawed on cognate-pairs in comparison, on the one hand, with his translation of non-cognates, and on the other, with the performance of the controls. As will be seen on pp. 156–62, Christopher's translation of connected text is anomalous in containing an abnormally high proportion of contextually inappropriate lexical items. These include errors involving cognates, as in example 6; errors involving ambiguous lexical items, where the inappropriate reading is chosen, as in 7; and errors involving items which are conceptually appropriate but not linguistically correct or related, as in 8:

6 Translating from Swedish, he rendered 'knä' as *knee*, instead of the appropriate *lap*

7 Translating from Hindi, he rendered 'magar' as *but*, instead of the correct *crocodile*

8 Translating from German to French, he rendered 'die in seine Richtung hinaufblickten' as 'qui dans son direction *passaient*', instead of the correct *regardaient*

The range of these examples and the complication caused by the potential use of different strategies for the translation of texts, as opposed to the accessing and translation of listed individual lexical items, makes the formulation of an explicit hypothesis rather problematic. None the less we prepared the test on the assumption that his performance would cast further light on the similarities and differences between him and normal second language learners.

The test material   The test consisted of a single list of lexical items to be translated from French into English. There were in all 372 randomly ordered words and short phrases, of which 199 were cognates (*faux amis*) and the rest (173) were non-cognates. On the basis of the results elicited from Christopher and the controls, these items can be allocated to various different categories as illustrated in 9:

9   Examples of Christopher's translations on the 'cognate' task and how
     they were scored

A	*enfant* – 'child'	Correct, etymologically unrelated[10]
B	*orphelin* – 'orphan'	Correct, etymologically related
B'	*actuel* – 'present'	Correct, subset of B where the English cognate was successfully avoided
C	*formellement* – 'formally'	Marginal, not wrong but highly dis-preferred[11]
D	*candidement* – 'candidly'	Wrong, because of false morphological identity: i.e. an archetypal example of a '*faux ami*' cognate.[12]
D'	*attirer* – 'wear'	Wrong, subset of D where the (non-cognate) English translation was caused by a cognate synonym
E	*songe* – 'care'	Wrong, for reasons independent of cognateness
F	*borne* – '——'	Unknown and not guessed: i.e. a blank response
F'	*fat* – '——'	Subset of F where an English look-alike was not chosen

For various reasons the 'cognate' status of some of the examples is not self-evident. First, some of them, such as *crudités*, have both an etymologically connected meaning ('crudities', 'coarse remarks') and an etymologically unconnected one ('snacks consisting of raw fruit and vegetables'). In a simple (decontextualised) translation exercise, either interpretation is possible. Second, some of the examples, such as *rat* have a preferred interpretation which is equivalent to the English congener, as well as various metaphorical subsidiary meanings. Third, some examples, e.g. *fabrique* ('factory' rather than 'fabric'), were treated by Christopher in a way that avoided the problem presented by classical *faux amis*, as he translated it as a verb ('makes') rather than the noun which usually occasions the problem. To achieve some measure of objectivity we have included as 'cognates' in our calculations all and only those items which appear as *faux amis* in Kirk-Greene (1990). As a result, some of the words included, e.g. *pendant*, are not treated as cognates here, even though they have obvious look-alikes in English.

A final complication as regards the scoring and interpretation of the results is that in some cases subjects obviously fell into the 'trap' afforded by the cognate, in other cases they did not: most obviously when they simply omitted any translation at all. This important point is obscured by the fact that we have scored mistakes and omissions equivalently: that is, we have ignored the distinctions within categories A,B,C and D,E,F in 9. We have, however, taken cognisance of such differences in the relevant parts of the discussion. As controls, we used fourteen adults whose exposure to and fluency in French varied considerably. Eleven of the controls were native English speakers, one was a native-speaker of French, and two others were not native speakers of English and had French as their second language. Appendix IV specifies for each of the controls his/her highest formal or other qualification in their L2 French.

Results and discussion   Full details of the results appear in Appendix IV. There are three salient aspects of these results which are in need of explanation. First, whatever processes are responsible for the pattern of errors discovered, they are clearly the same for Christopher as for normal subjects, as it is striking that his results are entirely comparable with, though in general somewhat better than, those of the controls. He ranks fourth best, and does signally better than several subjects with an A-level qualification. Second, everyone performed *worse* on cognates than on non-cognates. Third, polymorphemic items elicited systematically more mistakes than monomorphemic items. Intuitively, the last two phenomena are attributable to the facilitatory effect of transparent morphological structure and of cognateness. In the case of *faux amis*, the facilitatory effect of cognateness is misleading essentially by definition, and structural transparency enhances the effect. We need to develop a formal account which will accommodate these intuitions.

We begin with the last point: the fact that the set of cognates consisted of both monomorphemic items, such as *cane* ('duck'),[13] and polymorphemic ones, such as *candidement* ('ingenuously'), a distinction which underlay a major difference in Christopher's errors. Specifically, he gave a correct translation of less than a quarter (23 per cent) of polymorphemic cognates, but of over half (54 per cent) of monomorphemic cognates. Results from a sub-set of the controls indicate a similar discrepancy, although the percentages are generally lower, due to Christopher's greater success in the task overall. We assume that this is a reflection of the processes in the lexical component that are responsible for decomposing lexical items and assigning them a representation in terms of affixes and stems. Within lexical phonology there has been considerable discussion of the properties of such internal structure under the rubric of 'level-ordering' (Siegel, 1977; Kiparsky, 1982, 1983).

Levels of affixation are defined on the basis of the nature of the change (phonological or morphological) that is effected on the stem, on the degree of productivity of the relevant rule, and so on. Using this theory, Gordon (1989) investigated first language acquisition data in the domain of morphological affixation, paying particular attention to questions of productivity and overgeneralization. He argued that, to accommodate a number of false predictions of the theory, it is necessary to redefine the *domain of application* for Level 1 processes and allow for a *merger* of stem and affix into a single morph. He assumes that the redefinition, which essentially allows iterated Level 1 affixation in words like *direct-ion-al-ity*, is responsible for the constraints imposed on further morphological processes, while 'merger' determines which items count as *words* and which as combinations of stem + affix. Thus, *#directionality#* is a simplex, while *#Darwin#ism#*, for instance, is a complex, equivalent to two 'words'. These boundary distinctions are ultimately determined by the nature of the processes involved (e.g. depending on whether affixation causes phonological changes or not) which in turn constrain further morphological operations.

This suggests that in our cognates test the crucial distinction underlying the different rate of success for simple and complex words is the nature of the lexical representations involved. Presumably, simple items are represented as *words* (to which no morphological rules have applied), while complex items involve a representation including internal *boundaries* separating the stem from any affixes. Assuming that the lexical representations of the first and subsequent languages are included at a single location within the same component, matching the addresses of polymorphemic items in different languages would consist in identifying the sub-components specified in the lexical representation of the input and putting them into a one-to-one relation with the output. That is, the input and output lexical representations should, as far as possible, be identically structured. For example, *candidement* would be represented as *#candide#ment#*, and *candidly* would be similarly represented as *#candid#ly#*, where in each case the structure results from the operation of a Level 2 process. However, if the 'error' in the cognate-pair were due exclusively to the morphophonological properties of the stem, the difference in success rate between simple and complex cognates would not be clear.

In Cristoffanini et al.'s (1986) study it is argued that decomposition of the input form into a stem and affix complex takes place prior to address activation. Their claim is based on similar results obtained from derivationally and inflectionally complex words as well as cognates. The morphological analysis is understood in the light of the affix-stripping model of Taft and Forster (1975), which makes identification of the stem possible prior to activation of the corresponding address. In view of the difference in the success rate between simple and complex cognates, the assumption that morphological analysis precedes lexical activation is problematic. Although the lexical representation involved may differ, as suggested by the lexical theory of level-ordering outlined above, and although morphological decomposition may be available, it does not appear that these two assumptions have consequences for the on-line processing of lexical items, at least not in terms of temporally ordered operations. In other words, Carroll's claim that the morphological analysis may occur simultaneously or after lexical activation, but not prior to it, seems to give rise to a more plausible account of these results.

Given the above considerations, we tentatively suggest that lexical activation in the case of complex cognates involves not only morphophonological triggering, as in the case of simple cognates, but also mapping of the affixal element to the corresponding L1 item. If morphological decomposition is necessarily part of the activation and selection process, it is natural to assume that the feature specifications on both the stem and any affixes are brought into play as well. One consequence of identifying this information is the activation of requirements occasioned by the bound nature of affixes. In accessing terms this could be interpreted as a search for the appropriate host category. On the assumption that such processes are triggered automatically on the basis of a perceptual input, the activation of the (incorrect) cognate-pairing because of shared morphophonological properties would give rise to a representation where the stem + affix are immediately selected. Note that accessing information about the affixal or non-affixal nature of a morpheme is necessary to exclude cases where the affix is phonologically identical to a non-affixal morpheme in the language. For example -*hood* and -*ship* in *neighbourhood* and *relationship* should activate the entry for the affix and not that for the noun. Assuming that knowledge of the morphological identity of a given affix is already part of the learner's second language, and given that affixes in productive derivational and inflectional processes belong to the closed class, access and selection of the appropriate address in the first language should be regulated by whatever morphological rules of affixation govern the well-formedness of stem + affix complexes in the first and second languages respectively. Simple cognates, on the other hand, require mapping of primitive rather than complex forms, and are thus activated by exclusively morphophonological properties. The implication is that, *ceteris paribus*, if a complex cognate in the second language does not correspond to a lexical representation of the same level in the first language, then cognate-pairing should not be equally facilitated, and so success rate should increase. This prediction, however, requires further evidence which goes beyond the scope of the current discussion (see Tsimpli and Smith, 1994).

As we have documented, Christopher's performance is, overall, above average. This result further supports our earlier claim that his lexical component is 'enhanced' in the sense that the knowledge or information stored in this system is intact and its retrieval is uninhibited by any deficits associated with central operations. With respect to the ratio between the cognate and non-cognate items, Christopher's results are equivalent to those of the controls. In other words, as is the case with the controls, his 'errors' with cognate-pairs are significantly more than those with non-cognate items. This implies that whatever processes are operative in accessing the *addresses* of lexical items in the first and second languages of normal speakers are also implemented in Christopher's parallel performance. Furthermore, the results obtained are consistent with the suggestion that the lexicon of the second language is part of a lexical component which includes *all* lexical information of both native and nonnative languages.

Syntax

As documented in the previous chapter, Christopher's syntactic competence in his first language is comparable to that of any other native speaker, except for the dislocation and topicalization structures discussed on pp. 48–57. Moreover, given his evident awareness of the morphological properties of words in his various second languages, we concentrated on dimensions along which the structure of these languages differs from English. The major phenomena we concentrated on were variations in word-order, the possibility of null subjects, *that*-trace effects, extraction possibilities in wh-movement and focus-constructions, clitic-doubling and clitic left dislocation (CLLD) constructions.

In Smith and Tsimpli (1991) and Tsimpli and Smith (1991) we discussed Christopher's second language learning in relation to the pro-drop parameter (Rizzi, 1986, 1990) which is assumed to involve the correlation of three properties; null subjects, apparent violations of *that-t* effects and postverbal subjects (but see Chao, 1980; Brandi and Cordin, 1989; Abangma, 1992, for various problematic cases). His performance does not jibe well with the standard formulation of the parameter in question: while null subjects appear to be well integrated into his grammars of Greek, Spanish and Italian, he consistently rejects the effects of the other two properties: the possibility of postverbal subjects and the extraction of a subject out of an embedded clause introduced by an overt complementizer.

In our account of his performance we remained agnostic about the possibility of parameter resetting in second language acquisition, but entertained the possibility that his second language learning was like that of ordinary second language learners, the implication being that a general theory of second language acquisition could account for Christopher's performance as well. Although there appears to be supporting evidence for this claim, we remain sceptical about the generality of this solution for the following reasons (see also the discussion on pp. 35–6). In order to justify any specific suggestions about the availability or otherwise of parameter resetting in second language acquisition in the usual case of an adult second language learner (as well as in Christopher's case) we need to compare data from more advanced stages of the development of the second language, and define the similarities in these. All else being equal, an average second language learner can attain considerable fluency, in many cases approximating near-native competence. At the very least, it is possible to define for such speakers developmental stages pertaining to their performance in specific syntactic domains. It is not obviously possible to do this in Christopher's case. For example, during the last four years of his exposure to Greek, involving considerable spoken and written input (including occasional explicit instruction), Christopher's Greek has demonstrably improved in terms of his vocabulary, his fluency in spontaneous conversation and the incidence of his morphological errors. Yet his judgements on phenomena such as clitic-doubling, the possibilities of variant word-orders, and the structure of relative clauses (among other things) remain as flawed as at the beginning of the study. Similar observations hold for other languages in which Christopher was tested both at the early stages and later on in the project. Moreover, a definitive comparison between Christopher's second language learning and the second language learning of normal subjects would have to involve holding constant the nature of the input, the setting and method of exposure to the new language, and so on, none of which can be controlled in this case. It also appears that Christopher's case involves a processing or pragmatic deficit, as is suggested by his performance on *inter alia* metalinguistic negation, garden-path constructions and translation (see pp. 62–3, 57–60, 156–64). Accordingly, whatever the underlying cause for this deficit may be, it is clear that in his case it could interact with second language learning. In other words, there are enough superficially language-related differences between Christopher and normal second language learners to make any conclusions drawn from similarities in the early stages of second language learning necessarily tentative. With these caveats about the difficulty of generalizing conclusions derived from the study of Christopher to the normal case out of the way, we turn to the details of his syntactic performance.

Data collection

Christopher was tested on the syntactic phenomena mentioned above in a number of ways (see the discussion of his knowledge of English, pp. 44–60). In grammaticality judgement tasks, he was asked to give his reaction to each of the sentences presented and, if he was able, to correct those he considered ungrammatical. He was also presented with pairs of sentences, one of which was grammatical and one ungrammatical, where his task was simply to identify them appropriately. We also gave him sentence-completion tasks, where the missing items were functional elements, such as determiners, clitics, subjunctive and future particles, and so on. Finally he was presented with three or four versions of the same sentence, differing from each other only with respect to Case-marking of arguments or the use of functional categories (see Smith and Tsimpli, 1991), and Appendix V for examples).

Although translation was not usually required of him in these tasks, Christopher was always keen to provide a translated version of the sentences in either written or oral form (a typical example of his efforts is provided in figure 3.1). His general strategy in these tasks was to read the sentences to himself – he read aloud only when he was specifically asked to do so – and to perform the task in what seemed to us the quickest possible way. In other words, regardless of whether he considered the sentence grammatical or ungrammatical, there was usually no sign of delay or rehearsal in his reaction.

In the following examples illustrating the range of constructions he was exposed to, unannotated sentences are grammatical in the language concerned, while ungrammatical examples are indicated with a preceding asterisk. Christopher's judgements and corrections are given as in chapter 2 (note 1); that is, a following [R] indicates that Christopher 'rejected' or 'required a change' in the sentence; [OK] indicates that he found it

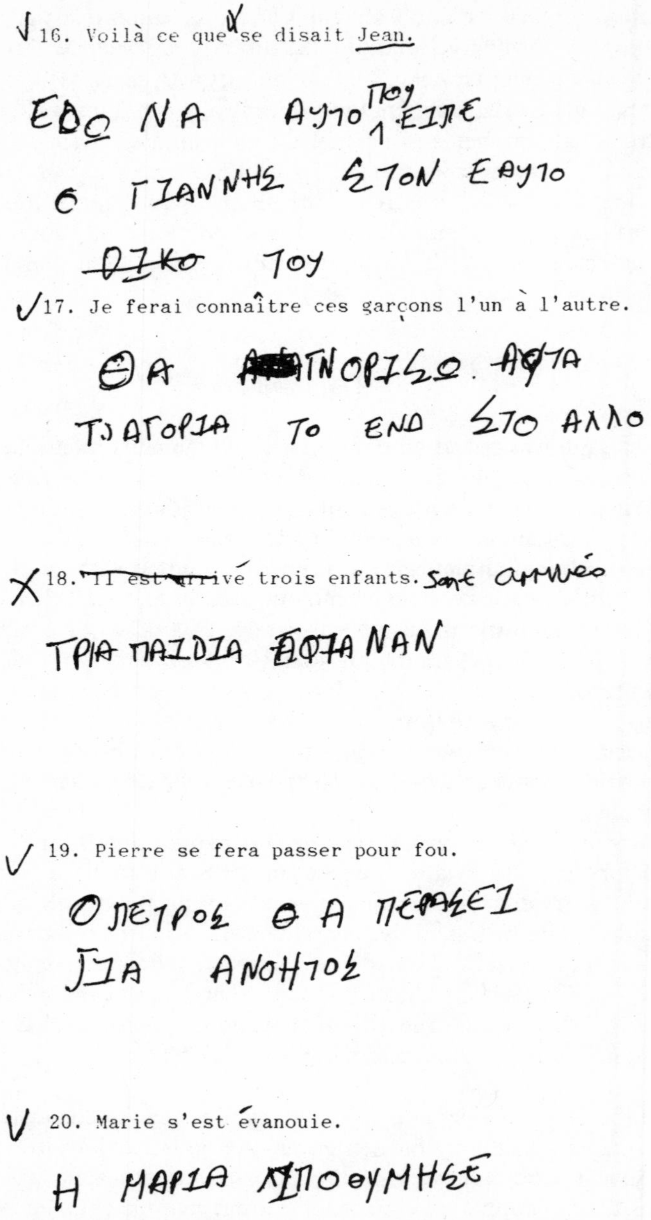

√ 16. Voilà ce que se disait Jean.

ΕΔΩ ΝΑ ΑΥΤΟ ^{ΠΟΥ} ΕΙΠΕ

Ο ΓΙΑΝΝΗΣ ΣΤΟΝ ΕΑΥΤΟ

~~ΔΙΚΟ~~ ΤΟΥ

√ 17. Je ferai connaître ces garçons l'un à l'autre.

ΘΑ ~~ΑΓΝΟΡΙΣΩ~~. ΑΦΤΑ

ΤJΑΓΟΡΙΑ ΤΟ ΕΝΑ ΣΤΟ ΑΛΛΟ

Χ 18. Il est arrivé trois enfants. ~~sont~~ arrivés

ΤΡΙΑ ΠΑΙΔΙΑ ~~ΕΦΤΑ~~ ΝΑΝ

√ 19. Pierre se fera passer pour fou.

Ο ΠΕΤΡΟΣ ΘΑ ΠΕΡΑΣΕΙ

JΙΑ ΑΝΟΗΤΟΣ

√ 20. Marie s'est évanouie.

Η ΜΑΡΙΑ ΑΠΟΘΥΜΗΣΕ

Figure 3.1 *Example of Christopher's judgement of sentences of French and their translation into Greek*

acceptable; and his own suggestions, marked by identical numbering but with prime notation, follow in inverted commas. We have also provided a literal and a free translation for all the sentences and, as before, Greek examples were presented to him in the Greek script.

Null subjects

Christopher uses and accepts null subjects in Greek, Spanish and Italian[14] both in spontaneous speech and in the tasks he was presented with throughout the course of the project. Representative examples from the three languages are:

Greek
10 Pote tha sas ksanadho?   [OK]
    when will you-see-1s
    When will I see you again?

11 Jirise piso jati ksexase ta klidhia tu   [OK]
    came-3s back because forgot-3s the keys his
    He came back because he forgot his keys

Italian
12 Era già andata quando ha telefonato a Luisa   [OK]
    was already gone when has telephoned to Luisa
    She had already gone when he/she telephoned Luisa

13 Sono andati via   [OK]
    are gone away
    They have left

Spanish
14 Creo que llaman a la puerta   [OK]
    think-1s that knock-3p to the door
    I think that they are knocking at the door

15 No quiero ver a alguien   [OK]
    not want-1s see to anybody
    I don't want to see someone

When explicitly asked about the possibility of subject-dropping in a number of languages Christopher's response was consistent, confident and appropriate:

16   La escribió Jorge a Juan   [R]
      it wrote-3s Jorge to Juan
      Jorge wrote it to Juan
16'   'Jorge la escribió a Juan'

      IT   Can you drop 'Jorge'?
      C   Not in English, but in Greek and Spanish.
      IT   In other languages?
      C   Italian
      NS   Berber?
      C   That as well
      NS   French?
      C   No

Given that Christopher's first language, English, has the negative setting for the null-subject parameter, the obvious question that is raised by these data is that of parameter resetting. Specifically, on the basis of Christopher's performance on relevant data from null-subject languages, it is plausible to conclude that his second language grammars have the appropriate target value. In particular, it should be noted that no 'transfer' errors were detected in this area and, as will be shown in the discussion of Berber and Epun in chapter 4, null subjects were assumed to be a possible option in these new languages, even though no input data included them. We return to this issue below.

That-*trace effects*

In general, Christopher consistently rejected wh-interrogatives involving subject-extraction out of an embedded clause introduced by an overt complementizer, in all of Spanish, Greek and Italian (see Tsimpli and Smith, 1991). This is a direct reflection of his judgements on the corresponding English data, which were appropriate in that he considered the sentences ungrammatical, and corrected them by deleting the complementizer (see pp. 44–8). However, although his reaction to such data was consistently to reject them, his correction strategy was not always the same, as can be seen in the following examples:

Greek
17   Pjos ipan oti paretithike?   [R]
      who-nom said-3p that resigned-3s
      Who did they say resigned?

17'   *'Pjos ipan oti aftos paretithike?'
      who said-3p that he-nom resigned

Immediately after the above (ungrammatical) correction, Christopher translated 17 into English:

C   'Who did they say that disappeared?'
IT   'Paretithike' means 'resigned'
C   'If it's 'ipan' [said-3p] it should be 'paretithikan' [resigned-3p] to go with 'ipan'.

18   Pjos ipan oti emine monos tu ekino to vradhi?   [R]
      who-nom said-3p that stayed own his that the evening
      Who did they say stayed alone that evening?

18'   'Pjos ipe oti emine monos tu ekino to vradhi?'
      who said-3s that stayed-3s own his that the evening
      'Who said that he would be staying on his own that evening?'
      [Christopher's English translation of the corrected 18]

19   Pjos mu-ipes oti jirise?   [R]
      who me-told-2s that returned-3s
      Who did you tell me returned?

19'   'Pjos mu-ipe oti jirise?'
      who me-told-3s that returned-3s
      Who told me that he returned?

Spanish
20   ¿Quién dijo Andrea que se quedó solo?   [R]
      who said-3s Andrea that stayed alone
      Who did Andrea say stayed alone?

Christopher's rejection of 20 was followed by the discussion below:

C   Is it *a Andrea* [to Andrea]?
IT   No.
C   Andrea dijo que quién . . .
IT   Where would you put *quién*?
C   Before *se*.
      Andrea said . . . [this is C's first attempt to translate 20]
IT   But it's a question.

    C   Did Andrea say who was staying alone?
Ipe o Andreas oti pjos emene monos, moni?
[literally: *Did Andreas say that who stayed alone-masc.,
alone-fem.]

21   ¿Quién dijeron que se fue?   [R]
who said-3p that left-3s
Who did they say left?

21'(a)   '¿Quienes dijeron que se fueron?'
who said-3p that left-3p

  (b)   'Pji eleghan oti efighan?'
[C's Greek translation of the corrected 21]
Who-pl. say-imp-3p that left-3p
Who were saying that they left?

  (c)   'Who said they left?'
[C's English translation of the corrected 21]

22   ¿Quién pensó la maestra que era el mejor alumno?   [R]
who thought the teacher that was the best student
Who did the teacher think was the best student?

22'(a)   '¿Pensó la maestra que quién era el mejor alumno?'
thought the teacher that who was the best student

  (b)   'Nomise i dhaskala pjos itan o kaliteros mathitis?'
thought the teacher who was the best pupil
[C's Greek translation of the corrected 22]

  (c)   'The teacher thought who was the best pupil?'
[C's English translation of the corrected 22]

Similar findings were obtained with the Italian data (cf. Tsimpli and Smith, 1991: 177). As shown by the above data, there are according to Christopher basically two ways of salvaging the construction: either by changing the sentence into a yes–no interrogative and repositioning the wh-phrase to the embedded subject position (cf. 19 and 22), or by changing the agreement marking on the matrix verb to correspond to that of the verb in the embedded clause (cf. 18, 19 and 20). Notice, crucially, that in none of the examples did he delete the complementizer. In other words, although his judgements were identical to the ones he provided for similar English interrogatives, his corrections were not similar. This fact presumably indicates his knowledge that deletion of the (non-interrogative) complementizer is not allowed in these languages, at least not in the constructions discussed here. Thus the picture presented by Christopher's performance on this construction involves incorrect, but only partial, transfer from the English first language, that is, in considering *that-t* structures ungrammatical.

According to Rizzi (1990) the correlation between the availability of null subjects and apparent violations of *that-t* effects lies in the possibility, available in null-subject languages, of postverbal subjects and subject extraction from the postverbal position. As we have already seen, null subjects are accepted and produced by Christopher in the sub-set of null-subject languages he was tested on, while subject extraction is not possible. What remains to be seen is his performance in constructions that involve postverbal subjects.

Postverbal subjects

Given this formulation of the pro-drop parameter, postverbal subjects right-adjoin to VP, so in this section we shall concentrate on cases where the subject appears in VP-final position, that is, VOS structures. However, Christopher's reaction to word-orders other than SVO, patterns with his reaction to VOS structures, so whether post-verbal subjects should be regarded, in his case, as an instance of a more general constraint on word-order in his second languages or as related specifically to the null-subject parameter remains, at this stage, open. Consider the following examples:

Italian

23   Mi ha chiaramente visto Maria[15]   [R]
        me has clearly seen Maria
        Maria saw me clearly
23'   'Maria mi ha visto chiaramente'
        Maria me has seen clearly

24   L'ha buttato via Susanna   [R]
        it has thrown away Susan
        Susan has thrown it away
24'   Susanna l'ha buttato via

25   Ha letto il libro Susanna   [R]
        has read the book Susan

Susan has read the book
25′ 'Susanna ha letto il libro'
Susanna has read the book

26   Ha vinto le elezioni una studentessa   [R]
has won the elections one student-fem
A student won the elections
26′ 'Una studentessa ha vinto le elezioni'

27   Sono arrivate tre donne   [R]
are arrived three women
Three women have arrived
27′ 'Tre donne sono arrivate'

28   Non mi ha parlato mai il professore   [R]
not me has talked never the professor
The professor has never talked to me
28′ 'Il professore non mi ha parlato mai'
the professor not me has talked never

Spanish
29   Leyó el libro Juan   [R]
read the book Juan
Juan read the book
29′ 'Juan leyó el libro'
Juan read the book

30   Telefoneó María   [R]
telephoned Maria
Maria telephoned
30′ 'María telefoneó'
Maria telephoned

Greek
31   Stamatise to aftokinito brosta sto vivliopolio o Yanis [R]
stopped-3s the car in-front to-the bookshop the-nom Yanis
Yanis stopped the car in front of the bookshop
31′ 'O Yanis stamatise to aftokinito brosta sto vivliopolio'
the Yanis stopped the car in-front to-the bookshop

32   Aghorase fruta i Maria xtes stin aghora   [R]
bought-3s fruit the Maria yesterday to-the market

Maria bought fruit in the market yesterday
32'   'I Maria aghorase fruta xtes stin aghora'
the Maria bought fruit yesterday to-the market

33   Dhiavase tin efimeridha mesa sto treno i Katja   [R]
read-3s the newspaper in the train the Katja
Katja read the newspaper in the train
33'   'I Katja dhiavase tin efimeridha mesa sto treno'
the Katja read the newspaper in the train

33' was followed by the conversation below:

    C   I Katja dhiavase . . . (*Katja read* . . .)
    IT   Boris na to exis kapu allu? (*Can you have this* [the subject] *anywhere else?*)
    C   Sta Aglika (*In English* . . .) [pointing to the beginning of the sentence]
    IT   Sta Ellinika boris na to exis sto telos? (*In Greek, can you have it at the end?*)
    C   Sta Ghallika (*In French*)
    IT   Sta Ghallika boris. Sta Ellinika? (*In French you can. In Greek?*)
    C   I Katja dhiavase . . . (*Katja read* . . .)

As shown by the above examples, Christopher's corrections of sentences involving subjects in VP-final position is consistently to place the subject in clause-initial position.[16] To the extent that this aspect of his performance and his inappropriate rejection of *that-t* constructions in the same languages can be grouped together as properties of the null-subject parameter in Christopher's second language learning, the overall picture is obscure. In Tsimpli and Smith (1991) we suggested an account based on the assumption that Christopher's performance indicated that the grammars of his relevant 'second' languages did not involve parameter-resetting. Instead, the acceptability of null-subjects was associated with an alternative strategy adopted by the second language grammar, whereby the agreement morpheme has the status of a subject-clitic, which attaches to the verbal complex at the PF level (as with Kayne's, 1989, account of subject clitics in French). As this is a possibility made available by UG, we can maintain the claim that second language learning is UG-constrained both in general and in Christopher's case. In our earlier article, this strategy was assumed to be available in second and interlanguage grammars and Christopher's learning strategies were accommodated within this general approach. This conclusion was based on similarities between results from Christopher and from normal adult second language learners of null-subject languages (Liceras, 1989; Tsimpli and Roussou, 1991; White, 1985). Given the discussion above, we would like to maintain the idea that, in virtue of being UG-constrained, the account involving the agreement affix as opposed to the subject-clitic strategy can be argued to hold both in general and in Christopher's case. We will refrain, however, from drawing wider generalizations about second language acquisition on the basis of other aspects of Christopher's second language grammars, because of the disparity between his linguistic and mental abilities on the one hand and those of average second language learners on the other.

Word order

VS(O)   In Spanish and Modern Greek VS(O) order is, in general, an unmarked option.[17] Theoretically, the representation involved in such cases of postverbal subjects in non-interrogative structures can be captured either by verb-raising to Comp or by failure of the subject to move to Spec,IP (see Philippaki-Warburton, 1985; Tsimpli, 1990, for Greek; and Torrego, 1984, for Spanish). Note that in Spanish and Modern Greek, unlike languages such as Arabic (see Koopman and Sportiche, 1991), there is subject–verb agreement on both pre- and postverbal subjects. VS order is commonly found in the written as well as the spoken form of the language, and Christopher's familiarity with Spanish and (especially) Greek guarantees that his encounter with such input data has been frequent and regular. When presented with grammaticality judgement tasks, however, it appears that the acceptability level of postverbal subjects for him is very low, as witness the following examples:

Greek

34   *O Nikos simfonise na dhen pari o Petros ti dhulia   [R]
          the Nikos agreed sub. not take-3s the Petros the job
          Nikos agreed that Peter should not take the job
34'   'O Nikos simfonise na min pari ton Petro sti dhulia'
          the Nikos agreed sub. not take-3s the Petro to-the job
          Nikos agreed not to take Petro to the job/to work
34"   'Nick agreed not pari to (*take the*) . . . that he would not
          take Peter to work'
          [C's translation of 34]

Spanish

35   Vio Carlos la película   [R]

saw Carlos the film
Carlos saw the film
35′ 'Carlos vio la película'

Example 34 is ungrammatical because of the choice of the negator *dhen*, which is incompatible with the subjunctive marker *na* (see Tsimpli and Roussou, 1992). Christopher corrected the original cause of the ungrammaticality, but he also changed the case-marking of the postverbal NP from nominative to accusative, and the NP object into a prepositional phrase. Thus, the interpretation of the sentence involves a Control structure where the postverbal subject became an object and the direct object a locative prepositional phrase.[18]

That the above changes were not random but consistent with the interpretation intended by Christopher is obvious from his translation in 34″. In cases like this, where Christopher's corrections give rise to equally grammatical sentences, his performance may indicate his preference for preverbal subjects rather than his ignorance of the possibility of postverbal subjects in the language tested.[19]

There are, however, certain constructions in which the difference between preverbal and postverbal subjects gives rise to a corresponding difference of (relative) grammaticality. In such cases, Christopher's amendments result in (relatively) unacceptable sentences. The next examples involve Greek relative clauses which, in the unmarked case, do not allow any constituent to intervene between the complementizer and the verb:

Greek

36 I ghineka xeretise ton astinomiko pu gnorize o fititis   [R]
    the woman greeted the policeman that knew the-nom student
    The woman greeted the policeman that the student knew
36′ ??'I ghineka xeretise ton astinomiko pu o fititis gnorize'
    the woman greeted the policeman that the-nom student knew

37 O kleftis apantise tis erotisis pu rotise o dhikastis   [R]
    the thief answered the questions that asked the-nom judge
    The thief answered the questions that the judge asked
37′ ??'O kleftis apantise tis erotisis pu o dhikastis rotise'
    the thief answered the questions that the-nom judge asked

Another construction in which preverbal subjects are marginal, in that their interpretation is that of a topic, is adjunct clauses involving verbs in the gerundival form. In such constructions, if one or both subjects in the matrix and the adjunct clause are null, their interpretation is always coreferential.[20]

38   Fevgontas o Yanis apo to sinema, sinantise tin Maria   [R]
      leaving the-nom Yanis from the cinema met-3s the-acc Maria
      While Yanis was leaving the cinema, he met Maria
38'   ??'O Yanis fevgontas apo to sinema, sinatise ti Maria'
      the-nom Yanis leaving from the cinema met the-acc Maria

Further evidence of the strategy Christopher is adopting comes from the examples below, which are from sentence-completion tasks:

39   Ipe adio se olus fevgontas — Maria
      said goodbye to all leaving — Maria
      When Maria was leaving, she said goodbye to everybody
39'   'Ipe adio se olus fevgontas ti Maria'
      said-3s goodbye to all leaving the-acc Maria
39"   'He said to them leaving . . . He said goodbye to all, leaving Maria'
      [C's translation of 39']

Example 39' is ungrammatical because the verb in the adjunct clause is intransitive, so the only possible form of case-marking on the determiner is the nominative. Christopher's choice indicates two problems. The first involves a possible transfer from his first language, where the verb 'leave', unlike the Greek *fevgho*, allows either the transitive or the intransitive reading. The second problem is associated with his general performance on constructions which include postverbal subjects.

40   Vlepontas — Maria — apotelesmata ton eksetaseon, stenoxorethike poli
      seeing — Maria — results the-gen exams, upset-PA-3s very
      When Maria saw the results of the exams, she was very upset
40'   *'Vlepontas ti Maria ta apotelesmata ton eksetaseon, stenoxorethike poli'
      seeing the-acc Maria the-acc results the-gen exams, upset-PA-3s very
40"   *'Seeing Mary the results of the examinations, he worried a lot'
      [Christopher's translation of 40']

      IT   So, who saw Mary?
      C   He did (pointing to the verb *stenoxorethike* [upset], the man did.
           So, I put *aftos* [he] in front.

Christopher correctly assigned a coreferential reading to the two subjects, but he incorrectly assumed that both subjects are null, hence the ungrammaticality. The gerund *vlepontas* is incorrectly assigned two objects, as shown by the accusative marking on the respective determiners. That this is the only possible interpretation according to Christopher is further illustrated by 40' and the comment following it.[21]

In interrogatives, Christopher's acceptability judgements in his second languages are appropriate. In both wh-questions and yes–no questions, subject–verb inversion is the only choice available. Note, moreover, that when tested on interrogatives where the auxiliary (*have*) + participle construction is used, Christopher correctly places the subject following the participle, rather than between the auxiliary and the participial form as in English. In other words, there is no transfer effect in his judgement of these cases:

Greek

41   *Exi o Kostas grapsi tin ekthesi tu?   [R]
      has the Kostas written the essay his
      Has Kostas written his essay?
41'   'Exi grapsi o Kostas tin ekthesi tu?'
      has written the Kostas the essay his

42   *Exi i Katerina pai sinema?   [R]
      Has the Katerina gone cinema
      Has Katerina gone to the cinema?
42'   'Exi pai i Katerina sinema?'
      has gone the Katerina cinema

43   *Ixes esi mathi gallika sto sxolio?   [R]
      had-2s you learned French to-the school
      Had you learned French at school?
43'   'Ixes mathi esi gallika sto sxolio?'
      had-2s learned you French to-the school

44   *Exoun ta pedhia jirisi apo to sxolio?   [R]
      have-3p the children returned from the school
      Have the children returned from school?
44'   'Exoun jirisi ta pedhia apo to sxolio?'
      have-3p returned the children from the school

Spanish

45   *¿Ha Pedro leído el libro?   [R]
      has Pedro read the book

Has Pedro read the book?
45' '¿Ha leído el libro Pedro?'
45" 'Did Peter read the book?'
      [C's translation of 45']

According to Suñer (1987), the 'have' + participle complex in Spanish behaves like a single morphophonological unit, hence head-movement to Comp includes both the auxiliary and the main verb. In Greek the situation is not so straightforward: the auxiliary bears independent stress and, although the subject cannot intervene in cases of verb-raising to Comp, aspectual adverbials can:

46   Pjo vivlio exis sxedhon teliosi?
      which book have-2s almost finished
      Which book have you almost finished?

47   Exi idhi fighi o Petros?
      have-3s already left the-nom Petros
      Has Petros already left?

Christopher seems to be aware of this possibility in Greek interrogatives, as is evident from his reaction to the following sentences:

48   Exis pote dhiavasi afto to vivlio?   [OK]
      have-2s ever read this the book
      Have you ever read this book?

49   *Exi i Maria pai pote sti Kipro?   [R]
      have-3s the Maria gone ever to-the Cyprus
      Has Maria ever been to Cyprus?
49'   'Exi pote pai i Maria sti Kipro?'
      have-3s ever gone the Maria to-the Cyprus

We assume that Christopher's appropriate corrections to 'have' + participle constructions in Greek and Spanish indicate that transfer is not involved. This view is confirmed by the fact that other morphophonological properties of the construction, which differentiate Greek and Spanish, also appear to be integrated into Christopher's competence in the respective languages.

Clitic-left dislocation and clitic-doubling On pp. 48–54 we discussed Christopher's problematic performance in English dislocation and topicalization structures. The account suggested there is crucially based on the distinction between levels of representation relevant to quantifiers and operators, and those also involving coreferentiality between a constituent in an A'-non-operator position and an argument NP or CP. We considered dislocation, topicalization, and some cases of extraposition relevant to this level of representation, referred to as post-LF.

If we now turn to clitic-left dislocation (CLLD) constructions in Greek, Italian and Spanish, we find that Christopher's judgements are entirely consistent in that he invariably corrects these sentences, just as he did left dislocation (LD) structures in English:

Greek
50   Tis Elenis, o Yanis dhen tis-to estile to gramma   [R]
      the-gen Eleni, the-nom Yanis not her-it sent the letter
      Yanis didn't send the letter to Eleni
50'   'O Yanis dhen estile to gramma tis Elenis'
      the-nom Yanis not sent the letter the-gen Eleni

51   Tu pedhiu tu kani mathima i Maria   [R]
      the-gen child him-make-3s lesson the-nom Maria
      Maria teaches the child
51'   'Tu pedhiu kani mathima i Maria'
      the-gen child does lesson the-nom Maria

When asked to translate 51, Christopher replied: 'Don't know'.

Italian
52   Le notizie, Maria le ha sentite   [R]
      the news, Maria them has heard
      Maria has heard the news
52'   'Maria ha sentito le notizie'
      Maria has heard the news

Spanish
53   *A la película, Juan la vio[22]   [R]
      to the film, John it saw
      The film, John saw it
53'   *'Juan vio a la película'
      John saw the film

According to Cinque (1991), neither LD nor CLLD involve Operator-variable chains, but LD differs from CLLD structures in various respects: CLLD is associated with NPs (hence the obligatory presence of the clitic), it can apply to root and embedded clauses, and more than one NP in a single clause can be associated with a CLLD structure.[23] LD is mostly restricted to matrix clauses, and is associated with non-NPs, while the number of left-dislocated constituents is restricted to one. Despite these differences between LD and CLLD structures, the data above show that Christopher finds them equally unacceptable, be it in English, Greek or Spanish. In other words, despite the theoretically advocated structural differences between the two constructions, his performance is fairly consistent in so far as the assignment of degrees of acceptability is concerned. Note that there is no difficulty with regard to the interpretation of these sentences in either his first or subsequent languages. More specifically, both the sentential interpretation and the coreferentiality between the clitic element and the dislocated NP are appropriately established.

For clitic-doubling in languages like Spanish, the standard assumption is that the clitic doubles the argument NP, and absorbs the accusative case, resulting in the obligatory insertion of the preposition (Jaeggli, 1982). In Modern Greek, however, clitic-doubling does not involve the presence of a preposition to introduce the doubled constituent, and both direct and indirect objects can be doubled – by an accusative and a genitive clitic respectively. The only constraint on the latter is that the indirect object, when doubled by a clitic, has to surface as a genitive NP and not as a prepositional phrase: an option which is possible if no clitic-doubling is involved:

54   O Stefanos edhose to vivlio sti Maria/tis Marias
     the-nom Stefanos gave-3s the-acc book to-the Maria/the-gen Maria
     Stefanos gave the book to Maria

55   O Stefanos tis-to-edhose to vivlio tis Marias/*sti Maria
     the-nom Stefanos her-it-gave-3s the-acc book the-gen Maria/*to-the
     Maria
     Stefanos gave the book to Maria

Just as with CLLD structures, Christopher corrects sentences which involve right-dislocation or clitic-doubling.[24] Thus the majority of sentences like the Greek ones in 56–58 are corrected:

Greek:
56 O Petros mu tin ipe tin istoria	[R]

the Petros me-her-told the story
Petros told me the story
56' 'O Petros mu ipe tin istoria'
the Petros me told the story

57 Tin exo idhi dhiavasi afti tin efimeridha [R]
her-have-1s already read this the newspaper
I have already read this newspaper
57' 'Idhi exo dhiavasi afti tin efimeridha'
already have-1s read this the newspaper

58 To dhiavasa to vivlio [R]
it-read-1s the-acc book
I read the book
58' 'Dhiavasa to vivlio'
read-1s the book

59 Tis edhikses tis fotografies sti Maria? [R]
them-showed-2s the pictures to-the Maria
Did you show the pictures to Maria?
59' 'Edhikses tis fotografies sti Maria?'
showed-2s the pictures to-the Maria

60 O Petros tis to edhose to dhoro tis Marias [R]
the-nom Petros her-it-gave-3s the-acc present the-gen Maria
Petros gave the present to Maria
60' 'O Petros tis to edhose'
the-nom Petros her-it-gave-3s
Petros gave it to her

61 Mi tis to paris to vivlio [R]
not her-it take-2s the-acc book
Don't take the book from her
61' 'Mi tis paris to vivlio'
not her take-2s the-acc book

62 Tis aghorasa ena vivlio ja ta jenethlia tis, tis Marias [R]
her-bought-1s one book for the birthday hers the-gen Maria
I bought Maria a book for her birthday
62' 'Aghorasa ena vivlio ja ta jenethlia tis Marias'

bought-1s one book for the birthday the-gen Maria
62″ 'I bought her a book for her birthday of Maria . . . for Maria's
      birthday'
      [C's translation of 62']

Christopher's usual explanation for his corrections of such sentences is
fairly vague: for example, 'You don't need *tin* if you have "the story" ' (for
56, and his versions of the corrected sentences do not consistently involve
the same strategy. For instance, example 60' involves the deletion of the
doubled NP; while examples 58' and 62' involve the deletion of the clitic
which doubles respectively the accusative and genitive NP.

In all the examples presented above the coreferentiality between the clitic
and the NP is unambiguously marked by the identical case-marking on the
two elements. There are times, however, in which the case-paradigm fails
to exhibit a distinction between the nominative and the accusative: for
example, in the plural form of the neuter gender. This syncretism, in
conjunction with the possibility of subjects being postverbal, and of having
CLLD and clitic-doubling results in sentence 63 below being ambiguous
between the readings indicated:

63   Ta pedhia ta aghapane ta zoa
     the(nom/acc) children them-love-3p the (nom/acc) animals
     Children love animals/Animals love children

The first interpretation suggests that the clitic doubles the accusative NP,
'the animals'. In the second interpretation, there is CLLD, hence the
object NP 'the children' appears in initial position and the postverbal NP is
the subject. Christopher reacted to this example by deleting the clitic, as
shown in 63', and providing the two translations in 63″:

63′   'Ta pedhia aghapane ta zoa'
         the children love-3p the animals
         Children love animals
63″(a)   Animals are loved by children
   (b)   Children love animals

         IT   Can it mean 'animals love children'?
         C   No, 'animals are loved by children.'

Given the amended version in 63', where the clitic is deleted, the only
natural interpretation is 63″(b).[25] That Christopher failed to detect the
ambiguity in this example presumably results in part from his dislike of

CLLD structures and postverbal subjects, in part from his general avoidance of multiple interpretations (see chapter 5).

His judgements on constructions such as 63 are consistent with his judgements on LD, CLLD and topicalization structures in all the languages that we have investigated, including English, and, as will become apparent in the next chapter, including the newly learned language, Berber. His grammaticality judgements thus seem to be uniform even though his knowledge of the various languages is clearly not uniform: his Greek is considerably better than his Spanish and Italian, which in turn are much better than his Berber. This is obviously to be expected when one considers how long he has been exposed to each of these languages and how much contact he has had with them. However, his performance on dislocation and topicalization structures in his first language prompts the question whether his judgements in his various 'second' languages are a function of whatever constraint is responsible for the rejection of these similar (but not structurally identical) English sentences, or result from a constraint on the representations in his second (or interlanguage) grammars. In other words, should LD, CLLD, topicalization and clitic-doubling be grouped into a natural class on the basis of formal similarities specifiable at some (linguistic) level? In answering this question, we need also to bear in mind the fact that some of Christopher's non-native languages manifest word-order possibilities, for instance postverbal subjects, which are similarly problematic for him, but which differ from the other constructions in that they contain no overt pronominal element coreferential with that subject. Furthermore, VOS structures differ from VSO ones in that they involve a pro in the canonical subject position whereas VSO ones do not. Accordingly, any account of Christopher's performance which presupposes the impossibility of parameter resetting as a means of accommodating null subject languages would fail to cover his problematic performance on the VSO structure.

One solution would be to assume that whatever parametric option is responsible for the possibility of VSO word-order in languages like Spanish and Greek is not (re)set in the corresponding grammars of Christopher's second languages. Assuming that VSO word-order arises when the subject fails to move to SpecIP and involves nominative case-assignment via structural government from I to SpecVP, and assuming that this possibility is formulated in terms of a parametric choice[26] associated with properties of the I head, it could be argued that this parametric choice is not yet[27] part of the developing grammar.

A similar account could be given of his performance on CLLD and clitic-doubling or right-dislocation structures. If the resumptive pronoun strategy reflects a language-specific property dependent on the presence of an overt pronominal with a variable interpretation, it might be that this strategy is not available in the grammar of the second language. In each of these accounts, Christopher's second language learning is viewed as a phenomenon to be explained on purely linguistic (i.e. grammar-internal) grounds. We consider an alternative account, which goes beyond the exclusively syntactic, at the end of the chapter.

Syntactic focus and wh-movement Word-order variation can also be the result of syntactic focusing. Unlike English, languages like Modern Greek have syntactic focusing, which involves the movement of a focussed element to clause-initial position and obligatory subject–verb inversion. A typical example is given in 64, where capitals indicate stress:

64(a) Ta VIVLIA dhiavase o Yanis
        the-acc books read-3s the-nom Yanis
        It is the books that Yanis read

 (b) *Ta VIVLIA o Yanis dhiavase
        the-acc books the-nom Yanis read-3s

It has been argued that syntactic focusing has certain similarities to wh-movement in that both processes involve Operator-movement and verb-raising to a functional category higher than IP (Tsimpli, 1990, 1994; Agouraki, 1991). Unlike wh-phrases, however, focus phrases are assigned the feature [+f], which is realized as focal stress. A second set of elements that have been argued to bear this feature and that therefore move in the syntax like focus-phrases are Negative Polarity Items (NPIs) (Tsimpli and Roussou, 1993), as illustrated in 65:

65(a) TIPOTA dhen tha dhiavaso
        nothing not will read-1s
        I will not read anything

 (b) KANENAN dhen zitisa na dho
        nobody not asked-1s sub. see-1s
        I didn't ask to see anybody

The distribution of NPIs in Modern Greek overlaps with that of NPIs in English. They can appear in interrogative, conditional and negative sentences in both languages, and their interpretation as an existential or a negative/universal quantifier depending on syntactic context, is likewise similar. However, Greek NPIs, in virtue of being foci, differ from English ones in being subject to focus-movement, and their distribution in clauses lacking deictic tense reference appears to differ in the two languages.

We presented Christopher with sentences containing focused constituents in Greek, including examples which involve the focusing of complements in both matrix and embedded clauses, and NPIs moved to clause-initial position. As usual, he was in each case asked to give his judgement on them and suggest any necessary emendation, as shown in the following examples:

66   To YANI simbathi i Maria   [R]
       the Yani likes the Maria
       It is Yanis that Maria likes
66'   'I Maria simbathi to Yani'
       Maria likes Yanis

67   Su ipa ta VIVLIA oti agorase o Petros   [R]
       you told-I the books that bought-3s the Petros
       I told you that Petros bought the BOOKS
67'   *'Su ipa ja ta vivlia oti agorase o Petros'
       you told-I about the books that bought-3s the Petros
       I told you about the books that Petros bought

68   Na DHULEVI perisotero theli o Yanis   [R]
       sub. work-3s more wants the Yanis
       Yanis wants to WORK more
68'   'O Yanis theli na dhulevi perisotero'
       the Yanis wants sub. work more

69   To YANI thelo na dho   [R]
       the-acc Yani want-1s sub. see-1s
       It is Yani that I want to see
69'   'Thelo na dho to Yani'
       want-1s sub. see-1s the-acc Yani

All the sentences with focusing were presented to Christopher in spoken as well as written form in order to ensure that he could identify the stressed element. As is clear from his correction of 67, he failed to understand the sentence altogether, changing it into a relative clause.

His judgements on constructions involving NPIs were, in the majority of cases, appropriate:

70   Dhen akusa KANENA na sizitai politika   [OK]

not heard-1s anyone sub. discuss-3s politics
I didn't hear anybody discussing politics

71   Akuse kanis an tha vreksi?   [OK]
        heard-3s anyone if will rain-3s
        Did anyone hear if it will rain?

71'(a) 'Did anyone hear if it was raining?'
   (b) 'Did anyone hear if it will rain?'

72   An iha lefta, tha tu agoraza tipota ja ta jenethlia tu   [OK]
        if had money, will him-bought anything for the birthday his
        If I had money, I would buy him something for his birthday

Moreover, according to his (appropriate) judgements, NPIs in subject
position in Greek require the presence of negation, unlike in English:

73   *KANIS apofasise na dhosi lefta ja afto to idhrima   [R]
        NPI decided-3s sub. give-3s money for this the institution
        Nobody decided to give money to this institution
73'   'Kanis dhen apofasise na dhosi lefta ja afto to idhrima'
        NPI decided-3s sub. give-3s money for this the institution

When Christopher was asked what the interpretation of the polarity item
(PI) could be, he said it could mean either *nothing* or *something*. This
occasionally gave rise to incorrect judgements where the element *kanenas/
tipota* was interpreted as an existential quantifier but not a polarity item, as
in 74:

74   ??Ipe oti tha sinantisi kanena   [OK]
        said-3s that will meet-3s PI
74'   'She said she will meet somebody'
        [C's translation of 74]

Otherwise, the only cases in which his judgements were inaccurate were
where the NPI was preposed, i.e. as a focus-phrase:

75   TIPOTA dhen thelo na aghoraso   [R]
        nothing not want-1s sub. buy-1s
        I don't want to buy anything
75'   'Dhen thelo na aghoraso tipota'
        not want-1s sub. buy-1s anything

In addition to providing judgements for Greek data, Christopher was also asked for his reactions to Spanish sentences involving negative and existential quantifiers:

76   No detesto a nadie   [OK]
      not hate-1s to anybody
      I don't hate anybody
      'I don't hate anybody'

77   ¿Quién no quiere a nadie?   [R]
      who not love-3s to anybody
      Who doesn't love anybody?
77'   *'¿Quién quiere a nadie?'
      who love-3s to anybody

78   ¿No ha llamado nadie?   [OK]
      not has called anybody
      Didn't anybody call?
      'Did nobody call?'

79   *Guille cree que el comité va a echar a nadie[28]   [OK]
      Bill think-3s that the committee will throw-out to nobody
      Bill doesn't think that the committee will throw anyone out
      'Bill thinks that the committee will throw nobody out'

80   No quiero ver a alguien [= 15]   [OK]
      not want-1s see to somebody
      I don't want to see someone
      'I don't want to see somebody'

With wh-movement Christopher's judgements were in most cases appropriate, though structures involving island effects gave rise to some inconsistency in both Greek and Spanish:

Greek
81   Pjon thelisan na dhioksun apo ti dhulia tu?   [OK]
      whom wanted-3p sub. sack-3p from the job his
      Who did they want to sack from his job?

82   Ti dhen kseris an aghorase i Maria?   [R]
      what not know-2s if bought-3s the-nom Maria
      *What don't you know if Maria bought?

82'   *'Dhen kseris an aghorase i Maria?'
        not know-2s if bought-3s the-nom Maria
82"   'Do you not know if Mary bought . . . if Mary bought?'
        [Cs' translation of 82']

83   *Pjon se rotise o dhaskalos an idhes?   [OK]
        whom you-asked-3s the-nom teacher if saw-2s
        *Who did the teacher ask you if you saw?

Spanish
84   *¿Que película conociste al productor que la hizo?   [OK]
        what film know-2s-past the producer that it make-3s-past
        *Which film did you know the producer that made?
   (a) 'Do you know the producer who know that film?' [first attempt]
   (b) 'I got stuck'
   (c) *'Que película conociste al productor que hizo?'
   (d) *'¿Que película conociste al productor que la hizo?'
   (e) 'What film did you know the producer who made it?'

85   *¿Qué dijiste que María lo comió?   [R]
        what say-2s-past that Maria it-ate
        What did you say that Mary ate?
85'   '¿Qué dijiste que María comió?'

86   ¿Quién conoces a la chica que lo quiere?   [R]
        who know-2s to the girl that him-love-3s
        *Who do you know the girl that loves him?
86'   ¿Quién conoce a la chica que lo quiere?'
        who know-3s to the girl that him-love-3s
        Who knows the girl who loves him?
86"   'I put *conoce* because of *lo quiere* not *lo quieres*'

87   ¿Quién te preguntas si lo conoció?   [R]
        who you wonder-2s if him-knew-3s
        Who do you wonder if he knew?
   (a) '¿Quién te preguntas si conoció?'
   (b) '¿Quién te preguntas si lo conoció?'
   (c) 'It is correct'

As shown by the Greek and Spanish examples in 82–83 and 85–87
respectively, Christopher's judgements are not consistent. Confronted with
examples showing extraction out of a wh-island, he corrected only some of

them, and some of his corrections were inappropriate. What is not clear, for instance, is whether his reaction was based on the assumption that 82 and 87 are ungrammatical in Greek and Spanish because of their English equivalents, or whether his failure to correct the Greek example in 83 was based on an appropriate second language judgement. In fact, it is only in cases where his first and second languages differ that Christopher's judgements become inconsistent, and hence make conclusions about the status of his second languages difficult.

Christopher's judgements of focus-constructions as opposed to his reaction to examples of wh-movement can be attributed relatively uncontroversially to syntactic differences between his first and subsequent languages. Syntactic focusing in English occurs only in cleft constructions, and focal stress on syntactic constituents gives rise neither to syntactic movement nor to the restriction on the number of focused constituents characteristic of languages like Greek. If such differences are to be accounted for in terms of a parameterized property associated with [f]-assignment (as in Brody, 1990; Tsimpli, 1994) and the presence of specific features on the relevant functional head (C or F), then we are dealing with a difference between grammaticalized and non-grammaticalized options in Greek and English respectively. Christopher's rejection of such sentences could then be plausibly argued to be due to the absence of parameter-resetting.[29] As far as his performance on sentences involving wh-phrases is concerned, it appears that the problematic examples are those where the English equivalent of a grammatical L2 example would be ungrammatical, as well as those where both the L2 examples and their English congeners are ungrammatical. The fact that his performance is inconsistent in such cases may suggest that he has difficulty in providing (meta)linguistic judgements on 'knowledge' drawn from two distinct sources. That is, there is some kind of conflict between – on the one hand – his first language, which has been shown to be unimpaired and so should flag the example as ungrammatical without conscious deliberation, and – on the other hand – his second language, intuitions about which necessitate a process of conscious retrieval, at least with regard to morphological and lexical properties, and so may not give a clear decision. It should be emphasized that this assumption about the status of grammaticality judgements by normal second language learners is, for both theoretical and empirical reasons, by no means unproblematic.[30] However, it appears that with the exception of his morphological knowledge, Christopher's second language performance is explicitly influenced by his first language, as witness the fact that his immediate reaction to test sentences is to translate them into English. This being granted, the degree to which his first language influences his judgements and the nature of this influence remain obscure and as yet unresolved issues. It may be, as suggested previously, that the core of his second language knowledge is largely lexical and morphological so that the influence of his first language on his syntactic judgements is fairly direct. Alternatively, it could be that the grammatical representation of his (flawed) second language does include syntactic and semantic properties which are distinct from those of his first language (even including some instances of parameter-resetting), but that accessing this knowledge is inhibited, at any level beyond the purely lexical, by processing strategies that are based overwhelmingly on the first language.

Other aspects of Christopher's 'second' languages

Another way in which Greek differs systematically from English concerns *easy-to-please* constructions (see Chomsky, 1977, 1986a; Browning, 1987; Brody, 1994). This construction is generally impossible in Greek, as the subject of predicates like *easy* ('efkolos') has to be impersonal when a proposition is selected, and so the embedded subjunctive clause needs to have an overt object NP as shown in 88a. If the subject of the embedded clause appears in sentence-initial position, it is not a real subject, but a topic as indicated by the agreement on the adjectival predicate in 88b:

88(a) Ine efkolo na efxaristisis to Yani
       is easy-neuter sub. please-2s the Yani
       It is easy (for one) to please Yani

  (b) Ta mathimatika ine dhiskolo na ta mathis
       the-neut-pl maths is difficult-neut-sing sub. them learn
       Maths is difficult to learn

From Christopher's judgements, however, it appears that he considers *easy-to-please* constructions fully grammatical in Greek:

89 Ta Aglika ine dhiskola na ta katalavis   [R]
    the English is difficult sub. them understand-2s
    English is difficult to understand
89′ *'Ta Aglika ine dhiskola na katalavis'
    the English is difficult sub. understand-2s

90 To film itan efxaristo na to parakoluthis   [R]
    the film was pleasant sub. it watch-2s
    The film was pleasant to watch

90′   *'To film itan efxaristo na parakoluthis'
      the film was pleasant sub. watch-2s

91   *Afto to milo ine poli skliro na kopsis me ta dhontia su   [OK]
      this the apple is very hard sub. cut-2s with the teeth yours
      This apple is very hard to bite

92   To fajito ine etimo na to valume sto furno   [R]
      the food is ready sub. it put-1p in-the oven
      The food is ready to put in the oven
92′   *'To fajito ine etimo na valume sto furno'
      the food is ready sub. put-1p in-the oven

It is revealing that Christopher's corrections focus largely on the presence of the resumptive clitic rather than on the *easy-to-please* construction. Furthermore, in English the presence of the pronoun in constructions like 93 is unacceptable, but the clitic in the corresponding Greek examples such as 94 is either obligatory or, at the least, optional:

93   I have bought a newspaper to read (*it) in the evening

94   Aghorasa mia efimeridha na (tin) dhiavaso to vradhi
      bought-1s one newspaper sub. her read-1s the evening

Christopher's judgements on such constructions again reflected properties of his first language:

95   Aghorasa freska luludhia na ta valo sto vazo   [R]
      bought-1s fresh flowers sub. them put-1s in-the vase
      I bought fresh flowers to put in the vase

95′   'Aghorasa freska luludhia na valo sto vazo'
      bought-1s fresh flowers sub. put-1s in-the vase

96   Afisa to isitirio na to pari kapjos allos   [R]
      left-1s the ticket sub. it take-3s someone else
      I left the ticket for someone else to take
96′   *'Afisa to isitirio ja na pari kapjos allos'
      left-1s the ticket for sub. take-3s someone else

Abstracting away from the syntactic differences among the various constructions exemplified above (see Theophanopoulou-Kondou, 1986, and Tsimpli, 1994 for discussion), Christopher shows a consistent tendency to render second language data with as great a similarity to English as possible, even though he does not necessarily translate the examples (audibly) and then correct them. The same question arises as before: is his performance due to defective knowledge of the grammars of the second languages, or is it due to difficulties in accessing that knowledge as a result of his processing strategies?

Conclusion

The major points arising from the discussion of Christopher's knowledge of his non-native languages are, first, the difference between his mastery of lexical and morphological properties on the one hand, as opposed to his mastery of syntax on the other; and second, the influence of his first language which, except in the case of null-subject constructions, appears to give rise to inconsistent and hence incorrect judgements. As regards the first point, we suggest that whereas in normal cases lexical learning is just one aspect of linguistic achievement, in Christopher's case it appears to predominate over all other domains, leading to above-average results in one area but less impressive ones elsewhere. It could therefore be that the unusual speed which characterizes his second language learning and the ease with which he switches from one language to another reflect a process of access and selection taking place entirely within the lexical component. For the normal case it has been argued that lexical access and selection are automatic, mandatory and so putatively modular processes (Swinney, 1979; Marslen-Wilson and Tyler, 1987; Marslen-Wilson, 1987, 1989). By contrast, the process of integration, that is, the stage where an activated lexical entry interacts with contextual information, necessarily involves non-modular notions of 'appropriateness' and relevance. If Christopher's linguistic performance reflects unimpaired access to modular properties, but only limited access to interactive ones (as is also indicated by the results of the Hayling test discussed on pp. 171–2, for instance), it is plausible to conclude that both the extraordinary and the flawed in his performance can be accounted for by postulating that lexical accessing, as part of a modular process, is intact, but that the integration of the output of that process by the central system is inhibited or defective.

We turn next to the second point: the difference between Christopher's command of the syntax and the lexicon of his second languages. It is clear for two reasons that, to the extent that his judgements reflect his knowledge of second languages, that knowledge is defective. First, there is an obvious English influence on his grammaticality judgements of second languages; second, although his exposure to second language input has (at least for some languages) been very considerable, and presumably adequate to allow something close to near-native attainment, the analysis and integration of this input into a competence grammar has been less adequate, so that the development of his L2 syntax is 'stunted'. This is in marked contrast with the results of his exposure to second language lexicons, where his abilities appear to be unbounded and much closer to those of native speakers. We conclude that this grammatical inhibition, which eventuates in a syntactic plateau-effect, results from difficulties in processing the input, with the implication that the difference between the lexicon and the syntax in this case is due to differences in the processing load they impose.[31]

This flawed interaction of the modular and the central allows us to reconsider some of the word-order data we discussed earlier. Word-order variation crucially implements pragmatic functions, and as Christopher's linguistic judgement is deviant precisely in cases where such functions are necessarily involved (see also pp. 62–3 on metalinguistic negation and pp. 156–64 on translation) it seems to demand a mixed account. His understanding of word-order possibilities other than SVO and of structures where a clitic and a full referential NP are involved indicates that he has no problem in interpreting the sentences appropriately. This prompts us to ask whether his corrections of these second language constructions indicate a performance preference or a competence difference? There seems to be some evidence for both possibilities. Where his correction gives rise to an ungrammatical structure, it is plausible to conclude that his knowledge of the second language is flawed. However, where the correction gives rise to an equally grammatical sentence, it may be that he has competence in the second language but he assigns a higher degree of acceptability to one of the two possible structures. This is particularly plausible, given that his occasional lack of attention and concentration make it difficult to regard his performance on every task as a direct and pure reflection of his linguistic knowledge.

Whatever the correct balance between these two factors may be, there is little doubt that Christopher's second language grammars are not comparable to that of his first language, English. Abstracting away from lexical and morphological errors that indicate overgeneralization within a particular language, his syntactic competence is far from native-like in any of his second languages. It is furthermore striking that his problematic performance in constructions such as those discussed so far, is not restricted to just one of his non-native languages but to all the relevant ones. As we shall see in the next chapter, his judgements on data from languages with which he was already familiar, especially Modern Greek, Spanish and Italian, extend to 'new' languages to which he was first exposed in the course of the project. His flawed performance is due in part to his tendency spontaneously to translate any stimulus into English, with the result that the original data are often contaminated. Indeed, it is not too inaccurate to suggest that the 'contamination' is in fact more deeply rooted, and that Christopher's syntax is basically English with a range of alternative veneers. This raises a serious problem regarding his ability to provide reliable meta-linguistic judgements, if these presuppose the exploitation of a level of representation beyond the strictly grammatical, but this is a problem which is common to the use of grammaticality judgments by normal second language learners as well. Given that Christopher's spontaneous speech and conversation are anyway limited in ways we have already described, his grammaticality judgements (and his translation) constitute our basic source of information about his linguistic abilities.

Granted the interpretational difficulties raised by Christopher's case, both theoretical and empirical considerations suggest a fundamental distinction between the lexical and the syntactic components. This distinction is then directly reflected in Christopher's stunning ability in the former domain and his systematic problems in the latter one.

4

New Languages

Rationale

We began our study of Christopher because of his remarkable knowledge of a vast number of languages, a part of which we have documented in the preceding chapters. In order to gain deeper insight into the way he learns new languages, one part of our research was devoted to teaching him new languages with which he was completely unfamiliar, while controlling the nature and order of presentation of the input data. In the most general terms the idea motivating this exercise was that we could simultaneously investigate the kind of relationships obtaining between different aspects of his knowledge, and test the predictions made by the principles and parameters framework of current linguistic theory. Specifically, in a framework where there are no construction specific rules (cf. Chomsky, 1981a, 1986a) one might expect that acquiring knowledge of one (type of) construction should bring with it 'unlearned' knowledge of a range of other, parametrically related, constructions without overt exposure to the relevant data. However, our earlier work (Tsimpli and Smith, 1991) suggested that parameter-(re-)setting is an inappropriate characterization of Christopher's acquisition process, but that there are none the less interesting relationships among the rules he has acquired. We here extend these results to account for the controlled-input acquisition of Berber and for the acquisition (or non-acquisition) of an invented language (Epun) whose general conformity to principles of UG is combined with the possession of a number of 'impossible' constructions.

Controlled Input: Berber

Berber is an Afro-Asiatic language spoken in Morocco and adjacent countries. It is characterized by a rich morphology, VSO word-order, null subjects, *that*-t effect violations, etc. (for further details, see Ouhalla, 1988; Smith et al., 1993). Christopher was exposed to Berber, specifically the Tarifit dialect thereof, in both written and spoken form, over a period of some eight months. Before his meetings with a native speaker,[1] we prepared written material consisting of sentences, accompanied by a word-by-word gloss and a free translation, as illustrated in 1:

1   Yesha Mohand tafirast
     ate Mohand pear
     Mohand has eaten the pear

Each sentence was read in Berber by Jamal Ouhalla and in English by Neil Smith, with repetitions and explanations when Christopher requested them. We also left a cassette recording of the sentences with him so that he could listen to them again at his leisure if he so wished. Subsequent lessons were comparable, except that for some of them the input was exclusively written. In addition, we provided such information as that 'Mohand' is a boy's name, and we appended a brief paradigm of the 'subject markers' in 2 – a form of representation that, interestingly, occasioned Christopher no difficulty at all:

2   Subject markers
     Singular   *Plural*
     (a)   —gh   (a)   n—
     (b)   t—t   (b)   t—m (masc.)
                                         t—mt (fem.)
     (c]   y— (masc.)   (c)   —n (masc.)
           t— (fem.)   —nt (fem.)

Christopher's reaction to the new language was enthusiastic. He had no inhibitions in starting to read examples immediately, even though he was as yet ignorant of the phonetic values of the letters used in the transcription. He spontaneously drew parallels, both morphological and lexical, with Arabic; he seemed thoroughly to enjoy teasing out the details of the subject agreement system; and after a few minutes he was able to suggest the correct verb form to accompany a masculine as opposed to a feminine subject (converting 'teswa' to 'yeswa'), despite there having been only two relevant examples. This reaction is in marked contrast to what happens on the initial exposure to a new language of most learners, who typically ignore entirely the morphological details of the sentences they are confronted with. One aspect of Christopher's exceptionality resides precisely in his sensitivity to and learning of complex morphology.[2]

Our first task was to investigate the possibility of eliciting 'unlearned knowledge' of the kind mentioned in the 'Rationale' above. To this end we had two specific, relatively circumscribed, preliminary questions we wanted to answer: whether, in the absence of positive data, Christopher would assume that Berber had prepositions rather than postpositions, and whether he would assume that it was a pro-drop language, i.e. that it allowed null subjects. The existence of prepositions rather than post-positions in a VSO language follows either from simple typological generalizations of a Greenbergian kind (see e.g., Greenberg, 1963), or from standard theories of parameterization, specifically the head-complement parameter (Chomsky, 1986a: 88). The possibility of null subjects, while hardly theoretically subtle, is more closely tied to current theories of parametric variation and has the advantage of distinguishing Berber from English, so that explanations in terms of transfer from the mother tongue are excluded. In each case the answer seems to be that Christopher came to the correct (positive) conclusion.

None of the forty examples in the first lesson contained a preposition, but the sentences in the first exercise Christopher was given to translate included a number of prepositional phrases. To make this exercise possible, he was also provided with a list of new vocabulary in which simple translation equivalents were tabulated as in 3:

3   zi = from
    ag = with (company)

Christopher duly came up with the correct translations in (4):

4(a)   Munat arrived from London
       'Munat texdel zi London'[3]

 (b)   She met Mohand with Munat
       'Telqa Mohand ag Munat'

While suggestive, this result is also what one would expect if parametric values were irrelevant and Christopher was simply translating word-by-word from English with no influence from the grammar of Berber at all. That this might be his strategy is suggested by the fact that his translations, as in 4a, consistently diverged from the canonical VSO word-order of Berber. Such consistency is itself somewhat surprising, given that the verb preceded the subject in every example in the input except for two (copular) sentences, though it could be accounted for on the assumption that the learner simply transfers the superficial word-order properties of his first language even in the presence of positive evidence to the contrary.

Although we are sceptical about the possibility of parameter resetting at all (see Tsimpli and Smith, 1991), a parametric account of Christopher's predilection for prepositions could be constructed along the following lines. In the process of second language learning the value of the first language qualifies as the first choice, in the sense that it is the value the learner resorts to in the absence of positive evidence from the language being acquired. Equivalently, one could argue that in second language learning, the parametric value of the first language is the only possible choice, or that it ceases to be the unique choice only when positive evidence is both provided and recognized. This would account additionally for the consistency in Christopher's performance, but although positive evidence is adequate for first language acquisition, it is well known that it is not sufficient for the construction of the correct grammar of a second or subsequent language.[4] We return below to the question of parameter-resetting.

Whatever may have been the role of English on Christopher's learning of these prepositional examples, it is clear that the influence of the first language could not be directly relevant to the correct production of null-subject sentences, as English is not a null-subject language. It is therefore highly significant that he assumed that Berber is such a language. For instance, in a grammaticality judgement task, he showed no hesitation in accepting 5a (despite mistranslating it), and he immediately produced 5b and 5c as Berber translations of the English:

5(a) Y-effegh ithyaden   [OK]
      3ms-left last year
      He left last year
      'He left yesterday'

  (b) You gave the fig to Mohand
       'Tewsht tazet i Mohand'
       2ms-give-2ms fig to Mohand

  (c) They saw him in London
       'Yzrin t gi London'
       Correct version: Zri-n t gi London[5]

This suggests that Christopher has inferred, presumably on the basis of Berber's rich morphology, that the language does allow null subjects. It would again be possible to argue that he has reset the pro-drop parameter to its positive value – an issue to which we return below – but it is clear that neither direct influence from English nor overt evidence from Berber could be the source of such a resetting. We will look again at the issue of null subjects in the context of Christopher's treatment of Berber word-order.

Word-order

Although Berber is a VSO language, it allows SVO order freely in both matrix and embedded declarative clauses, as illustrated in 6:

6(a) y-zra Mohand Munat   (VSO)
   3ms-saw Mohand Munat
   Mohand saw Munat

 (b) Mohand y-zra Munat   (SVO)

 (c) Nna-n iharmoshen qa y-zra Mohand Munat   (VSO)
   said-3p children that 3ms-saw Mohand Munat
   The children said that Mohand saw Munat

 (d) Nna-n iharmoshen qa Mohand y-zra Munat   (SVO)

Moreover, presumably because it is a pro-drop language, Berber also allows the order V (XP) S, with an object or adjunct intervening between the verb and the subject, as can be seen in 7:

7(a) y-zra Munat Mohand   (VOS)
   Mohand saw Munat

 (b) Tedwer idnnat Munat   (V XP S)
   3fs-returned yesterday
   Munat Munat returned yesterday

Christopher's reaction to Berber word-order Christopher performed well on the VSO and SVO orders, but somewhat inconsistently on the V (XP) S order. Thus, as shown by 4a, he typically translated English sentences into Berber using the (English) SVO word-order, despite the fact that virtually all the Berber sentences he was initially exposed to were given in the canonical VSO word-order. Indeed, of the first twenty sentences he had to translate, the only one which he rendered with the verb initial was 8:

8 Mohand bought her the djellaba from York
 'Yesgha Mohand i jellaba zi York'

Moreover, when asked to translate new Berber sentences into English, and simultaneously to correct any mistakes these sentences might contain, he carried out the first part of the task reasonably efficiently, but systematically neglected to offer any corrections. For instance, when we gave him the examples in 9:

9(a)   Tedwer idnnat Munat [=7b]
       Munat returned yesterday

  (b) Yelqa Munat Mohand idnnat
       Mohand met Munat yesterday

  (c) Yufa Mohand amshish
       Mohand found a cat

we had expected him to change 9a to 10a, that is, 'V XP S' to 'V S XP', and 9b to 10b, that is, 'V O S XP' to 'V S O XP', while leaving 9c unchanged.

10(a)   Tedwer Munat idnnat
   (b) Yelqa Mohand Munat idnnat

In fact, he changed none of them: indicating that he noticed nothing wrong either with the initial position of the verb or, somewhat more surprisingly, with a structure in which XP intervenes between the verb and the subject. While Christopher was always happy to allow SVO order, even though the initial input contained virtually no examples of this sequence, he was less consistent with V (XP) S order. He accepted a few such examples, such as those in 9(a) and (b), but his usual strategy when he came across sentences where the subject was not adjacent to the verb was to remedy the situation by placing the subject in immediately preverbal or postverbal position. Typical examples are given in 11 and 12, with Christopher's unnecessary 'corrections' indicated as usual:[6]

11   T-arzem tawwart Munat   [R]
     3fs-opened door Munat
     Munat opened a door
     'Tarzem Munat tawwart'

12   T-emmut ithyaden tamghart tawessart   [R]
     3fs-died last year woman old

The old woman died last year
'Temmut tamghart tawessart ithyaden'

That he consistently produces Berber sentences with SVO word-order and does not correct VSO Berber test sentences implies that Christopher has correctly inferred that Berber allows both word-orders. His preference for the SVO order in production is presumably a reflection of his first language. Indeed, it is possible that despite speaking many languages, Christopher really has only one grammar, and the fact that he accepts VSO order could be a simple consequence of his exposure to sentences with VSO order in Berber – the form taken by the overwhelming majority of the examples he had heard and read in the language – rather than a direct reflection of his competence. That is, we need to distinguish between those aspects of his linguistic behaviour that are a function of his encapsulated language faculty and those that are a function of his very considerable encyclopaedic knowledge.

Analysis of the Berber word-order data   Whether this minimal position is correct or not, the fact that Christopher shows such facility with constructions which do not occur in English obliges us to provide an appropriate analysis. The standard analysis (see, e.g., Pollock, 1989; Ouhalla, 1991) for VSO word-order is one in which TNS is hierarchically higher than AGR, as shown in 13:

13

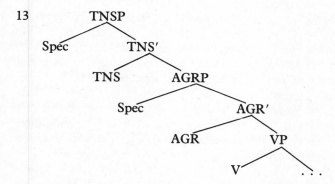

where the verb is raised successively to AGR and TNS, thereby accounting for the order of the morphemes in the verbal complex, and a variety of word-order facts. In particular, the fact that most VSO languages allow for the alternative word-order SVO is accommodated by assuming that preverbal subjects are generated as topics in the Spec of TNSP and are coindexed with a resumptive pro in the Spec of AGRP (for details, see

Ouhalla, 1991; Smith et al., 1993). The structure underlying SVO languages, on the other hand, is standardly taken to be one in which AGR is higher than TNS, as in 14:

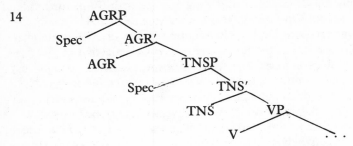

14

While accounting correctly for the order of morphemes in the verbal complex, the structure in 14 does not allow for the generation of subjects as preverbal topics to give VSO word-order, as the elements in the Spec of TNSP and the Spec of AGRP are in the wrong configurational relationship: specifically, the element in the Spec of TNSP does not m-command the coindexed resumptive pro in the Spec of AGRP. A putative advantage of this analysis is that it explains why SVO languages do not usually allow VSO as an alternative word-order.

On a parameter resetting account of the learning of a VSO language by the speaker of an SVO language, it would appear to be necessary to assume that the learner switches from a configuration like that in 13, where TNS c-selects AGR, to one like that in 14, where AGR c-selects TNS. However, in Tsimpli and Smith, 1991) we followed Ouhalla's (1991) claim that VSO order is also compatible with a configuration like that in 14, and suggested that, for subjects like Christopher who are speakers of a non-pro-drop first language learning a pro-drop second language, the Spec of AGRP is not really filled by pro in the grammar of that second language. Rather, morphological agreement is treated as a clitic which occupies the Spec of AGRP position and then cliticizes to the verb, as with French subject clitics. If such an analysis is valid, we can assume that a similar situation holds for Christopher's grammar of Berber, and an overt subject in postverbal position (VSO) is not in the Spec of AGRP but remains inside VP, as suggested by Koopman and Sportiche (1991). Thus we can accommodate Christopher's behaviour without having to have recourse to an assumption of parameter-resetting.

Christopher's normal avoidance of V (XP) S order, in contrast to his ready acceptance of SVO order, can be explained as follows. SVO order follows naturally both from the assumption that he assigns Berber sentences the structure in 14, that is, the canonical structure for SVO languages, and from the fact that his first language is an SVO one. In terms of the theory we are assuming, the subject occupies the Spec of AGRP position, while the agreement morpheme occupies the AGR position. This is licit if we allow for the possibility that the agreement morpheme can be analysed either as an incorporating subject clitic or as an AGR category. However, the derivation of the V (XP) S order depends on a dislocational process of subject-postposing which, in turn, depends on the ability of AGR to license a null subject, realized as pro, in the canonical subject position (see Rizzi, 1982; Chomsky, 1986b). The problem with this suggestion is that there is independent evidence that a dislocation analysis is implausible. The evidence comes from Christopher's usual rejection, even in English, of constructions involving dislocated elements and resumptive pronouns (see Tsimpli and Smith, 1993; and pp. 51–4) and our analysis accordingly excludes VOS order as well as VSO order. In other words it appears that Christopher's grammar of Berber can accommodate *only* the SVO order. This is consistent with his regular production of SVO Berber sentences and the absence from his output of sentences with VSO or VOS order. The fact that he finds VSO order acceptable is probably a result of his conscious awareness, given the input, that this order is possible; but this awareness is an example of encyclopaedic or meta-linguistic knowledge and is not strictly speaking to be taken as part of his linguistic competence in the technical sense.

Null subjects

As pointed out above and as illustrated further in 15, Berber allows null subjects in both matrix and embedded clauses:

15(a)   Y-zra Munat
        3ms-saw Munat
        He saw Munat

(b)   T-enna qa ad t-uggur zich
        3fs-said that will 3fs-leave early
        She said that she will leave early

As also mentioned earlier, the initial input to Christopher contained virtually no examples of null subject sentences yet, as shown in 5, he accepted and produced such sentences freely. As before, it would be possible to say that Christopher had reset the pro-drop parameter to its positive value (hence that AGR in Berber licenses a pro subject). However, in our discussion of other pro-drop languages which Christopher knows (namely, Modern Greek, Spanish and Italian; see pp. 95–102, and Tsimpli and Smith, 1991), we showed that, of the properties standardly associated with the pro-drop parameter, it is only the possibility of having a null subject that Christopher seems to have mastered. He rejects both constructions with inverted subjects and those which involve a violation of the *that*-t effect. It has been suggested by a number of authors that the pro-drop parameter is not a unitary property and should be split into two or more independent parameters. Thus Chao (1980) and Abangma (1992) cite Portuguese and Denya as allowing null subjects but disallowing inversion; and Brandi and Cordin (1989) cite the Trentino and Florentine dialects of Italian as allowing inversion but disallowing null subjects. Even if this separation is correct, and even if it is therefore possible that Christopher has indeed reset the (strict) null-subject parameter, it still leaves unanswered the question of why he should not have reset the parameters responsible for the other sub-parts of the original pro-drop parameter. In the light of these considerations, we continue to assume Rizzi's (1986) analysis of the phenomenon, and hold by our suggestion that the subject position is not filled by a pro subject but rather that agreement is treated, as in standard French, as a subject clitic, and that no appeal to parameter-resetting is therefore necessary.

Christopher's partial rejection of V (XP) S order thus conforms with our earlier findings in Modern Greek, Spanish and Italian, and in the next section we shall see that he also rejects Berber sentences which involve *that*-trace effects. Given that subject-postposing is a function of the ability of AGR to license a pro in the canonical subject position, Christopher's judgements imply a failure to reset the pro-drop parameter to the positive value. If this is indeed the case, it is unlikely that his representation of null-subject sentences involves a pro. An analysis which would be consistent with all these findings is one where the agreement morpheme in 5(a)–(c) is analysed as a subject clitic which incorporates into the verbal complex from the subject position. This, however, predicts incorrectly that dislocation constructions with a clitic subject should be possible for him. We have suggested an account of this problem (pp. 54–7), but it is significant that we have no need to appeal to parameter-resetting here either.

That-*trace effects*

Like null-subject languages in general, Berber allows violations of the *that*-t effect, as illustrated in the ambiguous examples in 16:

16(a) U ay t-nna Munat qa y-zra Mohand?
       who FM 3fs-said Munat that 3ms-saw Mohand
       Who did Munat say saw Mohand?
       or: Who did Munat say (that) Mohand saw?

(b)   Mi ay t-nni-t qa y-arez
       what FM 2s-said-2s that 3ms-broke
       What did you say has broken?
       or: What did you say (that) he has broken?

Because of his eagerness to translate any material he is presented with, it was difficult to elicit acceptability judgements from Christopher about sentences such as 16. Accordingly, to discover the status for him of such examples, we had to seek evidence from his translation. Presented with the sentence in 17, Christopher translated it incorrectly as indicated in 17':

17   U ay t-nni-t qa y-ssen Munat?
       who FM 2s-said-2s that 3ms-know Munat
       Who did you say knows Munat?
17'   'Whom did you say that Munat knows?'

That is, his version presupposes movement of the object rather than the subject, with 'Munat' being incorrectly construed as the subject, despite the fact that it does not agree with the embedded verb. This behaviour is consonant with his treatment of ambiguous examples such as 16(a), which he invariably translated as though the extracted wh-phrase was the object rather than the subject. Likewise, with sentences such as 16(b) containing verbs which can have either a transitive or an intransitive/ergative reading ('break'/*arz* in this case), Christopher's translations invariably conveyed the transitive reading, implying that the category extracted is the object not the subject.

These observations argue against the parameter-resetting hypothesis in two different, but related, ways. The ability of null-subject VSO languages such as Berber to violate the *that*-trace effect can be a function either of their having the structure given in 13 above, or the ability of their AGR to license a pro. Assuming Rizzi's (1990) definition of the ECP, where proper government is defined as government by a head within the single-bar domain, the subject position in 13 (Spec AGRP) is properly head-governed by TNS. The trace of an extracted subject will therefore always satisfy the ECP. The fact that Christopher rejects sentences containing *that*-trace violations implies, as concluded above, that he has not reset the parameter responsible for the order of TNS and AGR.

On the assumption that Christopher assigns Berber sentences such as
6(c) the structure in 14, the Spec of AGRP is not properly head governed.
The only potential proper head-governor is the complementizer 'qa', but
this is inert for government (see Rizzi, 1990), and the only legitimate way of
extracting the subject is from postverbal position. That is, wh-extraction of
the subject has to be preceded by subject-postposing to a properly head-
governed position, as in Standard Italian. However, this is an unlikely
strategy for Christopher as he tends to reject sentences with postposed
subjects, a fact which we explained above in terms of his failure to reset the
pro-drop parameter.

Corroborative evidence of the claim that Christopher's errors are due not
to parameter-resetting but are a joint function of transfer mistakes and the
exploitation of principles of UG comes from his reaction to wh-island
violations.

Wh-island violations

Like a number of null-subject languages – and, significantly, only null-
subject languages – Berber allows violations of wh-islands of the type
illustrated in 18, where the embedded subject has been extracted across a
wh-word in the Spec of CP:

18(a)   U ay ur t-ssn-t magha y-ukwta aqzin?
         who FM NEG 2s-know-2s why 3ms-hit dog
         *Who don't you know why hit the dog?

   (b)   Mohand ay ur ssn-gh magha y-ukwta aqzin
         Mohand FM NEG know-1s why 3ms-hit dog
         *It's Mohand that I don't know why hit the dog

In his treatment of comparable examples in Italian, Rizzi (1982)
concluded that these constructions do not involve extraction, but are
instances of the resumptive pronoun strategy, where the resumptive
pronoun is a pro licensed by the embedded AGRS element. Later (Rizzi,
1990) he suggests that the analysis of examples parallel to those in 16 can be
assimilated to that of sentences such as 17, which exhibit *that*-trace effect
violations, in that they both involve extraction from postverbal position.
On either account the preverbal subject position is filled with a pro licensed
by AGR.

Christopher's performance on these constructions was prone to error:
typically, his strategy in translating sentences such as 18(a) was to turn

them into yes/no questions, ignoring the wh-word entirely. For example, he translated 19 as a grammatical yes/no question rather than as the 'correct' but ungrammatical equivalent of the Berber (his mistranslation of the verb is irrelevant):

19 U ay ur t-ssn-t magha y-uggur?
    who FM NEG 2s-know-2s why 3ms-left
    *Who don't you know why left?
19' 'Don't you know why he came back?'

On a different occasion he translated the same sentence as in 20, where the form of the extracted wh-word (*whom*) shows that it is construed as the object rather than the subject:

20 'Whom did you not know why he left?'

Sentence 20 is not a possible translation of 19, as the Berber *uggur*, unlike its English counterpart 'leave', does not allow a transitive reading. However, while it is not easy to interpret his first attempt, as Christopher could perhaps not be expected to produce appropriate ungrammatical sentences to order, it is clear from his second attempt that he was avoiding translations which would involve a strong violation of the wh-island or the ECP. In this regard, it is important to recall that, in English, the extraction of a subject (or an adjunct) out of a wh-island yields a significantly worse result than the extraction of an object (see Huang, 1984; and Rizzi, 1990), among others).

This conclusion is confirmed by the results of a different test in which Christopher was asked to translate English sentences, some of which were ungrammatical, into Berber. When faced with 21, for example, his initial reaction was to translate it, correctly (and grammatically) as in 22a. However, he subsequently corrected his translation by crossing out the wh-word, thus turning the sentence into the yes/no question 22b:

21   *Who are you wondering when he arrived?

22(a) 'U t-xemmame-t melmi y-exdel?'
   (b) 't-xemmame-t melmi y-exdel?' [Do you wonder when he arrived?]

In the same exercise Christopher translated the English sentence in 23(a) as 24(a), whose status in Berber is considerably worse than that of its English counterpart. In this situation Berber strongly prefers the resumptive pronoun strategy, as illustrated in 24(b), where the resumptive pronoun is the '*t*' immediately following the embedded verb:

23   *Which book don't you know when Munat bought?

24(a)   *'Men lechtab ur t-ssne-t shem melmi t-esgha Munat?'
        which book not 2s-know-2s you when 3fs-bought Munat
   (b) Men lechtab ay ur t-ssnet-t (shem) melmi t-shgi t Munat?

Christopher's assumption that 24(a) has the same status as its English counterpart is presumably an instance of a transfer error.

As pointed out above, sentences such as 19 and 22(a) can be analysed as involving either a resumptive pronoun strategy or movement from postverbal position. The facts of object-extraction, where the resumptive pronoun strategy is strongly preferred, suggest the former, with the resumptive pronoun being a pro licensed and identified by AGR. One could then argue that Christopher's rejection of these sentences implies that pro is unavailable, suggesting in turn that the pro-drop parameter has not been reset. The same conclusion can be reached if 19 and 22(a) are analysed as involving extraction from postverbal position, as subject-postposing is determined by the ability of AGR to license a pro.

However, we have argued above that Christopher has the option of reanalysing the AGR morpheme as a subject clitic, which in the sentences under discussion could legitimately act as a resumptive pronoun, just as object clitic pronouns can. This may seem problematic, until one recalls that resumptive pronouns are excluded from the English counterparts of these sentences and, more generally, from sentences exhibiting (long) extraction. Thus, whatever is responsible for the exclusion of resumptive pronouns in the relevant environments in English can plausibly be said to be responsible for Christopher's rejection of the Berber constructions under discussion. In other words, this is another instance of transfer.

Conclusions

Christopher's partial acquisition of Berber has a number of interesting implications. First, there is evidence that the structural properties of the language led him to correct conclusions even in the absence of overt evidence of the relevant kind. Specifically, his assumption that Berber allowed null subjects, even though the input data had been deliberately designed to exclude any examples is striking, especially as transfer from English is obviously impossible. Even though pro-drop languages like

Chinese have an impoverished inflectional system, the major generalization in this domain is that the possibility of null subjects is a function of rich morphology. It is therefore presumably this aspect of Berber that led Christopher, via the pressure of UG, to make the correct inference. Second, despite this 'unlearned knowledge', there is no evidence in Christopher's performance for parameter-resetting as a mechanism for second language learning. Although the hypothesis of parameter-resetting predicts that learners should show such 'cascade' effects, where they end up knowing more than they have been exposed to, we have reason to exclude this as an explanation here. On the one hand, we have alternative (and more plausible) accounts for the phenomena described which make invoking parameter resetting unnecessary; on the other hand, Christopher precisely failed to manifest the clustering of properties that would have supported the hypothesis. Specifically, the usual correlation between the possibilty of null subjects and the existence of inverted subjects, of *that*-trace effects, and so on, was not in evidence. He mastered the appropriate use of null subjects, but remained irremediably 'English' in his responses to the other phenomena. Finally, given the asymmetry between his judgements of well-formedness and his own translations in so far as these involved SVO and VSO word-order, it is plausible to assume that some aspects of Christopher's second language learning do not result in a change in his encapsulated linguistic knowledge, his competence (in the sense of Chomsky, 1965), but rather that they are a function of his encyclopaedic knowledge allied, via his obsessional interest in languages, with the resources of UG.

Learning an Impossible Language: Epun

Similarly, knowing something about UG, we can readily design 'languages' that will be unattainable by the language faculty.
Chomsky, 1991b: 40

In the previous section our hypothesis had been that, if Christopher made mistakes in acquiring Berber, these would in the first instance be due to the different selection of particular parametric values made by Berber and English. By contrast, we predicted that he should find it impossible or extremely difficult to master those parts of a 'language' which, *ex hypothesi*, contravened universal generalizations and were therefore not describable in terms of parametric variation. We have argued that his status as a polyglot savant is accurately characterized – to a first approximation – in terms of his having an intact, or enhanced, language module in association with some impairment of his central, cognitive faculties. It follows that constructions which are attested in natural languages should afford him no insuperable difficulties, whereas unattested (and putatively linguistically impossible) constructions, even if conceptually simple and transparent, should occasion him severe problems.[7] However, on the assumption that second language learning may involve general inductive learning strategies as well as algorithms specific to language learning, it is plausible to assume that even the linguistically impossible could be learned via a 'central' process of inductive reasoning, provided only that the central system is not too impaired to cope.[8] In such a situation the order in which Christopher mastered different 'impossible' rules should be a joint function of their inherent complexity and their similarity to rules in languages that he already knows.

We are aware that it is problematic to describe some phenomenon as 'impossible'. What is deemed to be impossible today may well turn out to be not only possible, but commonplace, tomorrow. A striking example is provided by the debate over the existence of object-initial languages in the 1970s (see Smith, 1989: ch. 6), but we take it as axiomatic that (im)possibility is defined in terms of current theory. Accordingly, those constructions treated here as impossible are so described for two reasons: first, because neither we nor our colleagues know of valid counter-examples to the claim; second, because they are incompatible with some principle, or combination of principles, of current linguistic theory.

As a control we also attempted to teach a small group of four first-year linguistics undergraduates Epun, using exactly the same material and hence including exactly the same impossible constructions as those we tested Christopher with. Our expectation was that normal subjects would be more easily able to perceive the regularities in a linguistically impossible system and learn it by using their 'general intelligence' as a compensatory device for the inadequate, because irrelevant, language module. These predictions were partially confirmed, but the controls' performance was itself sufficiently complex to make any simple explanation of the results difficult.

Both Christopher and the controls were subjected to a variety of different structures,[9] both possible and impossible, with results which fell into three different categories. Structure-independent operations proved impossible for everyone. Structure-dependent operations which are empirically unattested and theoretically implausible were within the abilities of the control group but proved beyond Christopher in the initial stages, though he made some progress after prolonged exposure. Structure-dependent operations which are attested and plausible were within the capabilities of everyone, though Christopher made a range of 'unprovoked' mistakes which were distinct from anything produced by the controls, and which revealed something of his linguistic abilities.

The structure of Epun

Epun is an SVO language with a rich agreement system. Verbs inflect for past, present and future – specifically, the verb stem is prefixed by *ha-*, zero or *chu-*. The verb agrees with the subject in person, number and gender, where agreement takes the form of suffixes to the verb stem: *-u* for masculine singular, *-gu* for feminine singular, *-nis* for first-person plural, and so on. In the data given to Christopher, the subject consisted of a proper noun, or a common noun optionally preceded by either a determiner or a demonstrative. Demonstratives are invariable; the definite determiner (there is no indefinite determiner) agrees with the noun in number and gender, and also varies according to phonological context (cf. *'f'*, *'fa'* and *'afa'* in the examples in 25. The subject noun (proper or common) and any preceding adjective are marked with a nominative suffix (*'-in'*, following a consonant, or *'-din'*, following a vowel). The object noun and any preceding adjective are marked with an oblique suffix (*'-op'* or *'-p'*, again depending on the preceding phonological context). Pronouns show no case differences (i.e. have no nominative or oblique suffix). The phonological/orthographic system of the language is unremarkable and 'normal'. Additions to and variations from these patterns will be described below. Examples of all the above generalizations can be seen in 25:

25(a)   the (male) cat came – f imni-din ha-panib-u
              the cat-Nom Past-come-3MS

  (b)   a man will come – zaddil-in chu-panib-u
              man-Nom Fut-come-3MS

  (c)   the king returned – fa mideb-in ha-binap-u
              the king-Nom Past-return-3MS

  (d)   the girl returns today – afa zena-din binap-gu indid
              the girl-Nom return-3FS today

  (e)   we returned – ni-sa ha-binap-nis
              we Past-return-1Pl

(f)   we know that you will write many letters
      ni-sa jan-nis ef ho-za ch-erehel-oh nunu-p vlet-op-iz
      we know-1Pl that you Fut-write-2S many-OBL letter-OBL-Pl

Christopher took to the language happily, learning it with his customary speed and flair, and making a range of mistakes not uncharacteristic of second language learners. For instance, he had problems with the article system, he tended to omit the case endings, and he made a number of errors of vocabulary (for full details, see Smith et al., 1993). It was only after he had mastered these normal regularities of the language that we gradually introduced 'impossible' constructions.

Structure-independent operations

The syntax of emphasis   The archetypal example of impossible constructions is provided by structure independent operations (see Chomsky, 1972, for an early statement). We avoided these in the early stages of the experiment in case they made Christopher suspicious or caused him to give up trying, but after some nine months' exposure to Epun we thought that he was sufficiently accustomed to it not to be put off. Accordingly we confronted him with examples of emphatic sentences of the kind illustrated in 26, where the form and position of the emphatic element (*nog(in)*) are arithmetically rather than structurally determined:

26(a)   Fa zaddil-in ha-bol-u-*nog* guv
        The man-Nom Past-go-3MS-Emph yesterday
        The man *didn't* go yesterday

   (b)   Lodon-in ha-bol-u guv-*nog*
         Lodon-Nom Past-go-3MS yesterday-Emph
         Lodon did go yesterday

   (c)   Chi h-u-pat Lodo-p-*nog* to mi-za kakol?
         Who Past-3MS-Pos Lodo-Obl-Emph and I see
         Who did see Lodo and me?

   (d)   Mideb-in ha-panib-u *nogin*
         King-Nom Past-come-3MS Emph
         A king did come

The emphatic marker *nog* always appears suffixed to the third orthographic

word of the sentence – matrix or embedded – of which it is part. If there are
fewer than three words (as in example 26(d)), the form *nogin* occurs in final
position. Christopher had no idea what to do with *nog(in)*: his usual strategy
appeared to be to attach it to the verb as illustrated in 27(a)–(d), or to omit
it, as in 27(e) (where, as usual, Christopher's version is given last in
inverted commas):

27(a)   I wonder who *did* come
         Mi-za lokan-im [chi h-u-pat panib-*nog*]
         I wonder-1S [who Past-3MS-Pos come-Emph]
         'Mi-za lokan-im chi ha-panib-u-nog'

Note that in the correct version of this sentence the emphatic element is
suffixed to the third word of the [bracketed] constituent clause.
Christopher's version exhibits not only a problem with *nog*, but also a
consistent difficulty he had with the auxiliary system, even though this
system is perfectly possible, and indeed modelled in relevant respects on
that of English.

27(b)   Lodo *did* return
         Lodo-din ha-binap-gu *nogin*
         Lodo-Nom Past-return-3FS Emph
         'Lodo ha-binap-gu-nog'

27(c)   This dog *doesn't* catch them
         Osoze-u gub chegod-in-*nog* a-sa
         catch-3MS this dog-Nom-Emph them
         'Osoze-us-nog gub chegod-in a-sa'

(The ending *-us* is the plural congener of the correct *-u*).

27(d)   Which letter *did* Lodon and I write?
         Tik vlet-op h-oh-pat-*nog* Lodon-in to mi-za erehel?
         Which letter-Obl Past-2S-Pos-Emph Lodon-Nom and I write
         'Tik vlet-op h-erehel-us-nog Lodon to mi-za?'

(The anomalous form of the agreement marker will be discussed below.)

27(e)   The boy wonders whether Lodo *did* see a cat
         Fa makoh-in lokan-u [vem ha-gu-pat imni-p-*nog* Lodo-din kakol]
         The boy-Nom wonder-3MS [whether Past-3FS-Pos cat-Obl-Emph
             Lodo-Nom see]
         'Fa makoh-in lokan-u vem ha-kakol-gu Lodo imni-p'

Christopher's expected failure to master this structure-independent construction was confirmed in subsequent tests. First, he failed to correct 'ungrammatical' examples such as that in 28, which should have contained *nogin*:

28   Kov-in chu-panib-gu-*nog*
      Girl-Nom Fut-come-3FS-Emph
      A girl *will* come

even though he translated it adequately as: 'The girl will return (come)'. Second, he clearly associated the emphatic marker with the element it was suffixed to rather than with the clause as a whole, as witness his translation of 29:

29   U-za aveti-u gu-za-nog
      He love-3MS her-Emph
      He does love her
      'He loves her'

where his underlining shows that he realizes the emphatic nature of the suffix, even if what is focussed should not include only the object pronoun.

Like Christopher, the controls had no success in unravelling the mystery of *nog(in)*. Typical examples of their efforts are provided in 30(a) and 30(b), corresponding to the examples in 27(d) and 27(e) respectively:

30(a) Tik vlet-op ha-nis-pat Lodon-in to-nog mi-za erehel?
  (b) Fa makoh-in lokan-u vem ha-gu-pat-nog imni-p Lodo-din kakol

They all admitted to being baffled by the distribution of the emphatic marker and to having tried numerous (linguistically sensible) hypotheses as to what class or classes of constituent it attached to, to no avail. It may be that controls who were linguistically more naive might have had greater success, as they might have been more prepared to try 'logical' hypotheses.

A further type of 'impossibility' that we investigated fell on the border-line between structure-dependence and structure-independence. It consisted in testing Christopher's reaction to simple violations of principles of UG, such as (subjacency) violations of Ross's (1967) co-ordinate structure constraint, exemplified in 31. The instruction was to 'read the following Epun sentences and correct any that you think are wrong, then translate the corrected version into English'. As usual, he was given the Epun, including the hyphens, but no other information.

31(a)   Tik chegod-op h-oh-pat to pelik-op ho-za kakol?   [OK]
         Which dog-Obl Past-2S-Pos and tortoise-Obl you see
         Which dog did you see and a tortoise?
         'Which dog and tortoise did you see?'

  (b)   Tik chegod-op ch-u-pat u-za kakol pelik-op to   [R]
         Which dog-Obl Fut-3MS-Pos he see tortoise-Obl and
         Which dog will he see a tortoise and?
         'Which dog and tortoise will he see?'

He left 31(a) uncorrected, while translating it grammatically, and he
'corrected' 31(b) by indicating that the sequence *pelik-op to* should be
placed immediately before *u-za*. This links the sequence appropriately with
another noun phrase, but not the correct one, as is clear from the case
marking and from Christopher's translation. Unlike the purely structure-
independent 'emphatic' examples, these sentences exhibit partial violations
of structure, and seemed to occasion Christopher less difficulty, though we
have too few examples to be sure of his ability in this direction. Moreover,
his reaction to these exercises as being 'too difficult' indicated that it was
counter-productive to continue with them.

   The controls had no difficulty at all with these examples, both correcting
the Epun and providing appropriate English translations.

The morphology of agreement   The last example in this section of
phenomena unattested in natural languages involved morphological
agreement 'resolution rules' in the sense of Corbett (1991). The need for
resolution typically arises when a verb has to agree with a co-ordinate noun
phrase whose conjuncts have incompatible properties, such as masculine
and feminine or singular and plural. The rationale behind this choice was
the following. First, we wanted to test how difficult it is to learn forms
whose morphological properties are distinct from those in one's native
language. We hoped to show that differences between Christopher's
performance and that of the controls would support our earlier claim that
Christopher's second language learning is disproportionately dependent on
his sensitivity to morphological patterns. That is, his apparent fluency in
his non-native languages is a product more of his mastery of L2
morphology than of L2 syntax. Second, we wanted to see if there was any
difference between learning patterns which are merely distinct from those
in one's first language and those which are not only distinct but also
linguistically unattested.[10]

   Typically, the co-ordination of a first person singular noun phrase with a
third-person singular noun phrase results in first person plural agreement

on the verb. More specifically, Corbett gives the following three
generalisations: 'If the conjuncts include a first person, first person
agreement forms will be used' (1991:262); 'provided there is at least one
non-plural conjunct, plural agreement forms will be used'[11] (ibid.: 263);
and 'If all conjuncts are feminine, then the feminine form is used, otherwise
the masculine is used' (ibid.: 281). Accordingly we tested Christopher with
Epun examples in which the co-ordination of the first-person singular with
a third-person singular feminine noun phrase resulted in third-person
feminine plural agreement on the verb, and the co-ordination of a first-
person singular with a third person singular masculine NP resulted in
second-person singular agreement on the verb. Both possibilities are
exhibited in 32:

32(a)   She and I love tortoises
        Gu-za to mi-za aveti-*gus* pelik-op-iz
        She and I love-3FP tortoise-Obl-Pl

   (b) He and I love walruses
        U-za to mi-za aveti-*oh* vakvel-op-iz
        He and I love-2S walrus-Obl-Pl

Christopher translated 32(a) perfectly, and with the comparable example in
33:

33   Which letter did Lodo and I read?
     Tik vlet-op ha-*gus*-pat Lodo-din to mi-za hochik?
     Which letter-Obl Past-3FP-Pos Lodo-Nom and I read
     'Tik vlet-op ha-hochik-*gus* Lodo to mi-za'

his translation was correct in the relevant respect. That is, although he
made his usual mistakes of omitting the auxiliary and the nominative
marker on the proper name, the agreement marker was morphologically
correct. With 32(b) and similar examples, he interestingly generalized the
'impossible' pattern of 32(a) in the obvious way, using the third person
masculine plural marker on the verb, as illustrated in 34:

34(a)   'U-za to mi-za aveti-*us* vakvel-op-iz'   (cf. 32(b))

   (b) Which letter *did* Lodon and I write?
        Tik vlet-op h-oh-pat-nog Lodon-in to mi-za erehel?
        Which letter-Obl Past-2S-Pos-Emph Lodon-Nom and I write
        'Tik vlet-op h-erehel-*us*-nog Lodon to mi-za'

Of the controls, one got the agreement (impossibly) correct; the others regularized it as in extant languages and as illustrated in 35:

35(a)   Gu-za to mi-za aveti-*nis* pelik-op-iz   (cf. 32(a))

  (b)   U-za to mi-za aveti-*nis* vakvel-op-iz   (cf. 32(b), 34(a))

  (c)   Tik vlet-op ha-*nis*-pat Lodo-din to mi-za hochik?   (cf. 33)

  (d)   Tik vlet-op ha-*nis*-pat Lodon-in to-nog mi-za erehel?   (cf. 34(b)).

These data show that Christopher and the controls differed in their reaction to these constructions. Neither had any difficulty with aspects of the morphological paradigm which conformed to regularly attested patterns. Unlike the controls, however, Christopher correctly inferred one of the morphological resolution rules for number in Epun: specifically, that one violating the attested generalizations discussed previously. For the other rule, he incorrectly generalized the pattern of the first on the basis of *gender*, where in fact a new rule based on *number* was required. In neither case, however, did he impose the English pattern on the Epun data. By contrast, the controls simply generalized the pattern of their first language in both cases. In other words, our first prediction, that Christopher's second language learning is exceptional in its sensitivity to properties of the morphology, was confirmed. This contrasts with our findings *vis-à-vis* his syntax, where he regularly imposed the structure of his first language on his 'second' languages, implying that the learning of morphology, at least in his case, is different in kind from the learning (or acquisition) of syntax. The contrast between Christopher and the controls in their learning of morphology is not unexpected, given the rather exotic nature of the input and their relative inexperience with morphologically complex languages.

The results from the controls also seem to support the second prediction, that unattestedness leads to increased complexity, and so would have an inhibiting effect over and above that of mere unfamiliarity. Christopher's performance, however, indicates that, for him at least, morphological patterns are learned equally easily irrespective of their 'possibility'. While these results are suggestive, we remain agnostic about their deeper implications for the relation between Corbett's resolution rules and the notion of 'possible' vs. 'impossible' in morphology. Unless his generalizations are amenable to syntactic explanation (cf. note 11), differences in the learning of attested vs. unattested forms need not be attributed to the operation of UG, and the conclusion that unattested forms are *ipso facto* impossible is not legitimate. It seems clear, however, that structure-

independent processes are, in general and predictably, beyond Christopher's
capabilities.

Structure-dependent operations

While structure-independent operations represent the extreme of linguistic
'impossibility', it is also straightforward to devise constructions which are
theoretically illicit despite their normal structure dependence. We turn
now to two examples of such constructions in Epun.

The syntax of negation   In constructions without an auxiliary, Epun has no
overt negative morpheme, and negative sentences are characterized simply
by the verb preceding the subject. That is, we have a contrast between
SV(O) word-order in positive sentences and VS(O) word-order in negative
sentences. As will become clear below when we discuss the syntax of tense,
there are further complications, as the past tense is characterized by the
object being moved to initial position, as well as by the presence of the overt
prefix *h(a)*-. That is, Epun displays not just the basic SVO word-order
mentioned above, but the range of word-order patterns given in 36:

36   SV(O)   Positive (present and future)
     VS(O)   Negative (present and future)
     (O)SV   Positive (past)
     (O)VS   Negative (past)

However, the morphology is constant: i.e. subject and object are consistently marked as before, and the verb agrees with the subject as before.
Moreover, to make Christopher's task somewhat less difficult, he was given
the explicit information that: 'if the verb precedes the subject, the sentence
is negative; if the object precedes the subject the sentence is past'.

   A formal account of the peculiar negation described above presumably
has to have recourse to obligatory verb-raising in negative sentences. That
is, there is a NEGP projection immediately dominating AGRP, as
illustrated in 37:

37   NEGP
           /   \
       Spec   NEG'
               /   \
            NEG   AGRP
                    /   \
                 Spec   AGR' . . .

For reasons of recoverability, it is standardly assumed (see, e.g., Haegeman, 1995) that in a configuration of this type either the Spec of NEGP or the head NEG must be overt. Assuming further that NEG in Epun is a phonetically null affixal head, the verb has to raise to NEG at S-structure in order to satisfy Lasnik's Filter (see Pesetsky, 1989): a condition of UG. On the assumption that UG regulates the options available in second language acquisition, a representation with both the head and the specifier empty should in principle be excluded. As negatives in Epun involve a violation of UG in this way, the construction is considered to be 'impossible'.

Christopher had considerable difficulty with these anomalous negatives. After detailed exemplification, he was presented with eight negative sentences to translate into Epun, five of which he got wrong. In some cases it looked as if the subject incorrectly preceded the verb (e.g. 38(a)–(c)), though the nature of his mistakes makes it hard to be sure; in one he omitted the subject entirely (as though the language were pro-drop) (38(d)); one was wrong because of a mistake with the past tense (38(e)), and one was wrong because of morphological mistakes only (38(f)). Two sentences were correct, one transitive (38(g)) and one intransitive (39). As before, Christopher's version, when incorrect, is given last in inverted commas. No translation is provided in those cases where his version was completely correct.

38(a)   Cats don't look at tortoises
     hielo-gus imni-din-iz pelik-op-iz
     look at-3Pl cat-Nom-Pl tortoise-Obl-Pl
     'imnik-in-iz hielo-us peli-din-iz'

(It is not clear which NP Christopher intended to be subject: the word-order is wrong whichever is chosen.)

38(b)   That boy won't come today
     chu-panib-u heop makoh-in indid
     Fut-come-3MS that boy-Nom today
     'heop makoh-in chu-panib-u fa indid'

(Christopher explained that the underlining in his version of this sentence indicated that *chu-panib-u* should be in initial position; i.e. only the excrescent *fa* was incorrect.)

38(c)   We won't see the walrus tomorrow
     chu-kakol-nis ni-sa fa vakvel-op pa

Fut-see-1Pl we the walrus-Obl tomorrow
'Nisa chu-kakol-nis fa vakvel-op pa'

(Underlining as in example 38(b).

38(d)   We didn't see the walruses yesterday
        va vakvel-op-iz ha-kakol-nis ni-sa guv
        the walrus-Obl-Pl Past-see-1Pl we yesterday
        'ha-kakol-nis fa vakvel-op-iz guv'

38(e)   This woman didn't read the letter
        fa vlet-op ha-hochik-gu gub horu-din
        the letter-Obl Past-read-3FS this woman-Nom
        'ha-hochik-gu gub horu-din fa vlet-op'

38(f)   The cat didn't look at the tortoise
        fa pelik-op ha-hielo-gu af imni-din
        the tortoise-Obl Past-look at-3FS the cat-Nom
        'pelik ha-hielo-gu fa imnik-in'

(Note that the agreement on the verb is also incorrect, as Christopher has
used 'imnik' – a male cat, rather than 'imni' – a female cat.)

38(g)   Lodon doesn't love Lodo
        aveti-u Lodon-in Lodo-p
        love-3ms Lodon-Nom Lodo-Obl

39   This man didn't come yesterday
        ha-panib-u gub zaddil-in guv
        past-come-3MS this man-Nom yesterday

His translation from Epun into English was much better, with most of
the examples of negative word-order correctly interpreted, giving rise to
some completely correct sentences. There were none the less some
interesting mistakes: in three cases (out of eight) he failed to identify the
negative word-order, and in two cases he translated the Epun with an
English passive, thereby reversing the role of subject and object. Examples
of the last two phenomena are given in 40:

40(a)   fa mong-op ha-hielo-gu fa bozu-din
        the paper-Obl Past-look at-3FS the teacher-Nom

The teacher didn't look at the paper
'The teacher looked at the paper'

(b) miga-din imnik-in ch-osoze-gu makoh-op
     big-Nom cat-Nom Fut-catch-3FS boy-Obl
     A big cat will catch a boy
     'Big cat will be caught by the boy'

The fact that his translation from Epun into English was markedly superior to his translation in the other direction indicates that his comprehension, with the possibility of exploiting semantic and pragmatic information contained in the rest of the sentence, is in advance of his production ability. While a common enough phenomenon, this is interesting in the case of Christopher because of its implications for the integration of his syntactic and his non-grammatical knowledge.

Subsequent instruction in the language introduced Christopher to positive and negative auxiliary verbs (he systematically failed to master the auxiliary system, even though it was modelled closely on English). In these the word-order peculiarity of simple sentences was maintained and, after some considerable difficulty, Christopher seemed gradually to be mastering the Epun negative (at least 50 per cent of the time). An explanation for this can perhaps be derived from one of the options (see pp. 35–6) made available by the theory of second language acquisition we have adopted: namely, the second language learner may make use of inductive learning strategies. In other words, when faced with linguistic data that cannot be accommodated under UG, the learner formulates a hypothesis, using general learning mechanisms, on the basis of his observation of the data. To account for Epun negatives the relevant (linear) rule should look something like 41:

41 To construct a negative clause in Epun move the verb to a pre-subject position.

Some evidence that this is the correct explanation is provided by the fact that the controls made *no* errors with negation at all, presumably because of their superior ability to deploy central system mechanisms to solve linguistic problems. If this is correct, the same kind of observation should carry over to Christopher's and the controls' reactions to the past tense examples. We return to an alternative, semantic, explanation once we have looked at Christopher's reaction to the 'impossible' past tense.

The syntax of tense If Epun negation caused Christopher (perhaps temporary) problems, the peculiarities of the past tense proved totally insuperable. Just as the absence of an overt negative morpheme gave rise to a violation of a principle of UG – that governing the recoverability of deletion, the correlation between tense and word-order similarly gives rise to a problematic configuration in terms of UG. To account for past tense transitive sentences, with positive OSV and negative OVS word-order, it is necessary to provide some motivation for the movement of the object to initial position, and also to specify where precisely it moves to. There are in principle two possibilities: the movement could either be an example of topicalization, in which the object is adjoined to CP; or it could be an example of focusing, or operator-movement with the moved phrase substituting into Spec CP. In neither case is there any theoretical justification for the movement being obligatory, nor for the observed correlation with choice of tense.[12] Although there are documented cases in which, for instance, word order differences correlate with differences of aspect or 'perfect'-ness, there are to our knowledge no cases in which word-order is dependent on a choice of past vs. present or future.

Christopher's responses to these data were completely consistent: in the translation from English into Epun there were seven past tenses (six transitive and one intransitive), illustrated in 42:

42(a)   The queen looked at the king
        fa mideb-op afa mide-din ha-hielo-gu
        the king-Obl the queen-Nom past-look at-3Fs
        'Afa mide-din ha-hielo-gu mideb-op'

   (b)   The boy read the book yesterday
         fa tiktab-op fa makoh-in ha-hochik-u guv
         the book-Obl the boy-Nom Past-read-3MS yesterday
         'Fa makoh-in ha-hochik-u tiktab-op guv'

   (c)   A tortoise looked at the cat
         af imni-p pelik-in ha-hielo-u
         the cat-Obl tortoise-Nom Past-look at-3MS
         'pelik ha-hielo-gu fa imnik-in'

Christopher produced the wrong word-order with all and only the six transitives, usually using SVO instead of the correct object-initial order, as can be seen in his translations.

It is clear that the regular SVO pattern established for the present and future had become fixed for all tenses for Christopher. Neither the addition of auxiliaries, reinforcing the consistency of the anomalous word-order, nor the introduction of embedded sentences had any apparent facilitating effect. Thus, when given further sets of sentences to translate from and into Epun, Christopher systematically failed to put the object in initial position in the past tense. Instead he typically rendered them with SVO word order, i.e. like the Epun present/future, or indeed like English. In the twenty sentences he had to translate into Epun, there were seven past tense sentences, none of which he got right.

An interesting corollary of the grammar is that, where there is no overt case marking (i.e. on pronouns), there is the possibility of systematic ambiguity with, for example, 'what saw him?' and 'what did he see?' being translated identically. This allowed us to test whether Christopher would carry over patterns from, say, Modern Greek, which has the same pattern, as well as from English into his foreign language learning. At first, he failed to translate these sentences, but later gave unambiguous translations of examples like 43:

43(a)   tik h-u-pat u-za aveti?
       which Past 3MS Pos he love
       Which did he love?/Which loved him?
       'Which did he love?'

   (b)   mi-za lokan-im tak h-u-pat u-za kakol
       I wonder 1S what Past 3MS Pos he see
       I wonder what he saw/what saw him
       'I wonder what he saw'

In his version the object and not the subject has moved, confirming the tendency that we had earlier observed in both Berber and Greek. Again, his pattern of behaviour is consistent across languages, even where those languages allow for different interpretive possibilities, indicating that his L2 learning involves predominantly transfer effects.

In marked contrast to Christopher's failure to master the past tense peculiarity of Epun, the controls were overwhelmingly successful. Given that the correlation between the position of the object and the tense feature, [±past], on the verb is linguistically impossible, we have to assume that mastery of the phenomenon by the controls (only one of whom made a significant number of mistakes) is due to the use of some inductive strategy. A rule that could account for object movement in past tense sentences would need to include the information in 44:

44   To construct a transitive sentence in the past tense mark the verb with
     ha- and move the object to initial position.

This rule is more complex than the one suggested for the formation of negative sentences (41 above) in that it requires both morphological marking and movement. However, the movement part of both rules seems intuitively to be equivalent which, given Christopher's expertise with morphology, predicts that he should be able to master either rule with roughly equal facility. This, however, was not the case: object preposing in past-tense sentences appeared to be much more difficult for him to learn than negative formation.

A possible semantic explanation suggests itself. Specifically, negation has direct implications for the semantic, truth-conditional, properties of a sentence, and we have independent evidence that Christopher's semantics, both lexical and structural, is virtually intact. We would accordingly expect him to be sensitive to the distinction between positive and negative structures. On the other hand, the phenomenon of preposing in past-tense sentences has no effect on semantic interpretation. That is, given that the [±past] contrast is anyway morphologically marked by the presence of the prefix *ha-*, the semantic interpretation of the tense value of the sentence is already determined irrespective of the position of the object. The performance of the controls, who mastered both phenomena with comparable facility, indicates that the syntactic complexity of the rule is roughly the same and that their strategy is different from Christopher's. Specifically, we assume that the surface simplicity of the generalizations underlying both negative formation and past-tense formation was such that the controls could solve the problems they presented by non-linguistic (central) means, whereas Christopher's impoverished central system precluded his doing the same.

Innovative creations

Christopher's partial failure to master the structure of negative and past tense sentences illustrates the difficulty presented by 'impossible' configurations. Another aspect of his language learning at this stage was revealing for something like the opposite reason. That is, Christopher appeared to produce spontaneously configurations which are allowed by UG even though there was no direct evidence for them in the input.

Epun has neither subject nor object clitics, but when asked to translate English sentences containing subject pronouns into Epun, Christopher frequently dropped the pronoun and left just the subject agreement on the verb (cf. example 38(d) above). This apparently indicates that he considers Epun to be a null-subject language. Indeed, of the eleven sentences with subject pronouns that he was asked to translate, Christopher only included that subject in one sentence. Notice, however, that his omission of pronouns is not restricted to subjects. Seven sentences contained both subject and object pronouns, none of which Christopher included. However, in five of these seven, the verb ending which should have shown agreement with the subject appeared to be showing agreement with the object. For instance, in 45 Christopher gave the translations indicated in inverted commas, with the verb inflected correctly for tense and apparently marked for the gender of the object, but showing no subject agreement:

45(a) He loves her – u-za aveti-u gu-za
       he love-3MS she
       'aveti-gu'
       love-3FS

   (b) He loved her – gu-za u-za h-aveti-u
        she he Past-love-3MS
        'h-aveti-gu'
        Past-love-3FS

   (c) She won't love him – ch-aveti-gu gu-za u-za
        Fut-love-3FS she he
        'ch-aveti-u'
        Fut-love-3MS

   (d) He didn't love her – gu-za h-aveti-u u-za
        she Past-love-3MS he
        'ha-aveti-gu'
        Past-love-3FS

We think this provides evidence for the claim that Christopher treated agreement marking as a clitic-like element, along the lines suggested (pp. 131–6) for Berber and the other pro-drop languages that he speaks.

There was sufficient evidence to confirm that Christopher's performance was reasonably consistent, but we cannot be conclusive about the status of the object clitic/agreement in these cases. One possibility is to assume that the verb is marked for tense but, in the absence of subject agreement, the subject is a PRO. In a later grammaticality judgement task, when Christopher had become significantly more proficient in Epun, he correctly identified one example comparable to those in 45 as being ungrammatical, replacing *ha-smin-gu* (Past-kiss-3FS) with *u-za ha-smin-gu gu-za*, but he left three others uncorrected. It is hard to interpret these additional data as there was evidence that he was tired when doing the exercise: for example, he failed to notice an ungrammatical English sentence and miscorrected an Epun construction he otherwise habitually got right, but it seems clear that, at least at the stage concerned, Christopher was operating under the constraints of UG despite the absence of overt evidence for the structures he induced.

Conclusions

The point of teaching Christopher an invented language was in the first instance to provide indirect evidence for or against the validity of Fodor's modularity hypothesis. We anticipated a mismatch between his ability to cope with phenomena of natural language on the one hand and linguistically 'impossible' but logically simple phenomena on the other. Moreover, we expected that such a mismatch would not appear in normal control subjects who should be able to solve the problems by having recourse to central strategies of general intelligence. Although the data are rather complex, we think that these predictions are largely borne out. Structure independent operations proved beyond the capabilities of everyone and are therefore not particularly illuminating with respect to Christopher. None the less they are significant in that they suggest strongly that the fact that the input is linguistic may inhibit the activation of general learning mechanisms. Impossible structure-dependent operations, however, did separate Christopher from the controls in the manner anticipated, and accordingly lend support to the hypothesis being tested. Our prediction that learning attested constructions of natural languages should occasion Christopher 'no insuperable difficulties' rests on the assumption that such learning can take place on the basis of a combination of transfer, access to UG and the exploitation of morphologically defined inductive learning strategies. Christopher fails when inductive learning strategies are not based on morphologically marked items; hence the contrast between his success with resolution rules and his failure on negation, where there was no morphological evidence at all. We suspect that his defective exploitation of inductive learning strategies contributes indirectly to the 'plateau' effect we have observed throughout his second language learning.

The Epun data also corroborate our claim that the learning of morphology is different in kind from the learning of syntax. It is noteworthy that though Christopher was significantly inferior to the controls in learning arbitrary syntactic patterns, he was better than them in learning anomalous agreement paradigms where there was overt morphological evidence of the irregularity. Further, he seems, in his assumption that Epun was pro-drop and in his invention of a new object-agreement pattern, to give evidence of the continuing effect of UG in second language learning. This is in marked contrast to the absence of evidence for parameter resetting and further indication of the difference between first and second language acquisition. The picture is somewhat obscured by certain failures in his learning of Epun: specifically, he seemed quite unable to master the auxiliary system, despite the fact that it was modelled directly on English and so presumably 'possible', and putatively accessible on the basis of transfer. We can only speculate that other properties of Epun, such as its rich morphology, led Christopher to assume that it was pro-drop, and that there is an incompatibility between an auxiliary system of this type and the possibility of pro subjects in the SpecIP position (see Hyams, 1986, for some relevant discussion).

The combined results from the experiment to teach Christopher new languages under conditions of controlled input are more than suggestive. It seems clear that, while there is no evidence for complete mastery, there is support for the directing role of transfer from the first language and for the importance of UG; there is clear indication that the learning of the morphology and the lexicon is different in kind from the learning of syntax; there is evidence that, at least in this unnatural context, second language learning exploits inductive strategies as well as modular capabilities; and of course there is yet another demonstration of Christopher's remarkable talent in mastering (parts of) the structure of new languages.

5
Language and Mind

In this final chapter we attempt to develop a general model of the mind which is adequate to describe, and in part explain, the full range of Christopher's mental activities, as well as those of less interesting subjects. To do this, we return first to his flawed prowess at translation; we then construct a model of the mind on the basis of successive revisions to the model of Anderson we have developed previously; and we exploit that model to look in particular at the 'theory-of-mind' module and the problem of meta-representation.

Christopher's Translation

Introduction

Christopher first came to scholarly attention because of his remarkable ability to translate from one language to another, and we have already documented the range of languages at his disposal. A striking characteristic of his translation is its blending of the intelligent and the inept (see, for instance, Smith and Tsimpli, 1991: 323). While able to identify items from an awesome number of languages and provide a translation for them that gives at least clues about the content, Christopher regularly produces an output that is flawed to the point of incoherence. Moreover, he does this not only in languages where he has minimal competence, such as Finnish and Russian, but also in languages where he is reasonably proficient, such as French and Modern Greek.

Typical examples are provided by frequent errors of agreement, as in the French examples in 1, where the correct form is given in 1':

1   la course présent; une partie français; son direction
1'   la course présente; une partie française; sa direction

However, these are syntactically determined matters of inflectional morphology, and his command of (lexically based) derivational morphology is far better. This is shown most clearly in mistakes of overgeneralization, where he extends a correct, regular, pattern to irregular examples where it does not apply. Typical examples are given in 2:

2(a)   'examination' was translated as *examinação* (instead of *exame*) in Portuguese, and as *examination* (instead of *examen*) in French.

(b)   Italian *'rompersi'* ('to break' (reflexive)) was translated into Greek as the non-existent *spastike* ('broken-passive-3s') instead of the correct *espase* ('past-break-3s') on analogy with examples like *xtistike* ('built-passive-3s').[1]

(c)   Italian 'cominciarsi' ('to begin' (reflexive)) was translated into Greek as the non-existent *arxizonte* ('begin-pres.passive') on analogy with examples like *skotononte* ('killed-pres.passive').[2]

This asymmetry in his mastery of different aspects of morphology is a reflection of the general mismatch between his proficiency at word translation and his relative inefficiency at sentence translation, a contrast which is not unexpected given Linebarger's (1989: 203) observation that 'lexical and syntactic processes break down independently of one another'. In the next two sub-sections we look at the role of English and of other source languages in the mistakes Christopher makes.

The role of English

A recurrent feature of Christopher's translation is the pervasive effect of his first language, English, on the morpho-syntactic form of the various target languages he knows. The following examples are characteristic. In English, interrogative and relative pronouns share certain forms, giving rise to the partial syncretism seen in 3:

3(a)   *Who* is coming?
 (b)   The man *who* is coming is my friend
 (c)   *Which* would she like?
 (d)   The one *which* she would like is mouldy

and to the temporary ambiguity in 4, which can be construed either as a free relative (if followed by, e.g., 'depends on the context') or as a question (if followed by a question mark):

4   Which is chosen in these circumstances[3]

Presumably as a function of this property of English, Christopher regularly replaces relative pronouns by interrogative pronouns in languages where this is in fact impossible. Typical examples from German and Greek are given in 5:

5(a)   Und bei dem Zeitungskiosk ist ein Mann, *wer wer* käuft Melonen[4]
       [*wer* should be *der*]
       And by the newspaper kiosk is a man who who is buying melons.

  (b)   Ksehasa na su agoraso *ti* mu zitises
        [*ti* should be *afto pu* – 'that which']
        I forgot to buy you what you asked me

   Such examples can be attributed to a strategy of translation by word-for-word equivalent, but this is not a plausible explanation for other transfer phenomena, for example, his word-order mistakes, pro-drop phenomena, and so on. For instance, the subordinate clause in 5(a) should have the finite verb, *kauft*, in final position, and although Christopher showed on forced-choice tests that he knew the conditions under which German (and Dutch) have the verb in clause final position[5] (for example, in subordinate clauses and after auxiliaries), he systematically failed to implement that knowledge in his production, either in spontaneous speech or in translation. Examples of his judgements in forced choice tests are given in 6:

6(a)   Der Junge, der musste nach Hause gehen, ist hier   [R]
       Der Junge, der nach Hause gehen musste, ist hier   [OK]
       (The boy who had to go home is here)

  (b)   Wer kann deutsch sprechen?   [OK]
        Wer kann sprechen deutsch?   [R]
        (Who can speak German?)

  (c)   Mein Bruder hat gelernt albanisch   [R]
        Mein Bruder hat albanisch gelernt   [OK]
        (My brother has learnt Albanian)

and further examples of his mistakes in translation are given in 7, with the correct order given in the primed congeners:

7(a) Would you like to speak German?
      'Möchten Sie sprechen Deutsch?'
 (a') Möchten Sie Deutsch sprechen?

 (b) Can you give me more time?
      'Können Sie mir geben mehr Zeit?'
 (b') Könnnen Sie mir mehr Zeit geben?

 (c) Yesterday John said that Peter ate the apples
      'Gestern sagte Johann dass Peter ass alle Äpfel'
 (c') Gestern sagte Johann, dass Peter die Äpfel ass

An example showing that he has comparable knowledge of Dutch is provided in 8 where he corrected the ungrammatical (a) to the grammatical (b):

8(a) Mijn moeder heeft geroepen mijn broer
 (b) Mijn moeder heeft mijn broer geroepen
      (My mother has called my brother)

A half-way house between word-for-word and sentential transfer errors is provided by Greek examples like that in 9:

9   to oti i Eleni ine i kaliteri fititria to kserun oli
    Everyone knows that Eleni is the best student

which Christopher 'corrected' by deleting the definite article *to* immediately preceding the complementizer *oti*, presumably because the sequence 'the that' is ungrammatical in English.

The role of other source languages

In the preceding examples, it is clear that Christopher's native English is having a direct effect on his performance in other languages. The converse of this effect can also be seen in examples where Christopher's translation strategy results in his English translation being ungrammatical or inappropriate as a result of following the original unthinkingly. Examples are legion, as illustrated in 10, where (a) is Portuguese, (b) is Italian, (c)–(e)

are Norwegian, (f) is Swedish, (g) is Danish, (h) is French, (i)–(j) are
German, and (k) is Spanish:

10(a)   Os animais não riem, diz Hélder
        Animals don't laugh, says Hélder
        'The animals never laugh, says Hélder'[6]

  (b)   Mentre finiva di vestirsi
        While she finished dressing
        'While she was finishing to get dressed'[7]

  (c)   Petter gikk langsomt nedover trappene.
        Peter went slowly down the stairs.
        'Peter went slowly over, over the steps'.

  (d)   Det er jo ikke sikkert at han sulter i hjel om jeg glemmer å betala
        But after all it's not certain he will starve to death even if I forget to
            pay him.
        'It was not sure that he is jump, he is jumping, or I forget to pay'
        [Presumably 'jump' is due to contamination from French *sauter*]

  (e)   Når kommer Per hjem? Vanligvis til middag, litt over to.
        When does Per come home? Usually for dinner, just after two.
        'When is Peter coming home? Usually at midday, a little over two.'

  (f)   Katten spinner i hennes knä.
        The cat purrs on her lap.
        'The cat spins in her knee'.

  (g)   Mor ser ret bekymret ud.
        Mother looks rather worried.
        'Mother seems right worried'.

  (h)   J'appelai l'attention de ma famille sur ce poteau, et pendant le repas
            je pensai beaucoup à la fameuse bataille où le roi Henry V et sa
            petite armée vainquirent la chevalerie française.
        I drew my family's attention to this signpost, and during the meal I
            thought a lot about the famous battle in which King Henry V and
            his little army had defeated the French cavalry
        'I called the attention of my family on this signpost, and during the
            meal I thought much to a famous battle where the king, where
            Henry the fifth and his little army conquered the French
            knights'.

(i)   Die Wohnung war klein und befand sich im vierten Stock des
      Gebäudes.
      The flat was small and was situated on the fourth floor of the
      building.
      'The flat was small and found itself in the third, in the fourth floor
      of the building'.

(j)   Seine Verfolger wussten also, wo er wohnte.
      So his pursuers knew where he lived.
      'His followers knew also where he was living'.

(k)   Visiblemente complacido, Carmelo se ajustó las gafas, dio media
      vuelta y entrabrió las puertas correderas que communicaban con
      la pieza immediata . . .
      Looking satisfied, Carmelo adjusted his glasses, turned round and
      half opened the sliding doors that led to the next room . . .
      'Visibly pleased, Carmelo adjusted his glasses, put on a full speed
      and open windows which communicated with the immediate
      piece . . .'

Occasionally, his English mistakes seem to be a function of blending two
possibilities into one, as exemplified by the translation from the Greek in
11:

11   mou agorase ena forema
     he bought me a dress
     'He bought me a dress for me'

A striking example of Christopher's somewhat cavalier attitude to
translation, including an interesting combination of transfer effects from
both his first language and the source language is provided by his
translation into French of the German passage in 12.[8]

12   Bald bemerkte er jedoch vor einem kleinen Blumenladen, zwei
     Männer, die in seine Richtung hinaufblickten. Seine Verfolger
     wussten also, wo er wohnte.

     Soon, however, he noticed in front of a small flower-shop two men
     who were looking up in his direction. So his pursuers knew where he
     lived.

     'Tôt il est noticé une petite magasin en fleurs; deux hommes qui dans
     son direction passaient. Ses accomplices le savaient où il habitait.'

Apart from the errors of gender agreement, auxiliary selection and vocabulary, it is striking that Christopher coins the form *noticé* on the model of English, but keeps the verb-final German word-order for the relative clause.

Confirmation that on-line translation grossly underestimates Christopher's knowledge is provided by the kind of example illustrated in 13 where he is clearly attempting simply to provide a word-by-word equivalent of the English input, and makes mistakes (such as the translation of 'present' by '*présent*') where he demonstrably knows the correct form. In this case he had provided the translation 'present' for the French '*actuel*' just a few minutes previously.

13   . . . rests with how much effort you put into the present course
      '. . . reste comme beaucoup du effort qui tu mets dans la course
      présent'

Further examples are provided by Christopher's translations from Italian to Greek in 14:

14(a)   La nave affondò
        The ship sank
        *'to plio vithize'   (cf. the correct: to plio vithistike)
        the ship sank-active-3s   the ship sank-passive-3s

  (b)   I bambini si parlano
        The children talk to each other
        *'ta pedhja milunonte'   (cf. the correct: ta pedhja milune
        the children talk-passive-3p   the children talk-active-3p)

Similar results were obtained in a forced choice test of well-formedness, in which Christopher was confronted with the pair of sentences in 15:

15(a)   i bira pinete efxarista to kalokeri   [R]
        the beer drink-passive-3s with-pleasure the summer
        One drinks beer with pleasure in the summer

  (b)   *i bira pinei efxarista to kalokeri   [OK]
        'Beer drinks itself in the summer'

where he accepted the ungrammatical 15(b) and rejected the grammatical 15(a). He assumed wrongly that the passive affix *-ete* has a reflexive interpretation, hence his proffered translation. His choice of 15(b) as the correct version is a sign of transfer from English, where verbs in middle constructions show active voice morphology, unlike in Greek (see Tsimpli, 1989).

Preliminary explanation for Christopher's translation

In chapter 3 we presented an analysis of Christopher's performance on cognates, in which his scores were comparable with those of normal subjects. However, we suspect that Christopher's case differs from the normal in a number of respects. The results of the 'cognates' test that we described earlier (pp. 85–91) indicate that he has significantly greater difficulty with morphologically complex items than with simple (mono-morphemic) ones, but the most obvious difference between him and normals is his failure to integrate his lexical ability into his processing of sentence structure and a concomitant ignoring of contextual relevance. That is, Christopher stops short at the word recognition stage and provides a translation on a purely word-for-word basis, even though he may have the requisite knowledge to do better. A good indication of this strategy is provided by his translation of sentences into French, where it is essential to distinguish *savoir* and *connaître* ('to know' a fact or a person respectively), a contrast that he is consciously aware of. Despite this knowledge, he gave the translations in 16:[9]

16(a) I know the man is going home
       'Je sais que l'homme va chez lui'

  (b) I know the man who is going home
       'Je sais l'homme qui s'en ira chez lui'

When asked explicitly if he knew the difference between *savoir* and *connaître*, he gave an appropriate reply and proceeded to correct 16(b). It seems that once he has accessed a possible item, the recognition process comes to a full stop and he is content with whatever word constitutes a lexical equivalent of the input.

Christopher's translation, more than any other aspect of his flawed talent, makes it clear that there is some radical dissociation between the various components of his mind. Although his performance on nonverbal intelligence tests is depressed in comparison with his performance on verbal ones, his normal use of language in conversation and his overall ability and understanding are far higher than the examples in 10 or his acceptance of *n*th order approximations to English would lead one to expect, and his general ability is equally clearly far higher than that of

Laura (Yamada, 1990) or of Williams Syndrome children, who show a somewhat comparable mismatch between verbal and nonverbal skills. This patterning presents an obvious challenge to any attempt to provide a coherent model of the mind. We try to answer that challenge in the rest of the book.

A Model of the Mind

In this section we propose a model of the mind, sufficient both to characterize the full variety of Christopher's skewed talents and the less asymmetric abilities of normal subjects. The intention is that it be a competence model (where 'competence' embraces both linguistic and cognitive aspects of mentation), but that it also be specified in sufficient detail to make clear which components are accessed in various kinds of performance, and what the role of each of those components is.

Anderson revisited and revised

In what follows, we treat each of Christopher's various activities (spontaneous speech, conversation, translation, and so on) in turn, and see what each implies for the structure of a coherent model. The result will be both oversimplified and overly complex, but in the present state of ignorance this seems inevitable. Our account will be based loosely on Anderson's (1992a) theory of intelligence, that we have exploited previously (Smith and Tsimpli, 1993; ch. 1 above). We shall try to cover the phenomena listed in 17:

17(a)   Comprehension (including pragmatic inferencing)
        Production (spontaneous speech)
        Conversation (i.e. a combination of (a) and (b))

   (b)   Translation, both lexical and sentential

   (c)   Answering general knowledge questions
         Doing IQ tests, both verbal and nonverbal (including word/object recognition)
         Giving well-formedness judgements, in both English and other languages

   (d)   'Sally-Anne' and other theory of mind tasks

The two most obvious defects of the revision of Anderson's model given in Smith and Tsimpli (1993: 425; see also figures 1.5 and 1.6 above) are its failure to accommodate language production: that is, the fact that language is an 'output system' as well as an 'input system' (cf. Chomsky, 1986a: 14), and its failure even to mention the lexicon. We shall suggest a series of modifications to that model on the basis of a discussion of the various activities listed in 17.

First language activities (from comprehension to conversation)

Comprehension For comprehension the model previously described is adequate to a first approximation in that the language module does indeed act as an input system. Natural language input is analysed by the parser in conjunction with the grammar[10] and is further transformed at the interface via the verbal/propositional specific processor (SP2) into a form suitable for integration into the knowledge base, along the lines suggested in Relevance Theory (for example, by means of various kinds of strengthening, disambiguation, reference assignment, and so on). In order to make explicit the role of the specific processor, it is necessary to complicate the earlier diagram so that the arrow from the language module enters the knowledge base via the specific processor. There is also presumably a path connecting the SP2 and the language module, via the BPM, to allow the interaction necessary for pragmatic processes to augment the output of the language module. That is, as implied by figure 5.1, these processes are located inside the SP2 for the reasons given in Smith and Tsimpli (1993: 438–9).

Spontaneous speech In spontaneous speech, we assume something like the inverse of this process: a representation in the language of thought[11] (Fodor, 1975) is generated from the knowledge base via either (or both) the specific processors. This representation is transduced into a natural language representation via the basic processing mechanism and the interface (see pp. 25–7) between the central system and the language module. The linear separation of levels implicit in this characterization is misleading, and it may be more appropriate to think of the BPM as being a property of or a constraint on the functioning of each SP (and indeed of all components of the system). This would be one way of incorporating an element of parallelism into the system. Thus, given Anderson's minimal architecture, we can now ascribe differential abilities to different sub-parts of the overall system (see figure 5.1).

First, the transduction between the language of thought and natural

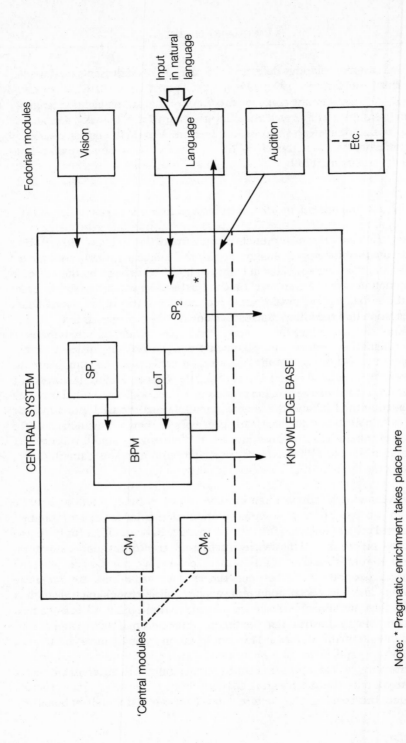

Figure 5.1 *Comprehension*

Note: * Pragmatic enrichment takes place here

language will be (for everyone) harder or easier, depending on whether the initial representation is mediated by the verbal or the spatial specific processor. That is, it is easier to express in natural language something which is closer to isomorphic with the language of thought, and we take it as axiomatic that verbal representations are closer to the language of thought than spatial ones are.[12] In Christopher's case, we hypothesize that his verbal specific processor is enhanced *vis-à-vis* his impaired spatial one, accounting in part for the severe asymmetry between his verbal and performance IQ results, as well as for his difficulty in finding his way around. This suggests a model of the kind in figure 5.2, where the size of the specific processors reflects their respective processing efficiency.

We attribute the monosyllabicity of much of Christopher's speech to his slowness in encoding ideas into the language of thought, except where these have been routinized. That is, although Anderson shows no direct connection between the knowledge base and the specific processors,[13] we assume that the initial stimulus for thought comes from outside the specific processors, and is ultimately expressed by first being encoded by them. (Whether the 'executive' function implicit in this assumption is located at the boundary between the knowledge base and the specific processor, or in the basic processing mechanism (as we suggested in Smith and Tsimpli, 1993: 426) is still an open question.) We further assume that some sequences occur ready-chunked in the specific processor and therefore occasion less difficulty for encoding, in that they obviate the 'cognitive overload' that inhibits much of Christopher's interaction. It is such chunks that are externalized in his bursts of verbal activity of the kind illustrated in Smith and Tsimpli (1991: 327). Just as the basic processing mechanism may be best thought of as a constraint on the operation of the rest of the system, it may be appropriate to think of the specific processors as 'internal' to the knowledge base. That is, the discussion immediately above presupposes that there is some sort of initial mentation 'prior' to the specific processors, but we actually view thought as emerging from systems (the knowledge base and the specific processors) that are orthogonal to each other in a multi-dimensional model.

This division of duties as between an executive and the specific processors may also permit an explanation for Christopher's normal ability to manipulate arguments like *modus ponens* (cf. ch. 2) and his reasonable control of non-truth functional connectives like *however*, beside his failure to use the latter in his spontaneous conversation in any language.

Conversation   If comprehension and spontaneous speech are characterized as above, conversation clearly involves both processes. The crucial difference between Christopher and normal subjects is that the operation of

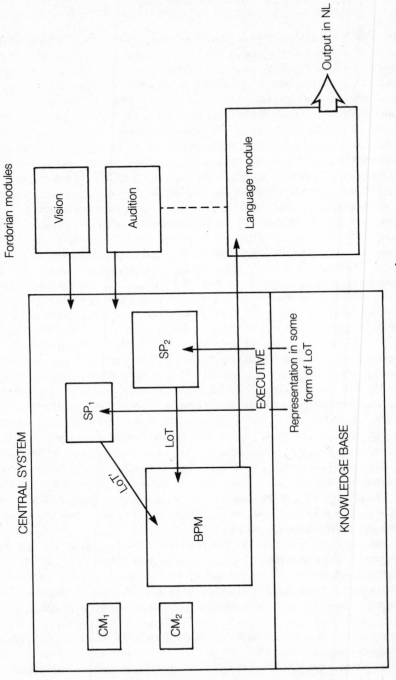

Figure 5.2 *Spontaneous speech*

the 'executive' is impaired, resulting in the inability of the system to deal with other than minimally complex sequences, unless they have been routinized. As the executive is a horizontal faculty (in Fodor's, 1983, sense) it is not subject to any constraint on the unidirectionality of information flow, but we assume that it does not have access to the internal computations of the language faculty. Accordingly, in language production and, *a fortiori*, in conversation, the executive checks representations in the BPM, and passes them on to the relevant output procedures. Presumably these processors must have immediate access to the morphological component of our lexicon, because of its interface status. Whether the cause of Christopher's somewhat impoverished conversational ability should be attributed exclusively to the executive, or whether it results from defects distributed throughout the system is not clear, as conversation necessarily involves more components than any of its constituent parts. However, the evidence from pragmatic tests, in particular Christopher's reaction to *n*th order approximations to English, seems to indicate that the executive is the most likely locus of difficulty.

Translation revisited

So far, the role of the interface has not been crucial, but it becomes so in two separate domains: in translation and in the mismatch between Christopher's morphological and lexical ability on the one hand and his syntactic ability on the other.

We claimed in earlier work (Smith and Tsimpli, 1993: 439–40) that Christopher's translation takes place in 'some domain which is not monitored appropriately' and that it does so at an 'interface level' in the sense of the discussion on pp. 25–7. This suggests a model in which the 'language faculty' and the knowledge base intersect, such that only part of our linguistic knowledge is constituted by the language module in Fodor's sense, and that part falls within the central system. The lexicon itself is also bifurcated to show the respective positions of the functional and conceptual components, and the (Chomskyan interface) components of PF and LF ($+LF'$) which lead off into the articulatory/auditory domain and the central system respectively.

This has the advantage of being compatible both with the standard psycholinguistic claim that lexical entries are subdivided into a 'lemma'[14] and the rest, and with Tsimpli's (1992) claims about the relation between the functional lexicon and the conceptual lexicon, and gives us a picture like that in figure 5.3.

Given this more complicated model of the mind, translation for

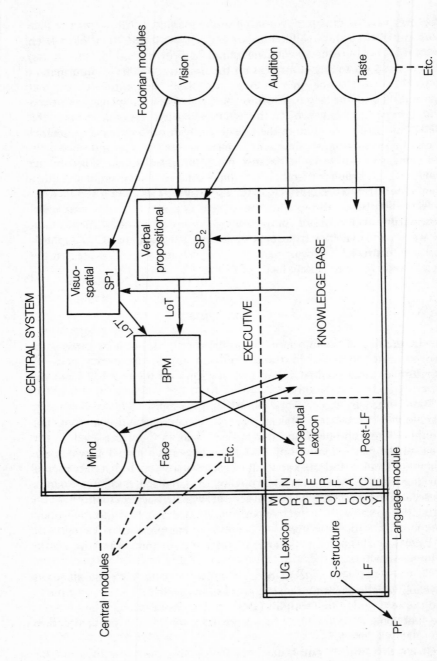

Figure 5.3 *A model of the mind*

Christopher then takes place as follows. Assuming a written input, the vision module inputs a signal which is transduced and fed via the verbal specific processor into the language module. The lexicon of the language module is partly multi-dimensional: that is, the entries in the conceptual part are paired/tripled, or whatever, in parallel, with *cat* associated with *chat, Katze, billi:*, Γατα, *koshka*, etc. Similarly, there may be multi-dimensional entries for some morphemes that correspond to functional categories, with {plural} associated with English {-s}, German {-en}, Greek {-es, -i}, depending on declension, gender, case, and so on. Crucially, however, the translation is partially insulated from the normal monitoring function of the executive on the one hand, and of access to the rest of the syntax of the language module itself on the other. Note that the idea of a monitoring function again supports postulating some kind of 'executive', presumably a sub-part of the 'central conceptual system' in Sperber and Wilson's words (1986: 90), as it is this which is most deficient in Christopher.

Tests of knowledge and intelligence

Although Christopher's general conversational ability is marked by a tendency to monosyllabicity and a reluctance to initiate exchanges, his answering of general knowledge questions is fast, fluent and accurate. We assume that the greater facility he shows in this domain is a result of the fact that there is minimal need to convert from the language of thought to natural language or vice versa. That is, a question requires only some *completion* of the logical form involved (see Sperber and Wilson, 1986: 252). In the case of a wh-question, such as 'What is the capital of Albania?', this basically involves substituting some noun phrase (*Tiranë*, in this case) for the item *What*, and leaving everything else unchanged. The implication of this is that question-answering of this kind takes place largely on the basis of a short-cut strategy which bypasses those parts of the system which are defective. Specifically, the information involved here is stored in the intersection of the conceptual lexicon and the knowledge base (under both 'Albania' and 'Tiranë') and can be retrieved without reference to the internal structure of the specific processor or any linguistic structure not present in the input. That is, the conceptual lexicon with its link to the memory store provides ready-made associations which can be activated with minimal central control.

Interesting confirmation of this hypothesis is provided by the results of the Hayling Sentence Completion Test (Burgess and Shallice, 1994).[15] This test of executive function has two sections, in the first of which the subject has to complete a number of sentences with the most appropriate item that comes to mind. Thus 'He posted the letter without a —' is typically and correctly completed with 'stamp'. In the second half of the test, the subject is instructed to complete a number of comparable sentences with a word which makes no sense whatever in that context. Thus 'Most sharks attack very close to —' might be correctly completed with 'eggs'. Christopher performed within normal limits on the first half of the test, but scored poorly on the second half.[16] The idea underlying the test is that the inhibition necessary to carry out the latter task successfully is crucially central (or 'system-wide') and accordingly occasions particular difficulty to patients with executive (typically frontal) problems. Within the framework we have been developing, we would like to suggest the following account. Successful completion of the first part of the test involves only the language module and the conceptual lexicon. Successful completion of the second half of the test involves not only these components but also the executive and a quasi-random search through the conceptual lexicon (see below) to access another, 'inappropriate' response. Christopher's results then provide corroboration for some aspects of our partial model of the mind, as also for some form of Fodorian modularity, where central control is defective.

The absence of this control function is shown particularly clearly in Christopher's reaction to nth order approximations to English that we cited on pp. 73–4. Christopher was asked to read these passages in English and then translate them into the language indicated. Sentence 18(a) is a seventh-order approximation, which he translated into French; 18(b) is a fifth-order approximation which he translated into Greek. (He translated after each sentence):

18(a)   The Pharaohs had enough stone to build enough papyrus, too, so there was nothing as large as floating islands. The papyrus a modest fifth of the Sphinx's length. Of the underworld of mummies and stood it made us realise what giant structures.

Les Pharaohs ont beaucoup de pierres pour, pour construire des papyrus, aussi, so il n'y était pas si grand comme le île flottante. Le papyrus, un modeste quinze – cinq de le longueur du Sphinx. Et je ne sais pas.

NS   What did you think of that passage?
C   Très bon, très bon.

18(b)   In the year 1786, an at the High Court in discovery. He was Sir

William an oriental scholar before reading, three years earlier, he had Sanskrit, the language in which texts of India are written, fourth to the sixth centuries, was no longer spoken but scholarship and literature.

Sto xrono 1786 enas sto anotato dhikastirio itan o lordhos Gulielmos
in-the year 1786 one in-the highest court was the lord William

enas kathighitis tis anatolikis epistimis prin na dhiavasi ixe sanskritika
one professor the-gen eastern science before sub. reads had sanskrit

ti glossa stin opia grafonte kimena tis indhias apo ton tetarto ston ekto
the language in-the which are-written texts the-gen india from the
    fourth to-the sixth

eona dhen miluse pja ma loghotexnia ke ipotrofia.
century not spoke anymore but literature and scholarship

Such examples raise interesting questions about Christopher's ability to provide well-formedness judgements of sentences in English and other languages. While purely modular activities, including linguistic ones, are 'reflex-like' (Fodor, 1983), the giving of well-formedness judgements presupposes the involvement of both modular and central processes, so we might again expect Christopher to experience some difficulty. Apart from the areas of difficulty we have already discussed (dislocation, topicalization, and so on: see pp. 51–4, 106–12), Christopher's grammaticality judgements in English are usually confident, consistent and swift. In other languages his reactions are not so consistent, and are often at variance with his spontaneous performance (see the discussion of German on pp. 158–9 above). If he is correctly characterized as speaking English in many different languages: that is, he has one syntax and many lexicons, then central considerations are essentially irrelevant for English, but are crucial for other languages. In other words, his well-formedness judgements, while revealing something of his competence (in the technical sense) in English, reveal more about his encyclopaedic knowledge of other languages.

Examples such as the nth order approximations also provide further illustration of the mismatch between Christopher's control of syntax and the lexicon. Although his vocabulary is (almost) adequate to the task of translation.[17] his syntax is not. On the assumption that parameter-resetting is impossible, his language module is intact but his syntax is frozen into

English. The morphological component, in virtue of being partially within an obsessive central system, is free to assimilate additions from arbitrary new languages essentially without restriction. This is illustrated by the difference between his flawed performance in sentential translation, as witness the examples on pp. 12–17 and 160–3, and his normal performance in lexical tasks. In this respect, consider both the original 'Peabody' tests carried out by O'Connor and Hermelin (1991: 677) and the French vocabulary test (contrasting 'faux amis' with other items) that we carried out ourselves (pp. 85–91), where Christopher scored at a level comparable to or above that reached by A level students. Given his excellent performance on these vocabulary tests (the aspect of language which tends to dominate 'verbal' IQ tests) Christopher's performance on theory of mind tasks is particularly interesting. According to Happé (1995: 850) verbal ability is 'a good predictor and a high correlate of theory of mind performance in young normal and autistic subjects. However, the autistic subjects appeared to require much higher verbal ability to pass theory of mind tasks than did either young normal or mentally handicapped subjects.'

To evaluate Christopher's performance on these tasks we need to discuss in greater detail the theory of mind (central) module in our model, as illustrated in figure 5.3. At issue are, first, the relation of this module to the language module and, second, the question whether what is defective in Christopher is simply this mind module or, given the differences among the various tasks, a general disability with second-order representation.

Theory of Mind and Meta-representation

The mind module

In chapter 1 and the preceding section, we outlined our view of the theory of mind, suggesting certain differences between our own position and Anderson's. We now return to this issue and attempt to cast light on Christopher's (dis-)ability in this area. We would like to begin by suggesting that Anderson's characterization of the theory of mind as a Fodorian module is inappropriate. While a theory of mind is, by hypothesis, domain-specific, and while it also has certain other 'modular' attributes (for example, its operation is fast, mandatory, subject to idiosyncratic pathology – as in autism, and so on), there are at least two considerations which lead us to consider that it belongs to the central system. First, it is clear that the nature of the representations over which the relevant computations are carried out is not perceptual, as with Fodorian modules, but conceptual. Second, the crucial characteristic of (Fodorian) modules is their informational encapsulation, whereby the direction of information flow is exclusively from the module to the central system, rather than vice versa (for interesting discussion, see Carston, 1988). Given the apparently inferential nature of operations of the theory of mind, it looks as if 'central' information is crucially involved. Accordingly, we think that the theory of mind (the 'mind module') should be located *within* the central system, as indicated in figure 5.3. That is, we are attributing a quasi-modular structure to the central system but one in which the vocabulary is derived from conceptual representations rather than from a domain-specific vocabulary.[18] Christopher's failure on theory of mind tasks is then to be interpreted as manifesting a central deficit (on a continuum with that evinced by true autists[19]), involving the inability to form and/or manipulate some second-order representations (or 'meta-representations') in the language of thought.

The range of phenomena which involve, or putatively involve, the mind module include both experimental findings and aspects of spontaneous behaviour. In the former category are the 'Sally-Anne', 'Smarties' and 'chocolate biscuit' tests, described in chapter 1, together with additional tests of our own devising, including the 'Shapes' and 'Tangerine' tests, described below. In the latter category are examples of pretend play and role adoption.

Although examples are few, we turn to these first, as it is important to document the fact that there have been rare occasions on which Christopher seems to show some evidence of an ability to project himself into non-actual situations. For instance, he is reported by his sister as having indulged in 'pretend play' as a child: specifically, during and after the Mexico Olympics he would dress up and pretend to be an Arab or a matador (see p. 1). Further, on a couple of occasions when he was reading constructed dialogues, of the kind exemplified in pp. 70–1, purportedly between a mother and child, he appropriately adopted a carping falsetto for the mother. This is in contrast with his usual (spontaneous) behaviour with dialogues in which he sometimes comes out with 'conversations' in which he speaks the words of both protagonists, as exemplified by the Greek dialogue in 19, with our English translation in italics:

19 'Greek conversation in a Greek kiosk.'
'Exete Aglikes efimeridhes?'
[*Have you got any English newspapers?*]
'Ne. Ja sena.'

[*Yes. For you.*]
'Egho, tha mu pite, tha sas po . . . ja Aglikes efimeridhes.'
[*I, you will tell me, I will tell you . . . about English newspapers.*]
'Dhiavasis, dhiavase tes oles . . . tis Aglikes efimeridhes ke gho
   dhiavaso tin Kathimerini.'
[*read, read them all . . . the English newspapers and I will read the
   Kathimerini*]
'Parakalo . . .'
[*please*]
'Ma aftos . . . afto to periptero dhen pulai i Kathimerini, jati dhen ine
   elliniko, ja sena.'
[*But this, this kiosk does not sell the Kathimerini, because it is not Greek,
   for you*]
'Adio.'
[*Goodbye*]

IT   Where did you learn that? Did you read this dialogue somewhere?
C   I . . . (have) that in my mind.

This seems to be a purely linguistic exercise without any social
component as he does it *exclusively* in languages other than English and, in
the example cited, there was no variation in his pronunciation of the
utterances of the putatively different speakers, the whole sequence being
spoken with a flat intonation. Examples of pretend play lie in Christopher's
remote childhood, the 'falsetto' examples are extremely rare, and the Greek
dialogue looks like a rehearsed exercise. All examples of this kind are
therefore difficult to adduce as evidence for or against the hypothesis that
Christopher has a defective mind module, so we need to have recourse to
experimental findings.

One of the tests we conducted involved Christopher in the prediction of
the shapes to be seen on either side of cards. For this experiment we
constructed a set of flash cards with various coloured shapes on each side.
With some cards the coloured shapes were the same on both sides
(matching cards), on others the shapes on the two sides were different (non-
matching cards). Sitting opposite Christopher at a table, we then showed
him the cards and asked him increasingly complex questions about what he
or we or a third person in various positions could or would see. We began
with matching cards and showed him both sides; then, holding the card
vertically so that he could see one side and we could see the other, we asked
the questions indicated in 20–22:

20   *Showing a card with a blue square on both sides:*

What can you see?
What can I see?

21   *Showing a card with a green circle on both sides*:
What can you see?
What can I see?

22   *Repetition of 20–21 with different examples of matching combinations.*

Christopher insisted on answering all the questions in French, but, apart from one or two mistakes of vocabulary, performed perfectly. We continued with matching cards, but showing him one side only, before interrogating him as in 23:

23   Showing one side of a card with a blue circle on both sides:
What do you think is on the other side?

After showing him the other side, demonstrating that he was right, we continued as in 22, with Ianthi sitting on the same side of the table as Christopher:

24   If we ask Ianthi, what will she say is on the other side?

Again, Christopher answered correctly. We then chose a non-matching card (with a red triangle on one side and a yellow pentagon on the other), showed him only the red triangle side and asked:

25   What do you think is on the other side?

After he had, naturally, answered with the factually incorrect 'un triangle rouge', we showed him the other side and proceeded as in 26:

26(a)   So what is on the other side?
  (b)   What did you think was on the other side?
  (c)   If we ask Ianthi, what will she say is on the other side?

Again he answered correctly, and when shown the yellow pentagon on another card was able to infer correctly that there was a red triangle on the other side, and could respond appropriately to questions such as those in 27:

27(a)   If you came round this side of the table what would you see?

(b)   What would Ianthi think you would see if you came this side of the
        table?

His responses were consistently correct, showing that he has no difficulty in
adopting a perspective different from his own; in recalling past, currently
invalid, states of affairs; and in projecting hypothetical states of affairs. His
only difficulty arose with ascribing counterfactual representations to a third
party. We showed him a matching card with a blue circle on each side and
then the blue circle side of another non-matching card with a blue circle on
one side and bells on the other. As expected, he assumed at first that the
other side would be 'the same'. After he had been shown that it was
different, the following exchange ensued:

28   NS   So what is on the other side?
      C   Bells
      NS   What did you think was on the other side?
      C   Blue circle
      NS   If we showed this to John, with a blue circle on each side, and
             then this one, with bells on one side [*showing the circle*] what is on
             the other side?
      C   Bells
      NS   What will John think is on the other side?
      C   Bells
      NS   You think John will think it's bells?
      C   Yes
      NS   OK How would he think that?
      C   Because they are two different sorts of bells

On repetition with other combinations, he responded in similar fashion,
saying that John would know there were hearts on the other side of a non-
matching card 'Because they are hearts'. It appears to be the case that on
this test Christopher has difficulty only with the imputation of false belief.
We return to a discussion of these results and of the results of a final
modification of the 'Smarties' test in the next section.

Competence models and performance models

In this section we shall look at some of the earlier research on theory of
mind, paying particular attention to the contrasting positions of Fodor and
Perner, and to Happé's discussion of the apparent correlation of theory of
mind deficits with verbal mental age. We shall then contrast Christopher

with normally developing children; we will discuss the role of the lexicon, and attempt to distinguish between a mind module deficit and a more general deficit in the ability to construct second order representations.

The basic generalization about normal children is that they demonstrate a stage-like discontinuity in their behaviour on a battery of tests. Whereas three-year-olds consistently fail 'false-belief' tasks of the 'Sally-Anne' and 'Smarties' variety, four-year-olds consistently pass them, correctly predicting the behaviour of uninformed or misinformed actors in the tests. (For summaries of the literature, see Wellman, 1990, and Perner, 1991). There are basically two different kinds of explanation for such behaviour: what one might think of as 'competence' theories and 'performance' theories, represented by Perner (1993) and Fodor (1992) respectively, where a competence theory claims that the younger child's conceptual ontology is essentially different from that of the older child or adult, and a performance theory claims that they are essentially the same.[20] That is, for a competence theorist, three-year-old children are characteristically described as not having a notion of 'false belief' (for example, because they cannot differentiate between belief and pretence: Perner, 1993: 3); or because they have a simple 'desire' psychology, rather than a 'belief/desire' psychology (Wellman, 1990). For a performance theorist, the three-year-olds' 'failure in the false belief paradigm does not imply that they have no concept of false belief . . . they prefer not to invoke the agent's belief to predict his actions' (Fodor, 1992: 291), where 'prefer' is a picturesque way of referring to the lack of 'computation space' that is really what inhibits the younger children from success.

Fodor (1992) is intent on demonstrating that apparent discontinuities in the developing child's theory of mind are due not to some radical difference between the child's and the adult's theories of mind, but simply to a difference in the computing resources available to each. He puts forward (1992: 286) a 'Very Simple Theory of Mind' (VSTM) which consists of the two clauses in 29:

29(a)   *ceteris paribus*, people act in a way that will satisfy their desires if their beliefs are true;
  (b)   *ceteris paribus*, people's beliefs are true.

He then claims (ibid.: 286–7) that three- and four-year-old children both exploit the heuristics in 30:

30(a)   H1   Predict that the agent will act in a way that will satisfy his desires.

(b)   H2   Predict that the agent will act in a way that would satisfy his
           desires if his beliefs were true.

The difference between the two age-groups is then that three-year-olds use
H1 'whenever it affords a unique behavioural prediction', whereas four-
year-olds and adults use H1 'whenever they think the beliefs that the agent
is acting on are true. If they don't know whether the agent is acting on true
beliefs, or if they think that the beliefs the agent is acting on are false, they
use H2.'

In the case of the 'Sally-Anne' test, the analysis works as follows. Four-
year-olds (and adults) do not use H1, because they perceive the agent's
belief as not being true; accordingly they use H2 to predict that the agent
will look where his desires would be satisfied *if* his belief were true: namely
in the place where he last saw the concealed item. Three-year-olds (and
Christopher) operate simply according to H1, as this '*affords a unique
behavioral prediction*' (Fodor, 1992: 287),[21] and therefore look where the
item actually is concealed. For the 'Smarties' and comparable tests, Fodor
(ibid.: 293–4) generalizes his heuristics to those given in 31:

31(a)   GH1   Assume that a representation has its unmarked value
              whenever doing so affords a unique prediction.
  (b)   GH2   Ascribe to x the appearance it would have *if* the beliefs that
              it causes *were* true.

For the older children it is clear that their appreciation of the falsity of
the agent's belief should lead to their predicting, correctly, that the agent
will think there are Smarties rather than a pencil in the tube. For the
younger children, the situation is not entirely straightforward. If the
unmarked representation of a Smarties tube is to contain Smarties, then
there should be a unique prediction, and GH1 should lead to the three-
year-olds also saying that the uninformed onlooker should predict that the
tube contains Smarties rather than pencils. This interpretation, however,
makes no distinction between three- and four-year-olds, and while it
accounts extensionally for Christopher's behaviour, it is, presumably, not
the interpretation Fodor intended. (It is interesting that Fodor gives no
worked-out discussion of this 'belief prediction' task.) To achieve such
discrimination it is necessary to interpret 'ascribe to x' in GH2 as pertaining
not simply to the Smarties tube, but to the subject's representation of it.
That is, knowing that the tube contains a pencil, the subject ascribes to it
pencil-producing-thoughts, and so predicts that the agent will describe it as
containing a pencil.

Under Perner's, 1993 'competence' analysis, the situation *vis-à-vis* normal children is straightforward, but there is again no obvious treatment of Christopher's case. He argues that 'young children do not distinguish between the state of affairs a belief is about and how this state of affairs is thought of' (1993: 1), and that more generally young children do not differentiate belief and pretence, but have a neutralized concept of 'prelief' unlike anything in the adult's ontology. On this account, the discrepancy between three- and four-year-olds follows equivalently on both the 'Sally-Anne' and 'Smarties' tasks: on the former, 'children cannot conceive of belief as misrepresenting where the chocolate really is' (ibid.: 7); on the latter, 'young children can't understand how a person can misrepresent the actual content of a box as being something different' (ibid.: 8).

Both the 'competence' and the 'performance' analyses (at least on one interpretation of them) predict that performance on 'Sally-Anne' and 'Smarties' will be matched: a prediction that is generally corroborated in both normal and pathological cases. Christopher's conflicting results from the 'Sally-Anne' and 'Shapes' tests on the one hand, and the 'Smarties' test on the other, therefore present a problem. As documented in the literature (see, e.g., Frith, 1989; Happé, 1995), autistic children usually fail both the Sally-Anne and Smarties tests, so Christopher's performance on the 'Sally-Anne' test is typical of autistic behaviour while his performance on the 'Smarties' test is atypical.[22] Moreover, recent work by Happé (1995) indicates that there is no significant age difference in successful performance on these two tests by normal children, so there is no obvious explanation for Christopher's differential behaviour in terms of his having reached a putative maturational stage intermediate between that necessary for passing the Smarties test and that necessary for passing the Sally-Anne test. Christopher's performance appears even more inscrutable when we take into consideration Happé's (1995) suggestion that verbal mental age (VMA) is (causally) correlated with performance in theory of mind tasks. On the basis of results from a large number of autistic, mentally handicapped and normal children, she observes that subjects with a VMA above a certain level 'X' always pass theory of mind tasks, whereas subjects with a VMA below a different level 'Y' (Y < X) never pass them. For subjects whose VMA lies between X and Y there is no correlation with theory of mind tasks, suggesting the configuration in 32:

32

$$| \textit{pppppppppp} \ | \ \textit{pppppppppp}$$
$$\text{Y} \qquad \qquad \text{X}$$
$$\textit{ffffffffff} \ | \ \textit{ffffffffffffff} \ |$$

where all those who pass (represented by the sequence of p's) have a VMA greater than Y, and all those who have a VMA greater than X pass; while all those who fail (represented by the sequence of f's) have a VMA less than X, and all those who have a VMA less than Y fail. That is, having a VMA greater than X is sufficient to pass theory of mind tasks, and having a VMA greater than Y is *necessary* to pass them. Equivalently, for a subject with a VMA less than Y success on such tasks is impossible, and a VMA greater than X guarantees that that subject has theory of mind.

A solution

We wish to argue for a mixed position. The phenomenon of 'cognitive overload', discussed in relation to Christopher's translation ability (see Smith and Tsimpli, 1993: s. 439–41, and pp. 165–7 above), supports an analysis in terms of performance constraints, specifically the absence of computational space of the kind Fodor appeals to. On the other hand, it is not at all clear how a performance account would allow a generalization of the results achieved with three- vs. four-year-olds to the autistic population, as autistic children can frequently perform at a complex level, suggesting that they dispose of plenty of 'computational space'. On the other hand, a competence explanation – for example, in terms of the absence or failure to mature appropriately of some component of the mind – would generalize to autistic subjects while still accommodating such computational versatility. That is, it may not be necessary, but it is highly desirable that whatever accounts for the difference between normal children at different ages should also account for the comparable difference between normal and autistic children. This is particularly so as, to a first approximation, autistic children and normal three-year-old children succeed and fail on (a sub-set of) the same tasks.[23] Moreover, a 'competence' theory looks more likely to be able to handle as a 'natural class' the various phenomena that fall together under the rubric of 'second-order' representation (see pp. 74–8), as the computational complexity of these different activities is not obviously comparable.

A striking feature of Christopher's case is the contrast between his verbal and nonverbal performance and, crucially for the current discussion, his VMA which is average: indeed, in the multi-lingual Peabody Picture Vocabulary Test devised by O'Connor and Hermelin (1991) and reported above (pp. 7–8), he scored well above average. Presumably this means that, in Happé's terms, his VMA is at level X or above, yet his performance in theory of mind tasks is not successful in the way this would predict.

Moreover, his performance in other domains involving meta-representations, such as the interpretation of figurative language and jokes, is also unsuccessful. On the parsimonious assumption that these phenomena are also attributable to a theory of mind deficit, it looks as if Christopher's case is atypical in two respects: first, given his average VMA, it is surprising that he should fail theory of mind tasks at all; second, given this failure, it is surprising that it is not uniform across different examples of such tasks.

As regards the former problem, it is clear that, while Christopher's theory of mind deficit may characterize him as 'autistic', this is not an exhaustive characterization of his central operations. While the average autistic individual has minimal or impoverished language, Christopher's linguistic competence in his first language is essentially intact. More accurately, his linguistic abilities are intact in so far as this pertains to formal properties of language including the lexicon, but not as it pertains to the further pragmatic processing of linguistic input. The case of Christopher, and perhaps of Asperger Syndrome subjects, suggests that language deficit in autism correlates with but is causally independent of the deficit in the theory of mind. Given the (quasi-)modular structure of each, there is in principle a dissociation such that both the theory of mind and language are impaired, or either one may be selectively affected while the other is intact. The fact that there *is* usually a correlation is accounted for if we assume that there is close to isomorphism between LF and the pragmatically enriched representations in the language of thought (that is, propositional form), and that representations in the language of thought, in particular second-order representations, are necessarily mediated by natural language representations; or at least that a deficit in Natural Language inhibits the operation of the theory of mind, even if this is itself intact. If this is correct then Christopher may provide a case of a theory of mind deficit largely independent of language.

It is interesting to evaluate this suggestion in relation to the performance of normal three-year-olds in theory of mind tasks: in this case, we are not dealing with a deficit but with a maturational constraint on the development of the theory of mind module. In other words, any correlation between VMA and performance on theory of mind tasks is explanatory neither in the case of normal three-year-olds nor of Christopher.

Further, it appears that Christopher's case casts doubt on the correlation suggested in Happé's account above, whereby it is not possible to have a VMA greater than X without thereby also having a theory of mind. Again, if our account above is correct we predict precisely this dissociation; that is, Christopher's performance illustrates the atypical 'autistic' behaviour whereby language is preserved but theory of mind is affected.

This issue raises related problems to do with the acquisition of the lexicon, which involve the use of ostension – that is, a form of ostensive communication – and pragmatic inferencing in general. If it turns out that the linguistic deficit in the average autistic child is partly the result of the impoverished nature of his or her communicative and pragmatic abilities, then the correlation between VMA and theory of mind tasks is further elucidated. The language deficit in this case is much less 'modular' in that the component affected is, in our terms, the interface, that is, it is not informationally encapsulated. Moreover, if conceptual and encyclopaedic information is crucial for successful performance in a theory of mind task and autistic children lack much of such information (Happé, 1995) because of their inability to use normal communicative strategies in word-learning, the correlation between VMA and theory of mind tasks is predictable. As discussed previously, Christopher's knowledge and speed of acquisition of lexical items in both his native and other languages is strikingly good. This implies that whatever communicative principle regulates inferencing and the learning of new vocabulary items, it is fully operative in Christopher but not in the average autistic individual. In turn, this crucially indicates that Christopher's performance in theory of mind tasks is purely a deficit in the domain-specific mechanisms of this central sub-component rather than in the linguistic medium by which it is expressed. If this line of reasoning is correct, it is possible to attribute failure in theory of mind tasks either to the inaccessibility (or unavailability) of the information used in implementing domain-specific algorithms in the theory of mind, or to theory of mind processes exclusively.

We return now to the asymmetry in Christopher's behaviour on different theory of mind tasks: that is, his puzzling success on the 'Smarties' test in conjunction with his failure on 'Sally-Anne' and the more advanced parts of the 'Shapes' test. Although the average autistic person fails both theory of mind tasks, there is a group of autistic people who perform below average in the Smarties test but pass the Sally-Anne test (Happé, in prep.). In other words, the results obtained from this class of autistic people are diametrically opposite to Christopher's results.

In solving this problem we shall need to consider whether a competence solution, a performance solution or some mixed solution is appropriate, and also take into consideration a range of other factors that may be involved in these tasks: their inherent complexity, notions of agency and modality, the possible contributory role of encyclopaedic information and, in the context of a 'competence' solution, the contrast between the theory of mind as such and the imputation of different kinds of second-order representation.

There are two factors which characterize the notion of second-order representation but which are not obvious in the formulation of H1 and H2 (example 30 above). The first is the notion of the 'agent' of an activity as distinct from the individual subject projecting the representation of this activity. More specifically, it is a necessary condition for second-order representation to project a thought (in the form of a proposition) as entertained by someone other than oneself (cf. Sperber, 1994a). The second factor is the nature of the predicate which expresses the attitude of the individual towards the actions, beliefs or desires of the agent. We can draw a distinction between predicates that can enter second-order representations and those that cannot. Predicates of the type *expect, believe, hope, think* and so on are typical of theory of mind processes in that they enable the speaker to project other people's view of reality on the basis of her understanding of the others' different informational relation to it (cf. Forguson and Gopnik, 1988). In false beliefs and second order representations in general, the proposition introduced by this type of predicate expresses the attitude of the individual towards it, thereby expressing not an actual situation, but a possible or desirable one. Assuming that this is precisely the effect of a *modality* reading, we can assume that second-order representations involve 'modal' predicates,[24] and that second-order representations project as shown abstractly in 33 and exemplified in 34:

33   [m thinks [x MODAL PREDICATE [that P]][25]
     where m is the subject, and x is some other person.

34   [Christopher thinks [that Alexia believes [that the tube has Smarties in]]]

The last point we would like to make regarding theory of mind processes relates to the source of the propositions involved in second-order representations. Specifically, we would like to draw a distinction between the roles of perceptually vs. cognitively derived input to theory of mind operations.[26] In this respect, consider the difference between the 'Shapes' task on the one hand, and the 'Sally-Anne' and 'Smarties' tasks on the other. In the former, the representation is that of a visual stimulus and the subject is asked to attribute to a different referent beliefs about this perceptual evidence. In the other two tasks, the proposition is derived either from the knowledge store or from immediate memory (with certain differences discussed below).

Importantly for our account it is possible that the 'Smarties' test need not give rise to a second-order representation. The 'Smarties' test, as opposed to the 'Sally-Anne' one, requires the retrieval (or accessing) of encyclopaedic information associated with Smarties tubes, namely that they contain Smarties. Recall that this type of information is part of the conceptual entry in the mental lexicon, which includes both idiosyncratic and non-idiosyncratic information. In the case of the Smarties, we are dealing with non-idiosyncratic (that is, widely shared) encyclopaedic information. The 'Sally-Anne' and 'Shapes' tests, on the other hand, are context-bound in that the proposition embedded in the second-order representation is not retrieved from any part of the mental lexicon but from premisses formulated in the current situation.

In principle, there are two possible ways of describing the process involved in a performance task such as the 'Smarties' one. The first possibility, is that, as with the 'Sally-Anne' test, what is involved is the projection of second-order representations by the subject. The second possibility is that the subject does not form any second-order representation, in that he does not consider any of the evidence of the other person's knowledge which may be available. Rather, the subject retrieves encyclopaedic information from his general knowledge store and projects it either as unattributed or as attributed to himself at a time prior to present. Note, however, that in this case we are not dealing with a standard second-order representation as one of the conditions defining them is that the attribution of the belief, expectation, and so on, involves someone *other than oneself*. On this interpretation, when Christopher was asked what he (or anyone else) thought was in the Smarties tube before he (or they) knew what was in it, he gave an intuitively sensible answer on the basis of his general knowledge about what is usually contained in Smarties tubes. That is, he provides the same answer regardless of whose opinion is being tapped. In other words, his response does not take into consideration any information related to the referent other than that available in the encyclopaedic entry of the objects concerned (in this case, Smarties), which is presumably the same across individuals. The availability of this interpretation then depends on two factors: first, the presence and easy accessibility of the conceptual entry and its sub-components, and second, the construal of the agent in the representation as the subject himself, in which case it is not a second-order representation in our sense of the term.

Our suggestion, then, is that Christopher's successful performance in the 'Smarties' test is due precisely to the construal of a representation which does not employ theory of mind processes in the sense specified above. Evidence for this assumption comes from Christopher's reaction to subsequent questions minimally different from those in the original test in that the belief was explicitly attributed to a contrasting subject. When asked what Alexia, as opposed to John, would think was in the Smarties tube, Christopher replied with a confused 'Don't know'. Assuming that the repeated change in the referent would force the construal of a second-order representation, the prediction is that a theory of mind deficit would be reflected in the response, which is precisely what happened. In this case the 'Smarties' and the 'Sally-Anne' tests are both theory of mind tasks and Christopher's performance becomes less puzzling. His partially successful performance in the 'Shapes' task can be accounted for in a similar fashion. More specifically, the early stages of the test do not necessarily involve the construal of a second-order representation in that the subject's response can be based on his own previously established inferences, that is, prior to his having been presented with the new evidence. The new referent in this case may be replaced by the subject. In the later stages of the test, however, which (on the usual analysis) involves the imputation of false belief, there in no non-contradictory way of substituting the ego for the agent.

With respect to the group of autistic individuals who performed successfully in the 'Sally-Anne' task but failed on the 'Smarties' test, we can tentatively assume that what inhibited successful performance in the latter was the retrieval of encyclopaedic information from the conceptual lexicon. In other words, if VMA is associated with the implementation of pragmatic inferencing during the acquisition of lexical items, failure in the 'Smarties' test can be attributed to a deficit in the source of appropriate information.[27] In sum, Christopher's failure on the 'Sally-Anne' and 'Shapes' tests is to be interpreted as a central deficit (on a continuum with that evinced by true autists), which amounts to the inability to form and/or manipulate second-order representations in the language of thought. His success on the 'Smarties' test is a function of the salience of the encyclopaedic information associated with the objects concerned. This analysis predicts that otherwise identical tests with objects lacking the encyclopaedic salience of Smarties should be treated quite differently: that is, presented with a nondescript box with some unexpected item in it, Christopher (and little children) should assume that uninformed subjects identify the item according to reality.

To test this prediction we subsequently asked Christopher to guess at the contents of an unremarkable, round, opaque, plastic container. It was in fact similar in appearance to one in which we had given him some mastika (a Greek sweet) a year or two previously, and he accordingly guessed 'mastika'. We then opened it to reveal that it actually contained a tangerine. On being asked what an absent friend would say was in it he responded 'tangerine'. He was able to remember what he had previously guessed was in the box, and his reaction was consistent whether he was asked what someone else would *say* or *think* was in it. He was similarly consistent on a number of further trials involving other items, or no item at all, leading us to believe that this is strong corroboration of our analysis.

Summary and Conclusions

We opened the chapter with a consideration of Christopher's translation, remarkable both for its fluency and its imperfections. We take this to suggest that for him it is a non-communicative enterprise: a linguistic exercise independent of central control. It also highlights the mismatch between his lexical and morphological prowess on the one hand, and his syntactic and pragmatic limitations on the other. His lexicon is normal or, in some dimensions, enhanced; his other linguistic abilities are inhibited by problems of processing load. This dissociation, in conjunction with the findings from earlier chapters, led us to suggest a revised model of the mind.

We took Anderson's model of the mind as a point of departure and modified it in various ways, with the result that the overall structure of our new version is radically different from his. Some of these differences are simply the result of our fleshing out his somewhat skeletal suggestions: for instance, we have ascribed a range of broadly linguistic functions to the verbal/propositional specific processor, which Anderson had left inexplicit. Other divergences are more basic. Anderson is silent about the role of an 'executive',[28] but our evidence suggests that an 'executive deficit' is the correct characterization of some aspects of Christopher's behaviour. Corroboration of this view was obtained from the results of the Hayling test in which he showed himself unable to inhibit the appropriate responses in a sentence-completion task. A yet more radical departure is represented by our location of the language 'module', more accurately the language faculty, as intersecting with the central system. This suggestion, in conjunction with our proposals (building on Tsimpli, 1992) about the morphological interface, enables us to account for the various mismatches in Christopher's performance, while accommodating Chomsky's (1986a: 14) objection to Fodor's treatment of language as an input system. Our division of the lexicon within this module is also compatible with work in pragmatics and the philosophy of language on the characterization of concepts.

One area where we depart from Anderson is in our claim that 'theory of mind' is a 'central module',[29] whereas he puts it with the other input systems. Given Christopher's failure on 'Sally-Anne' and some (but only some) other tasks normally diagnostic of autism, it is clear that his performance in this domain is defective. We confirmed our earlier results with new tests involving the imputation of false belief on a 'Shapes' task, and suggested a solution to the problem raised by his apparently inconsistent behaviour on the 'Smarties' and similar tests. Our proposal crucially involved a marriage of 'competence' and 'performance' theories, and built on our previous treatment of second-order representations and the availability of encyclopaedic knowledge.

Our understanding of Christopher's mental processes is still sketchy, but the model we have put forward allows for a consistent and coherent treatment of a satisfyingly wide range of his behaviours, both linguistic and non-linguistic.

Epilogue

A being darkly wise, and rudely great
(Pope, *Essay on Man*)

Christopher is still unique, but we now understand him a little better. After four years' intensive investigation, the nature of his talent and its limitations are becoming clearer, and are simultaneously casting light on the nature of the mind more generally. Whatever greater understanding we now have has been achieved because of the dissociation of abilities that is so starkly manifest in savants in general and in Christopher in particular. Such dissociation has implications for several different domains. The disparity between Christopher's linguistic talent and his impaired performance, especially his performance on so-called 'intelligence' tests, makes it abundantly clear that intelligence is not a unitary notion. On the positive side, he provides evidence for less unsophisticated theories of intelligence couched within a more general theory of mind. We have tried to spell out some of those implications. The same dissociation provides further evidence for the modularity hypothesis, which precisely predicts the kind of discrepancy found in Christopher. Although there are still deep and interesting problems surrounding Fodor's position, it is no longer plausible to talk of 'cognitive prerequisites' to language. This has been apparent on the basis of many studies, especially of Williams Syndrome children. Christopher's case confirms it, most strikingly in his ability to master the complexities of many languages, but his inability to cope with the linguistically impossible – but logically simple – characteristics of an invented language.

A different dissociation apparent within Christopher's linguistic behaviour provides evidence for particular constructs of linguistic theory. It is worth emphasizing that the fact that abnormal cases are even amenable to description within a framework devised for normal ones constitutes striking confirmation of the validity of that framework. If we have been able to provide a consistent account of Christopher's knowledge of English and other languages, we have thereby provided evidence for the theories we have exploited. Examples are legion, but we mention two: the asymmetry in Christopher's performance on lexical and syntactic tasks reinforces the validity of a theory that draws a radical distinction between them. Similarly, the fact that a number of phenomena fall together under the rubric of second-order representation provides support for whatever theory predicts that they constitute a natural class – for instance, in terms of a (defective) theory of mind module.

As well as its implications for linguistic and pragmatic theory, Christopher's case has potential, but somewhat more problematic, implications for the theory of second language acquisition. Central issues in this domain are the roles of UG, of parameter-resetting and of transfer effects motivated by the first language. With regard to the first of these, Christopher's case seems to confirm that UG underlies all language learning processes. As regards the second, to the extent that the various properties of particular parameters fail to cluster in the performance of second language learners, as with Christopher, so is that view called in question. The evidence here is no more than suggestive, however, precisely because Christopher's case is so different from normal. The last issue is the clearest. The most striking characteristic of Christopher's 'second' language acquisition is the overwhelming effect of transfer from his first language and, on occasion, even from other source languages. By 'transfer' in this context we are not referring to translation, but to his spontaneous production, his judgements of well-formedness, and his reaction to forced choice tests. In all of these the effect of English is pervasive, confirming the suggestion that he has a single dominant grammar – that of his mother tongue – and a phenomenal facility for acquiring the morphology and lexical items of a host of second languages.

Christopher has provided us with a wealth of evidence about the nature of mind and language. He has also provided us with insight into the nature of humanity, and in the process he has enriched our lives.

Appendix I:
Word and Object Test

This test consisted of the twenty-five items in 1 below. Christopher and the controls were told that the stimuli could be either words or objects, and if words, in either English or Greek. In 1, CAPITALS indicate an object, lower-case roman indicates an English word, and italic indicates a Greek word. That is, there were ten 'objects', eight English words, one numeral and six Greek words.

1	TELEPHONE	weary	squid	*telos*	FLOWER
	CHRIS	STAR	grocer	*lathos*	DIAMOND
	SCISSORS	SIEVE	*karavi*	CLUB	uncle
	HAND	*pleno*	1962	*selida*	AEROPLANE
	ABSURD	WRENCH	ARROW	HEART	*fagito*

It is clear from the detailed results in Smith and Tsimpli (1993) that the test was not optimal, not only in that some items were inherently easier than others, but in that some items fail to differentiate the various subjects. None the less, the results, as presented in table 1, are sufficiently clear-cut for us to be confident that they reveal, on the one hand, a consistent difference between Christopher's verbal and pictorial ability and, on the other hand, the absence of such a difference in the parallel abilities of normals.

Table 1: Word/picture recognition

	Christopher	*Control (average)*	
English	6.4	8.25	($n = 16$; range 5.4–10.2)
Greek	7.8	6.3	($n = 3$; range 4.8–7.2)
Objects	13.9	6.1	($n = 16$; range 4.4–8.5)

The averages in table 1 are merely suggestive, so we calculated the subjects' rank for each of the test items (excluding the Greek examples for which there were too few subjects). The average ranks are given in tables 2(a) and 2(b).

Table 2(a):   Average rank for objects

Chris	C1	C2	C3	C4	C5	C6	C7	C8
4.69	11.94	9.19	10.06	10.25	6.81 ·	8.37	8.69	11.94
	C9	C10	C11	C12	C13	C14	C15	C16
	8.19	9.44	11.50	10.25	11.62	7.81	4.12	8.12

Table 2(b):   Average rank for objects

Chris	C1	C2	C3	C4	C5	C6	C7	C8
14.55	10.30	8.10	8.45	10.70	7.95	7.80	8.05	13.05
	C9	C10	C11	C12	C13	C14	C15	C16
	7.55	7.55	7.35	13.05	6.75	4.70	7.45	9.65

The correlation between the score on words and the score on pictures is highly significant, whether Christopher is included in the calculations or not. Spearman's rank correlation is 0.78 (including Christopher) and 0.87 (for the controls only): $p < 0.005$.

If we then calculate the difference between the average rank for words and the average rank for objects, we get the display in Table 2(c), with Christopher dramatically different from all the controls. (The figures show the average for the recognition of objects subtracted from that for words.)

Table 2(c):   Difference between the average ranks for word and object recognition

Chris	C1	C2	C3	C4	C5	C6	C7	C8
−9.86	1.64	1.09	1.59	−0.45	−1.14	0.57	0.64	−1.11
	C9	C10	C11	C12	C13	C14	C15	C16
	0.64	1.89	4.15	−2.80	4.87	3.11	−3.33	−1.53

Appendix II:
Representative examples of Christopher's well-formedness judgements (English)

Out of the many thousands of examples we have collected, we give here a small but reasonably representative sample of Christopher's well-formedness judgements on a range of English constructions. No marking on a sentence means that it was explicitly accepted as correct by Christopher. The judgement was indicated either by his ticking a written representation of the sentence, or by his assenting verbally that it was 'all right', 'good', 'you can say that', and so on. An [R] following a sentence means that Christopher rejected it as 'bad' or 'ungrammatical' or required some change (see the discussion on pp. 44–8), again either by marking it with a cross or by commenting on it. Where sentences occur in pairs they were presented to Christopher in the order given. Where sentences which were judged to be ungrammatical occur singly, we give Christopher's suggested emendation (if any) in inverted commas. In some cases we also reproduce Christopher's further comments or reactions to our questions about problematic examples.

For one or two exercises we asked Christopher to specify how sure of his judgement he was, as indicated in sentence 1, where he had to specify whether the sentence was 'good' or 'bad' and also say whether he was 'very sure', 'quite sure' or 'unsure' of that judgement:

1 Here is the newspaper that the boy looked at it this morning.
                [   ] good   [   ] bad
         [very sure____ / quite sure____ / unsure____ /

We didn't persist with this practice, as Christopher was invariably 'very sure'.

My shoes is dirty [R]
'My shoes are dirty'
Mary put the books on the shelf
John gave a gift Susan [R]
'John gave a gift to Susan'
Are your glasses new?
John put the car to the garage [R]
'John put the car in the garage'
John sent a letter to Mary
The Mary is very intelligent [R]
'Mary is very intelligent'
John was given a book by Peter
The door is closed by John
'How come you goed home so early?' [R]
'How did you go home so early?'
Mary didn't know if Peter was coming
Me thought that nobody would like this film [R]
'I thought that nobody would like this film'
Which you thought was an interesting idea? [R]
'Which have you thought was an interesting idea?'
Who did you say Mary met at John's party? [R]
'Whom did you say Mary met at John's party?'
Who do you think left? [R]
'Who do you think has left?'
What you think is this new book about? [R]
'What do you think is this new book about?'
Who did you say that arrived yesterday? [R]
'Who did you say arrived yesterday?'
I'm sure that Peter will remember what to say in the interview
I wonder that Mary was so upset [R]
'I wonder why Mary was so upset'
Remember Susan to feed the dog [R]
'Tell Susan to feed the dog'
If I went home what will you do? [R]
'If I went home what did you?'
You can answer these questions, can't you?
The weather today is beautiful, is it? [R]
'The weather today is beautiful, isn't it?'
The door is open by Peter [R]
The door is opened by Peter
John wants no apples
John wants not apples [R]

Not to make mistakes is unnatural
To not make mistakes is unnatural   [R]
Anybody can go in this room
Anybody can't go in this room   [R]
Neither John believed this story neither Mary   [R]
'Neither John believed this story nor Mary'
What did you go to London to see?
What didn't you go to London to see?   [R]
Don't you think that this is unfair?   [R]
'Do you not think that this is unfair?'
There seems to be a man in the garden
It seems to be a man in the garden   [R]
It is easy to make John laugh
John is easy to make Peter laugh   [R]
Which books did you throw away without looking at?
Which books did you throw away without looking at them?   [R]

    IT   Can you say that?
    C   Some people do.

If I had had enough money, I would have bought a car   [R]
'If I had enough money, I would have bought a car'
That this is the wrong answer is obvious
That this is the wrong answer it is obvious   [R]
John shaved himself this morning
Mary thinks high of himself   [R]
'Mary thinks high of herself'
She considers her to be clever   [R]
'She considers herself to be clever'
John saw Mary's picture of herself   [R]
'John saw Mary's pictures of himself'

    IT   So who was in the picture?
    C   John.

Himself believes John to be happy   [R]
'He believes John to be happy'
John and Susan often write to each other
Who did you say that they saw him leaving the station?   [R]
'Who did you say that they saw leaving the station?'
The person that John insulted him in the meeting was his boss   [R]
'The person that John insulted in the meeting was his boss'

How many have you bought shoes? [R]
'How many shoes have you bought?'
John tried Peter to escape from prison but he didn't succeed [R]
'John tried with Peter to escape from the prison but he didn't
   succeed'
I don't want for Peter to fail the exams [R]
'I don't want Peter to fail the exams'
He has suddenly realised that he was wrong
He suddenly has realised that he was wrong [R]
The candidate who I was told that they rejected him is Peter [R]
'The candidate who I was told that they rejected is Peter'
So difficult the exam questions were that everybody failed [R]
So difficult were the exam questions that everybody failed
Leaving small children alone at home is not a nice thing to do
John seems to have enjoyed his holidays
Do you remember the last time we meet? [R]
'Do you remember the last time we met?'
It is impossible John to pass the exams [R]
'It is impossible for John to pass the exams'
Peter likes fish and chips but Mary didn't [R]
'Peter likes fish and chips but Mary doesn't'
What a nice dress Mary was wearing!
John driving is very dangerous [R]
'John's driving is very dangerous'
I promised to him that I will go to the meeting [R]
'I promised to him that I went to the meeting'
Seems that John left the party because he wasn't feeling well [R]
'It seems that John left the party because he wasn't feeling well'
The girl who that you saw this morning is John's sister [R]
'The girl who you saw this morning was John's sister'
You will come with me, aren't you? [R]
'You will come with me, won't you?'
This is the woman who John knows very well [R]
'This is the woman whom John knows very well'
The book I have read many times is the Bible
It is reading newspapers that I like most [R]
'It is reading newspapers that I like the most'
Never before have I seen such a scene!
John kisses often Mary [R]
'John often kisses Mary'
That this is the wrong answer is obvious
That this is the wrong answer it is obvious [R]

Who did you say that they saw him leaving the station?   [R]
Who did you say that they saw leaving the station?
It is Mary that has passed these exams   [R]
'It was Mary that has passed these exams'
John is not as tall as I thought he is   [R]
'John is not as tall as I thought he was'
John is easy to please him   [R]
'John is easy to please'
John to go to France would be very difficult because he has
    no money   [R]
'For John to go to France would be very difficult because he has
    no money'
Who did you say that arrived?   [R]
'Who did you say arrived?'
Carol was hit by a car while she was crossing Oxford Street   [R]
'Carol was hit by a car when she was crossing Oxford Street'
Honesty frightens Mary
To not consult the doctor when you feel ill is irresponsible
Peter loaded fruit on the truck   [R]
'Peter loaded fruit onto the truck'
John no want apples   [R]
'John does not want apples'
Peter is the man who decided to join the police force   [R]
'Peter was the man who decided to join the police force'
A president is Peter   [R]
'Peter is a president'
Had Peter joined the team we would have won the match
    very easily   [R]
'Had Peter joined the team we would have won the match
    very easy'
Nobody can forget the army's destruction of the cathedral
Bought John this book?   [R]
'Did John buy this book?'
There arrived three men yesterday   [R]
'Three men arrived yesterday'
They seem very proud of theirselves   [R]
'They seem very proud of themselves'
What did John say that Mary thought that Peter had
    misunderstood?   [R]
'What did John say Mary thought Peter had misunderstood?'
Susan promised Steven to take her to the theatre   [R]
'Susan promised Steven to take him to the theatre'

What did Peter ask who left behind?   [R]
'What did Peter ask who was left behind?'
Learning how to drive will not take John long   [R]
'Learning how to drive will not take John very long'
That he hasn't called yet worries me a lot   [R]
'That he hasn't called me yet worries me a lot'
It is possible that it rains   [R]
'It is possible that it will rain'
The car stopped for to let the children cross the road   [R]
'The car stopped to let the children cross the road'
Difficult though it may look it is not impossible   [R]
'Though it may look difficult it is not impossible'

Appendix III:
'Garden-path' sentences

1(a)	He put down the child	[OK]
1(a)'	'il a mis l'enfant' [*sic*]	
2	He put the child down	[R]
3	He put down the child that had sat down	[OK]
4	He put the child that had sat down down	[R]
5	While Mary was mending the sock fell on the floor	[R]
6	The horse raced past the barn fell	[R]
7	They told the girl that Ian liked the story	[OK]
7'	'Ipan sti kopela oti o Ian agapise tin istoria'	
	[They told the girl [that Ian loved the story]]	
8	Fred told the man that he hired a story	[OK]
8'	'O Friderikos ipe ston anthropo oti proselave mia istoria'	
	[Fred told the man [that he hired a story]]	
9	Susan convinced her friends were unreliable	[?]
9'	'I Susana pistike oti i fili tis itan anaksiopisti'	
	[Susan was convinced that her friends were unreliable]	
10	Without her contributions would be inadequate	[R]
11	We gave the man the book we wrote because he had written a similar one last year	[OK]
	Dhosame ton anthropo to vivlio pu grapsame epidhi ixe grapsi ena idhio persi.	
12	We gave the man the book was written by a copy of this one we had written	[R]
13	Ianthi found the answer to the problem in the book	[OK]
	'I Ianthi vrike tin apantisi tu provlimatos sto vivlio'	
14	Ianthi found the answer to the problem was in the book	[R]
	'I Ianthi vrike tin apantisi tu provlimatos sto vivlio'	
14'	Ianthi found the answer to the problem in the book	

15	Because of the blizzard the guests left before the evening meal was finished	[OK]
16	Because a blizzard had been forecast the guests left before the evening meal	[R]
17	Though Chris kept on reading the story Ianthi frightened him	[OK]
18	Though Chris kept on reading the story really frightened him	[R]
19	It's obvious that Holmes suspected the son of the banker was guilty	[OK]
20	It's obvious that Holmes suspected the son of the banker right away	[R]
21	It's obvious that Holmes realised the son of the banker was guilty	[OK]
22	It's obvious that Holmes realised the son of the banker right away	[OK]
23	Have the students take the exam today!	[R]
	'Have the students to take the exam today'	
24	Have the students taken the exam today?	[OK]
25	Have the students put their books away!	[OK]
26	Have the students put their books away?	[OK]
27	Since Ianthi can swim a mile it seems like a very short distance to her	[OK]
28	Since Ianthi can swim a mile seems like a very short distance to her	[OK]
29	Neil gave her earrings today	[OK]
	'Simera o Neil tin edhose skularikia simera'	
30	Neil gave her earrings away	[OK]
	'O Neil edhose ta skularikia tis allou'	
31	Alexia put the sweet on the table in her mouth	[OK]
	'I Alexia evale to gliko sto trapezi sto stoma tis'	
32	Susan convinced her friends were unreliable	
33	John persuaded him friends were unreliable	
	m in 'him' circled as wrong	
	'O Yanis tu epise oti i fili itan anaksiopisti'	
34	The children painted with bright paint all morning	[OK]
	[Illegible Hindi]	
35	The children painted with bright paint were delighted	[R]
36	John knew the men and the women were strangers	[OK]
37	John gave the boy the dog bit a bandage	[R]
38	Fred told the man that he hired a story	[OK]

39	Fred told the man that he hired to leave	[R]
40	The man told that the crowd was angry was upset	[R]
41	The man told Bill that the crowd was upset	[OK]
42	Neil gave her earrings yesterday	[OK]
43	Neil gave her earrings to Anna	[OK]
44	The lawyer thinks his second wife will claim the inheritance	[OK]
45	The second wife will claim the inheritance belongs to her	[R]
46	The second wife will claim that the inheritance belongs to her	[OK]
47	After the child had visited the doctor prescribed some medicine	[R]
48	After the child had sneezed the doctor prescribed some medicine	[OK]
49	Which book did John read to the children last night?	[OK]
50	Which book did John read to the children from last night?	[R]
51	Which prisoner did the policeman march to the jail?	[OK]
52	Which prisoner did the policeman march with to the jail?	[R]
53	The man left is a mystery	[R]
54	Who left is a mystery	[OK]
55	What did Neil say that Ianthi ate?	[OK]
56	Which picture of himself does Bill think Fred was embarrassed by?	[R]
57	The defendant examined by the lawyer turned out to be unreliable	[OK]
58	The evidence examined by the lawyer turned out to be unreliable	[R]

Appendix IV:
Results of the Cognates Test

	Right	*Wrong*	*% correct*
Chris			
Faux-amis	77	119	39 ($n = 196$)
Others	153	19	89 ($n = 172$)
Control 1 (native French speaker)			
Faux-amis	126	71	64
Others	159	15	91
Control 2 (O-level only)			
Faux-amis	28	171	14
Others	82	91	47
Control 3 (native speaker of German, BA in French)			
Faux-amis	76	122	38
Others	148	25	86
Control 4 (GCSE only)			
Faux-amis	40	159	20
Others	113	61	65
Control 5 (native speaker of Italian, GCSE equivalent in French)			
Faux-amis	62	136	31
Others	108	63	63
Control 6 (A-level plus much travel)			
Faux-amis	132	68	66
Others	164	9	94

	Right	Wrong	% correct
Control 7 (A-level)			
Faux-amis	58	142	29
Others	132	40	77
Control 8 (GCSE only)			
Faux-amis	21	179	10
Others	68	104	40
Control 9 (A level)			
Faux-amis	58	141	29
Others	116	57	67
Control 10 (A level + Special paper)			
Faux-amis	52	147	26
Others	108	65	62
Control 11 (A level grade A)			
Faux-amis	67	134	33
Others	142	31	82
Control 12 (GCSE only)			
Faux-amis	49	150	25
Others	114	59	66
Control 13 (O level)			
Faux-amis	37	162	18
Others	85	88	49
Control 14 (A level)			
Faux-amis	107	92	54
Others	160	12	93

Ratios: *Faux-amis* % correct: Others % correct

Chris	C1	C2	C3	C4	C5	C6	C7	C8
39:89	64:91	14:47	38:86	20:65	31:63	66:94	29:77	10:40

C9	C10	C11	C12	C13	C14
29:67	26:62	33:82	25:66	18:49	54:93

'slightly autistic and obsessional behaviour' (1991: 675), but they also note the 'lack of any social hesitancy . . . along with his willingness to initiate social contacts' (ibid.).

10   We are grateful to Alexia Antjaka for her help with this test.

11   We are grateful to Justin Cormack for writing the program for this experiment.

12   We are grateful to Ivan Smith for detailed help and advice in the administration and interpretation of this test.

13   The Greek examples were included for only that small sub-set of the controls who knew the language.

14   Specifically: Arabic, Basque, Bengali, Catalan, Chinese, Czech, Dutch, Finnish, Gaelic, (Modern) Greek, Old Greek (sic), Hausa, Hebrew, Hindi, Hungarian, Icelandic, Italian, Japanese, Korean, Luxemburg (sic), Mongolian, Norwegian, Polish, Rumanian, Serbian, Spanish, Turkish, Urdu and Welsh. His 'failure' to identify others is probably due to lack of attention, as he didn't notice some languages, such as Danish and Swedish, that he is reasonably competent in; and on other occasions he has correctly identified Serbo-Croat, Swahili, Ukrainian, etc.

15   We are not distinguishing here between 'learning' and 'acquiring'. See Smith et al. (1993: fn.2) and chapter 4 below.

16   The items in square brackets either do not exist (ΚΑΤΑΤΡΟφΗ), or are mis-spelt (ΟφΙΣ, ΚΟ̲Σ, φΟ̲ΤΑ).

17   'Thekatria' is the Greek for thirteen; 'ps' is a possible initial cluster in Greek, whereas 'sn' is not. The reverse, of course, is true for English.

18   For simplicity of exegesis, we use the term 'innateness hypothesis' even though we are aware of the controversy surrounding the expression. We accept Chomsky's position that 'there is no such general hypothesis' (1991a: 15) but 'there are specific hypotheses about what is innate' (ibid.), and that 'what is required is further evidence . . . and some theoretical understanding of what the innate resources of the mind actually are' (Chomsky, 1991b: 34). This book represents an attempt to provide such evidence and understanding.

19   For discussion, see Chomsky (1991a); Piattelli-Palmarini (1989). For a useful summary and hostile critique of arguments for innateness, see Sampson (1989).

20   As best embodied in Fodor's First Law of the Nonexistence of Cognitive Science: 'the more global . . . a cognitive process is, the less anybody understands it' (Fodor, 1983: 107).

21   For a contrary view, see Marslen-Wilson and Tyler (1987), who claim that not all linguistic processing is stimulus-driven. Following Carston (1988), we consider that the results reported in Swinney (1979) are sufficiently robust to withstand their criticism.

22   As will become apparent in chapter 5, we do not necessarily subscribe to all aspects of Anderson's model. For instance, we think it is necessary to postulate some kind of 'Executive' and, as a result, it may be best to characterize the BPM itself as a 'horizontal faculty' (see Fodor, 1983: 11), which crosses

content-domains, and hence acts as a constraint on the operation of other parts of the system, rather than being any kind of module in its own right.

23   Anderson also proposes (1992a: 194) a third class of modules, but these are left too inexplicit to be usefully exploited here.

24   The extent of the transfer of L1 values to L2 data is a debatable issue. Eubank (1993) argues for a 'moderate-transfer' account, while Schwartz (1993) takes the strong position of transfer being characteristic of initial stages of interlanguage grammars.

25   As will be discussed later, Christopher's sensitivity to morphological constraints is much greater than his sensitivity to syntax proper, i.e. syntactic variation attributed to parametric differences. Nevertheless, our findings do not suggest that Christopher's knowledge of his non-native languages is not UG-constrained (see chs. 3 and 4).

26   We ignore the phonological dimension, where different considerations may obtain.

27   As suggested explicitly by Van der Lely and Stollwerck (in prep. a: 15), who write that 'the SLI children have "no knowledge" of binding principles but appear to attempt to "obey" the principles by using relatively well developed central system knowledge and processes'. We are sceptical about the possibility of the cognitive penetration of the language module by the central system which seems to inhere in this formulation.

28   Specifically, number, gender, animacy, mass/count, proper names, tense and aspect.

Chapter 2:   The First Language

1   The stimulus sentence – for example, 1 – is given first and is followed by Christopher's judgement in square brackets: either '[OK]' if he found it acceptable, or '[R]' if he rejected it for some reason. In the latter case, it is followed by Christopher's suggested emendation in inverted commas, with the same number primed – e.g. 1′ – as the stimulus. Examples where Christopher was given alternative stimuli are numbered with additional letters – e.g. 1a, 1b – with an indication of which he accepted and rejected, but with no further emendation.

2   We do not discuss A-binding or control structures in detail for two reasons: first, as can be inferred from Appendix II, Christopher's judgements on these constructions correspond to those of other native speakers in all relevant respects; second, by concentrating on A′-dependencies the difference in Christopher's judgements can be reduced to the presence vs. absence of an Operator-like element.

3   Note that 'pure' topics can also appear in similar constructions (see Reinhart, 1983).

4   One problem with this analysis is that QR, which is standardly assumed to involve adjunction to IP, falls outside the configurational definition of operators, an undesirable result.

5   Alternatively, if we assume (following Lasnik and Stowell, 1991) that the empty category is a null epithet, i.e. an empty category which is [-anaphor, -pronominal] and [-variable], we can still maintain the desired result that there is no Operator–Variable structure (see Tsimpli, 1994, for discussion).

6   The unnecessary 'correction' in 47' is a typical example of tense harmony to which we return on pp. 65–7. It has no bearing on the present discussion.

7   By 'sufficient' contextual information we mean that, whereas in the absence of context, dislocation and topicalization may appear stylistically marked, the context rendered the constructions entirely natural.

8   Note that, while cleft constructions are 'marked' in the sense described here, they are syntactically 'complete' in that they contain an additional clause. Co-indexation then links the element in the higher clause to the Operator in the Spec-CP position of the embedded clause. Like relative clauses, the analysis of clefts involves predication (Chomsky, 1982).

9   As before, we ignore corrections irrelevant to the issue at hand.

10 The translations into various languages which Christopher volunteered cast light on which is the preferred (or more accessible) interpretation of ambiguous examples.

11 Full data appear in Appendix III.

12 This reading is the preferred interpretation on the assumption that satisfying the processing principle of 'minimal attachment' takes precedence over satisfying 'late closure' (see Frazier and Rayner, 1982; Flores d'Arcais, 1988).

13 Indeed, he also rejected the possibility of substituting 'him' for 'her', indicating unambiguously that he interpreted the sequence [her friends] as a constituent.

14 In fact, in both English and Greek it is possible to contradict the intended rhetorical force of a question as in:

A.   'Who has ever lifted a finger to help me?'
B.   'I have, you ungrateful wretch!'

But B's answer trades precisely on the rhetorical intention behind A's utterance. For Greek, Tsimpli and Roussou (1993) have argued that the co-occurrence of wh-phrases and polarity items is not possible (because of syntactic constraints), but in rhetorical questions this co-occurrence is possible, and the value of the wh-phrase is that of a negative quantifier (see also Progovac, 1994).

15 Notice that any question can be interpreted (pragmatically) as rhetorical. The claim here is that in the case of a wh-question with a polarity item, this is the *only* possibility.

16 In Reichenbach's (1947) theory, the difference depends on whether the event time (ET) of the embedded clause is linked to the ET of the matrix clause or to speech time (ST). In the former case, the time of speaking Berber may in fact precede the time of thinking. See Hornstein (1990) for detailed discussion.

17 These examples were devised on analogy with the k-limited stochastic sources

discussed in Miller and Chomsky (1963: 427ff), though we have ignored word-frequency.

18   These translations are given on pp. 172–3.
19   See Smith (1989: ch. 8) for an analysis of such jokes.

Chapter 3:   'Second' language

1   In earlier discussion of the status of Christopher's 'second' languages, we investigated the possibility of his being a prodigy who learns each new language as though it was a 'first' language (Smith and Tsimpli, 1991; Tsimpli and Smith, 1991; Smith et al., 1993). We concluded that this suggestion could not be supported, for two reasons: first, because there is a clear contrast between his competence in English and in other languages; second, because the mistakes he makes in production and comprehension are similar to those of typical second language learners of the various languages involved.
2   We are grateful to Saras Smith for her help with the Hindi data.
3   These are the appropriate subject markers for Berber verbs, see p. 124.
4   It is instructive to consider the Subset Principle in this context (Berwick, 1985; Manzini and Wexler, 1987; Wexler and Manzini, 1987). It aims in essence to restrict grammar-construction to what is possible on the basis of positive evidence alone and can accordingly be understood as a constraint excluding overgeneralization in the domain of syntax proper.
5   This assumption is neutral as between continuity and maturational approaches (see Tsimpli, 1992, for discussion).
6   Again, see ibid. for discussion.
7   The contrast between Christopher's mastery of the lexica of his second languages and his relatively inadequate syntax may have to do with the greater processing complexity of sentential as opposed to lexical material. We have some independent evidence that complex structures, such as multiple embeddings and garden-path constructions, cause him difficulty, confusion and even distress (see pp. 57–60). Comparable observations may pertain to his translation strategy, which appears to concentrate on lexical entities rather than on the sentence (see pp. 156–64.
8   Carroll (1992) suggests that differences in the *modality* of the input may result in triggering phonological rather than morphological information. This is consistent with the experimental findings of Browne (1982) which indicate that 'errors' in cognate-pairs differ depending on the nature of the input, i.e. visual vs. auditory.
9   In this respect 'cognate-pairing' is reminiscent of the context-independent accessing of homophonous pairs described by Swinney (1979).
10   This was one of several examples where Christopher avoided an etymologically related form. Another was provided by his translation 'good' for *brave*.
11   Note that it is often unclear which 'correct' category an item should be assigned to: e.g. *son* was given sundry correct translations, all of which avoided the *faux ami* interpretation.

12 Words were assigned to C or D only if neither Kirk-Greene nor the Collins Robert Dictionary mentioned Christopher's suggested translation.

13 It is not always clear which category a particular item comes in: for instance, *vivace* ('hardy') with its cognate *vivacious*, and *truculent* ('colourful, racy') are transparently adjectival, but their putative internal structure is (synchronically) opaque.

14 We are grateful to Maria Black, Carmen Curcó, Andrea Moro and Marcela Mora y Araujo for their help with the Italian and Spanish data.

15 The word-order in this and the following examples is acceptable only contrastively.

16 Examples 31 and 33 involve subjects in sentence-final position: that is, following not only the object but a VP-adjunct as well.

17 There are cases where to have the subject in preverbal position is the only possibility: for example, in generics and in cases where there is a clausal subject. The contrary situation also obtains: namely, where it is obligatory to have the subject postverbal: for example, bare indefinite subjects of passive, middle and ergative predicates (Roussou and Tsimpli, 1993).

18 Whether control involving a PRO subject is the appropriate analysis for Christopher's correction is moot. Given the obligatory presence of agreement morphology in Greek, it could alternatively be argued that the coreference involves a pro subject in the embedded clause.

19 This is an inevitable problem with the interpretation of grammaticality judgement tasks, not only in Christopher's case but in general (see Birdsong, 1989; Cook, 1993 for discussion). In particular, it is not clear whether the judgement provided indicates preference between two acceptable alternatives or absolute choice between an acceptable and an unacceptable sentence. See also pp. 42–3.

20 In fact, it is not clear that gerund clauses of the type exemplified in 38 allow topicalization or dislocation at all. If this turns out to be the case, the topic interpretation of the preverbal subject can be analysed as topicalization of the subject of the matrix clause.

21 In view of his generally perfect performance in his first language, it is somewhat surprising that Christopher had no hesitation in providing the ungrammatical English translation of 40′ given in 40″. We assume that this is the result of two interacting factors: his frequently flawed translation strategy and his inability to construe the postverbal NP as a subject.

22 This sentence is ungrammatical because only animate objects are preceded by the preposition 'a': that is, each of 53 and 53′ would be fully grammatical if the 'a' were omitted. It is of interest that Christopher failed to correct this mistake although he immediately 'corrected' the word-order in his usual fashion.

23 Note that subjects can appear preceding dislocated constituents as in (i):

(i)   O Petros, tin Maria, dhen tin idhe
      the-nom Petros the-acc Maria not her-saw-3s
      Petros didn't see Maria

We assume that in such cases the subject is also left-dislocated and is coindexed with a pro in subject position (Tsimpli, 1990). In this respect, subjects are unlike object NPs in CLLD structures for two reasons: first, there are no subject clitics in Modern Greek, and second, pro is available in subject but not in object position.

24 We will remain agnostic on whether right-dislocation and clitic-doubling are distinct options in Greek (see Agouraki, 1993).

25 It is possible to have a focus interpretation in which the preverbal NP is an object which has been focus-moved to clause-initial position. However, given that there is no oral (emphatic stress) or orthographic (e.g. capitalized) indication that would point to this possibility, Christopher's translation of the corrected version is the unmarked one.

26 For the purposes of the current discussion, the possibility of alternative accounts of the derivation of VSO order is not crucial. We assume that, whichever account is suggested within the principles and parameters approach, cross-linguistic variation involving the presence or absence of VSO word-order will stem from a parametric difference.

27 As Christopher's Spanish is not as fluent as his French or Greek, it might be suggested that parameter-resetting for Spanish could be achieved later on in the learning process. However, his contact with Greek has been sufficiently regular, prolonged and intensive to make it unlikely that his intuitions about VSO word-order can still develop to become more native-like. We accordingly remain sceptical about the possibility of parameter-resetting at all.

28 To be grammatical this sentence would need the negative 'no' before 'va'.

29 It might be that the parameter associated with this functional category is 'unset' in the sense that English may not have a negative specification for focus-movement. In other words, if the lack of a grammaticalized feature implies the absence of the corresponding functional category from syntactic represen-tations, then it may not be accurate to claim that parameter-setting is involved at all.

30 See the references of note 19 above, White (1985b) and especially Bley-Vroman et al. (1989) which claims that Korean advanced learners of English are sensitive to subjacency violations in the language they are learning. As there is no basis for such judgements in their own first language, the assumption is that they have some sort of access to UG.

31 It is clear that if this is true then it implies that Christopher's second language learning is crucially different from his first language learning, as processing load cannot have caused any significant problem when he was learning English. It might be suggested that his processing deficit was developmental, hence affecting only some aspects of his learning of some of his second languages, but in this case one would not expect the cross-linguistic uniformity which is characteristic of his judgements.

Chapter 4:   New Languages

1 We are grateful to Dr Jamal Ouhalla of Queen Mary and Westfield College for his collaboration on the Berber component of the project.

2 It is worth mentioning, however, that when he began Epun (see pp. 139–54) Christopher's initial translations into the new language were marked by the frequent omission of articles and affixes: precisely those morphological elements that he excelled at in Berber.

3 As before (and with the same caveats), Christopher's reactions are indicated by '[OK]' and '[R]' for acceptable and unacceptable examples respectively, and his own contributions are given in inverted commas.

4 See Clahsen and Muysken (1986) for relevant discussion of this issue in the context of the varying stages in the acquisition of German as a second language.

5 Christopher has generalized the y- prefix characteristic of the third-person masculine singular to the plural.

6 The written version of the sentences given to Christopher contained no morpheme boundaries.

7 We considered at some length the ethical problem of deceiving Christopher about the status of Epun, and concluded that our actions were justifiable. Christopher has mastered fragments of many languages, several of which he has never had the opportunity of speaking, and which, in the absence of specific stimulus, he shows no particular interest in pursuing. In these circumstances, we did not think that he would be harmed in any way by learning bits of a (twentieth) language, of which he will never encounter speakers other than us. It might also be suggested that it was cruel to teach him an 'impossible' language, but his enthusiastic reaction to the language over a period of a year or more indicates that he was in no way upset by it.

8 Alternatively, if normal second language learning involves only access to UG, with or without parameter-resetting, while general learning mechanisms are irrelevant, Christopher's defective attainment (discussed in chapter 3 and the first part of the present chapter) could be attributed in part to his employment of inductive learning strategies to analyse linguistic data which are inherently resistant to such a strategy. That is, one part of Christopher's exceptional second language learning, specifically the plateau effect visible in his non-native languages, might be a function of his need to exploit inductive learning strategies.

9 Full details of the Epun data, together with Christopher's and the controls' reactions to them, can be found in Smith et al. (1993).

10 Note that we do not think Corbett's generalizations show that the unattested patterns are linguistically impossible in the sense defined by UG. As the morphological forms that enter into subject–verb agreement in conjunction structures are not necessarily syntactically motivated, the learning of this part of the L2 morphology can be viewed as independent of UG and parameter-ization. This is consonant with the claim that the morphological component,

even though it clearly interacts with the syntax, is in fact autonomous. Thus, learning the lexicon and the lexical rules regulating derivational and inflectional morphology in the second language does not directly reflect the core functioning of the language module.

11 This form of words is necessary to account for the impossibility of agreement with the dual, in those languages where the dual is distinct from the plural.

12 Focusing with the use of an emphatic marker does occur in the language, but Christopher had not as yet been exposed to such examples.

Chapter 5: Language and Mind

1 The sentence containing this example was:

> Quel vaso era già rovinato anche prima di rompersi
> This vase was already spoilt before it was broken
> Afto to vaso itan ioi katestrammeno prin akoma spastike.

2 *Spastike* and *Arxizonte* don't exist, because the verbs are subject to the ergative/causative alternation, which allows only active morphology.

3 The use of *who* in a free relative is slightly archaic, but is widely exemplified in literature: 'Who steals my purse steals trash'.

4 This example was given as part of a description of a picture and did not involve overt translation.

5 His knowledge of the correct form of the relative pronoun was also better when explicitly tested than it was in spontaneous speech or in translation. However, when forced to choose between two sentences one of which was ungrammatical in virtue of containing an interrogative rather than a relative pronoun, and the other of which was ungrammatical in virtue of having the finite verb in non-final position, he chose the former, as indicated in (a):

> (a) Ich kenne einige Leute, wer gut tanzen können   [OK]
>   Ich kenne einige Leute, die können gut tanzen   [R]

The correct form is given in (b):

> (b) Ich kenne einige Leute, die gut tanzen können

Christopher did not accept the invitation to provide a correct alternative to both examples.

6 The preceding context, which Christopher had just translated, made it clear that a generic interpretation was intended.

7 This was a rerun of a previous attempt at translating this passage (see pp. 14–15 above, and Smith and Tsimpli, 1991: 323).

8 Christopher had originally translated this passage into English for O'Connor

and Hermelin (see their 1991: 675). He had no recollection of having seen it before when we asked him a year later to translate it first into English and then into French.

9   The examples were not presented one after the other as here, hence the change in tense is not surprising. These examples occurred as part of an exercise designed to test his look-ahead facility by presenting him with minimal pairs of this kind and others like those in (a) and (b):

(a)   Have the boys leave!
(b)   Have the boys left?

Unfortunately he refused to accept (a) as a possible sentence of English, although he was perfectly happy with (c):

(c)   Make the boys leave!

10   We are ignoring many interesting issues in the relation between grammars and parsers. For discussion, see Flores d'Arcais (1988); Koot (1990).
11   Although not universally accepted, the idea that there is a language of thought in Fodor's sense is common to a majority of researchers working on mental representation in general and theory of mind in particular. See, for instance, Leslie (1988: 32): 'the cognitive mechanisms that form the basis of the child's capacity to construct a theory of mind exploit the systematic formal relations that hold between sets of meta-representational expressions in the language of thought.'
12   Isomorphism between the language of thought and natural language is not complete as natural language contains elements such as pro-forms and empty categories that are alien to the language of thought, and the latter exploits non-verbal, e.g. imagistic, categories that are alien to natural language.
13   For Anderson, *thinking* consists in the 'implementation of an algorithm generated by a specific processor' (1992b: 17–18).
14   The 'lemma' embraces the semantic and syntactic properties of words but excludes their morpho-phonological properties (see Caplan, 1992: e.g. 106 – following *inter alia* Levelt, 1989). We are not committed to this precise demarcation but we are sympathetic to the principle of such a distinction.
15   We are grateful to Paul Burgess for discussing Christopher's performance on this test with us.
16   Full details of the results are given in Appendix VI.
17   He gave up the translation of 18(a) with 'et je ne sais pas' because he didn't know the French for the items 'underworld' and 'mummies'.
18   This suggestion is in the spirit of Shallice's claim (1988: esp. ch. 12) that specific dissociations, such as those manifest in acalculia or selective semantic memory loss, provide evidence for the non-equipotentiality of the central system. More recently, Sperber (1994b) has suggested that the human mind is 'modular through and through' with virtually every concept defining its own

module. While we are unconvinced that this suggestion is fully supported
by performance mechanisms, we are sympathetic to his general position,
especially the vast importance he attributes to the 'metarepresentational
module'.

19 For perceptive overviews of 'the autistic continuum' and the need 'to
differentiate various forms of autism', see Frith (1991) and Wing (1991).

20 We are grateful to Amahl Smith for discussing these issues with us.

21 We are not convinced that Fodor's uniqueness requirement is well motivated.
It seems that the appropriate generalization is that young children will follow
H1 unless they are given explicit evidence that the agent's desires are thwarted.

22 Happé (1995) documents a number of cases in which children are
differentially successful on the two tests, but the most striking generalization is
that performance on the two tasks is correlated. Given, on the one hand, that
Christopher's performance in the two tasks does not match that of the average
autistic person, and on the other, that there exist cases where the performance
of autistic individuals differs in relation to their success in the two tests, we
assume that there is a difference in complexity between the two tasks. We
return to this issue below. We are grateful to Uta Frith and Francesca Happé
for helpful discussion on this issue.

23 This is oversimplified; see, e.g., Baron-Cohen (1993) and Happé (in prep.) for
more adequate characterizations.

24 We need to make an auxiliary assumption: namely, that modality necessarily
entails non-actuality. This implies that, although it is necessarily true that the
actual is possible, possibility in modal readings does not include the actual.
This becomes clear in relation to the difficulty (or impossibility) of assigning
truth-values to the proposition embedded under a modality predicate of the
type discussed here.

25 The first verb need not necessarily be 'think', but we wish explicitly to exclude
simple examples of indirect speech from the representation given in 33.

26 This distinction has been addressed by Perner and Leekam (see Perner, 1991:
312, for brief discussion), where the crucial consideration is whether the deficit
manifest by autistic children (and by Christopher) generalizes to cases of non-
mental representation. They tested for this by using a modification of
Žaitchik's (1990) photo task and compared it with a matching false-belief task.
The autistic children were better at the former than the latter; normal children
were better at the latter than the former, so Perner concludes that 'this suggests
that autism is not characterised by a general metarepresentational deficit'
(ibid.). If theory of mind tasks are differentially affected by perceptually vs.
cognitively derived representations, as we suggest, then Perner's conclusion
can be remotivated in the sense specified here.

27 There are numerous other considerations that need be taken into account in
relation to this non-average autistic group: for example, their performance in
tests involving figurative language, jokes and, in general, any cognitive task
implementing second-order representations. The point is that, if successful
performance in theory of mind tasks involves the construal of second-order

representations *and* the accessibility of a source from which the propositions are derived *and* VMA within certain specifiable limits, then there is an increasing number of alternative combinations giving rise to atypical performance. Detailed discussion of such findings is beyond the scope of this study.

28 In personal communication he has suggested that it may be an emergent property dependent on both modular and central factors. While sharing his doubt about the possibility of 'locating' an executive in the kind of box and arrow diagram we both use, we feel that it is necessary to include it explicitly in our ontology, whatever metaphysical problems it may raise.

29 In personal correspondence it has become clear that our difference here is not as profound as appears on the surface.

References

Abangma, S. (1992) *Empty Categories in Denya*. University College, London, PhD thesis.

Agouraki, Y. (1991) 'A Modern Greek complementiser and its significance for Universal Grammar'. *UCL Working Papers in Linguistics* 3: 1–24.

Agouraki, Y. (1993) *Spec-Head Licensing: The Scope of the Theory*. University College, London, PhD thesis.

Anderson, M. (1992a) *Intelligence and Development: A Cognitive Theory*. Oxford: Basil Blackwell.

Anderson, M. (1992b) 'Intelligence'. In K. Brewin (ed.), *Handbook of Human Performance*, London: Academic Press, vol. 3, pp. 1–24.

Andrews, A. (1988) 'Lexical structure'. In F. Newmeyer (ed.), *Linguistics: The Cambridge Survey*, Cambridge: Cambridge University Press, vol. 1, pp. 60–88.

Atkinson, M. (1992) *Children's Syntax: An Introduction to Principles and Parameters Theory*. Oxford: Basil Blackwell.

Baker, M.C. (1988) *Incorporation: A Theory of Grammatical Function Changing*. Chicago, Ill.: Chicago University Press.

Baron-Cohen, S. (1993) 'From attention-goal psychology to belief-desire psychology: the development of a theory of mind and its dysfunction'. In S. Baron-Cohen, H. Tager-Flusberg and D.J. Cohen (eds), *Understanding Other Minds: Perspectives from Autism*, London: Oxford University Press, pp. 59–82.

Baron-Cohen, S., A.M. Leslie and U. Frith (1985) 'Does the autistic child have a theory of mind?' *Cognition* 21: 37-46.

Baron-Cohen, S., H. Tager-Flusberg and D.J. Cohen (eds) (1993) *Understanding Other Minds: Perspectives from Autism*. London: Oxford University Press.

Belletti, A. and L. Rizzi (1986) 'Psych-verbs and theta-theory', Lexicon Project Working Paper no. 13. Cambridge, Mass.: Centre for Cognitive Science, Massachusetts Institute of Technology.

Bellugi, U., Marks, S., Bihrle, A.M. and Sabo, H. (1993) 'Dissociation between language and cognitive functions in Williams Syndrome'. In D. Bishop and K. Mogford (eds), *Language Development in Exceptional Circumstances*, Hove, Sussex: Lawrence Erlbaum, pp. 177–89.

Berwick, R. (1985) *The Acquisition of Syntactic Knowledge*. Cambridge, Mass.: MIT Press.

Birdsong, D. (1989) *Metalinguistic Performance and Interlinguistic Competence*. New York: Springer.

Birdsong, D. (1992) 'Ultimate attainment in second language learning'. *Language*, 68: 706–55.

Blakemore, D. (1987) *Semantic Constraints on Relevance*. Oxford: Basil Blackwell.

Bley-Vroman, R. (1989) 'What is the logical problem of foreign language learning?' In S. Gass and J. Schachter (eds), *Linguistic Perspectives on Second Language Acquisition*, Cambridge: Cambridge University Press, pp. 41–68.

Bley-Vroman, R., S. Felix and G. Ioup (1989) 'The accessibility of Universal Grammar in adult language learning'. *Second Language Research*, 4: 1–32.

Borer, H. and K. Wexler (1987) 'The maturation of syntax'. In T. Roeper and E. Williams (eds), *Parameter Setting*, Dordrecht: Reidel.

Borer, H. and K. Wexler (1988) 'The maturation of grammatical principles'. University of California at Irvine, MS.

Bowerman, M. (1987) 'The "no negative evidence" problem: how do children avoid constructing an overly general grammar?' In J. Hawkins (ed.), *Explaining Language Universals*, Oxford: Basil Blackwell.

Braine, M.D.S. (1963) 'The ontogeny of English phrase structure'. *Language*, 39: 1–13.

Brandi, L. and P. Cordin (1989) 'Two Italian dialects and the null-subject parameter'. In O. Jaeggli and K. Safir (eds), *The Null-subject Parameter*, Dordrecht: Kluwer, pp. 111–42.

Brody, M. (1990) 'Some remarks on the focus field in Hungarian'. *UCL Working Papers in Linguistics*, 2: 201–25.

Brody, M. (1994) *Lexico-logical Form: A Radically Minimalist Theory*. MS University College London (to be published Cambridge, Mass.: MIT Press).

Brown, R. and U. Bellugi (1964) 'Three processes in the child's acquisition of syntax'. In E. Lenneberg (ed.), *New Directions in the Study of Language*, Cambridge, Mass.: MIT Press, pp. 131–61.

Browne, R. (1982) 'Aural and visual recognition of cognates and their implications for the teaching of cognate languages', Harvard University PhD, distributed by UMI Dissertation Information Service.

Browning, M. (1987) *Null Operator Constructions*. PhD thesis, Massachusetts Institute of Technology.

Burgess, P.W. and T. Shallice (1994) 'Fractionation of the frontal lobe syndrome'. *Revue du Neuropsychologie*, 4: 345–70.

Burton-Roberts, N. (1989) *The Limits to Debate: A Revised Theory of Semantic Presupposition*. Cambridge: Cambridge University Press.

Burton-Roberts, N. (1993) 'On preservation under negation'. *Newcastle and Durham Working Papers in Linguistics*, 1: 18–41.

Caplan, D. (1992) *Language: Structure, Processing and Disorders*. Cambridge, Mass.: MIT Press.

Carroll, S.E. (1992) 'On cognates'. *Second Language Research*, 8: 93–119.

Carruthers, P. (forthcoming) *Language, Thought and Consciousness*. Cambridge: Cambridge University Press.

Carston, R. (1988) 'Language and cognition'. In F. Newmeyer (ed.), *Linguistics: The Cambridge Survey*, Cambridge: Cambridge University Press, vol. 3, pp. 38–68.

Carston, R. (1993) 'Conjunction, explanation and relevance'. *Lingua*, 90: 27–48.

Carston, R. (1994) 'The pragmatics of negation'. University College London, MS.

Chandler, M., A. Fritz and S. Hala (1989) 'Small-scale deceit: deception as a marker of two-, three-, and four-year-olds' early theories of mind'. *Child Development*, 60: 1263–77.

Chao, W. (1980) 'Pro-drop languages and non-obligatory control'. *University of Massachusetts Occasional Papers in Linguistics*, 7: 46–74.

Chapman, S. (1993) 'Metalinguistic negation, sentences and utterances'. *Newcastle and Durham Working Papers in Linguistics*, 1: 74–94.

Choe, H.S. (1987) 'Restructuring parameters and scrambling in Korean and Hungarian'. Massachusetts Institute of Technology, MS.

Chomsky, N. (1965) *Aspects of the Theory of Syntax*. Cambridge, Mass.: MIT Press.

Chomsky, N. (1972) *Language and Mind*. New York: Harcourt Brace Jovanovich.

Chomsky, N. (1977) 'On wh-movement'. In P. Culicover, T. Wasow and A. Akmajian (eds), *Formal Syntax*, London: Academic Press, pp. 71–132.

Chomsky, N. (1981a) *Lectures on Government and Binding*. Dordrecht: Foris.

Chomsky, N. (1981b) 'Principles and parameters in syntactic theory'. In N. Hornstein and D. Lightfoot (eds), *Explanation in Linguistics*. London: Longman, pp. 32–75.

Chomsky, N. (1982) *Some Concepts and Consequences of the Theory of Government and Binding*. Cambridge, Mass.: MIT Press.

Chomsky, N. (1986a) *Knowledge of Language: Its Nature, Origin and Use*. New York: Praeger.

Chomsky, N. (1986b) *Barriers*. Cambridge, Mass.: MIT Press.

Chomsky, N. (1991a) 'Linguistics and adjacent fields: a personal view'. In A. Kasher (ed.), *The Chomskyan Turn*, Oxford: Basil Blackwell, pp. 3–25.

Chomsky, N. (1991b) 'Linguistics and cognitive science: problems and mysteries'. In A. Kasher (ed.), *The Chomskyan Turn*. Oxford: Basil Blackwell, pp. 26–53.

Chomsky, N. (1991c) 'Some notes on economy of derivation and representation'. In R. Freidin (ed.), *Principles and Parameters in Comparative Grammar*, Cambridge, Mass.: MIT Press, pp. 417–54.

Chomsky, N. (1993a) 'A minimalist program for linguistic theory'. In K. Hale and S.J. Keyser (eds), *The View from Building 20*. Cambridge, Mass.: MIT Press, pp. 1–52.

Chomsky, N. (1993b) 'Language from an internalist perspective'. Massachusetts Institute of Technology, draft MS.

Cinque, G. (1991) *Types of A'-dependencies*. Cambridge, Mass.: MIT Press.

Clahsen, H. and P. Muysken (1986) 'The availability of Universal Grammar to adult and child learners: a study of the acquisition of German word-order'. *Second Language Research*, 2: 93–119.

Clark, W. (1991) *Relevance Theory and the Semantics of Non-declaratives*. PhD thesis, University College London.

Collins-Robert (1978) *French–English, English–French Dictionary*. London: Collins.

Cook, V.J. (1993) *Linguistics and Second Language Acquisition*. London: Macmillan.

Corbett, G. (1991) *Gender*. Cambridge: Cambridge University Press.

Cossu, G. and Marshall, J.C. (1986) 'Theoretical implications of the hyperlexia syndrome: two new Italian cases'. *Cortex*, 22: 579–89.

Courchesne, E., R. Yeung-Courchesne, G.A. Press, J.R. Hesselink and T.L. Jernigan (1988) 'Hypoplasia of cerebellar vermal lobules VI and VII in autism'. *New England Journal of Medicine*, 318: 1349–54.

Cristoffanini, P., K. Kirsner and D. Milech (1986) 'Bilingual lexical representation: the status of Spanish–English cognates'. *Quarterly Journal of Experimental Psychology*, 38A: 367–93.

Cromer, R.F. (1991) *Language and Thought in Normal and Handicapped Children*. Oxford: Basil Blackwell.

Culicover, P. (1991) 'Topicalisation, inversion and complementisers in English'. MS.

Curtiss, S. (1977) *Genie: A Psycholinguistic Study of a Modern Day 'Wild Child'*. London: Academic Press.

Eisenmajer, R. and M. Prior (1991) 'Cognitive linguistic correlates of "theory of mind" ability in autistic children'. *British Journal of Developmental Psychology*, 9: 351–64.

Eubank, L. (1993) 'Sentence matching and processing in L2 development'. *Second Language Research*, 9: 253–80.

Fay, W.H. (1993) 'Infantile autism'. In D. Bishop and K. Mogford (eds), *Language Development in Exceptional Circumstances*. Hove, Sussex: Lawrence Erlbaum, pp. 190–202.

Felix, S. (1984) 'Maturational aspects of Universal Grammar'. In A. Davies, C. Criper and A. Howatt (eds), *Interlanguage*, Edinburgh: Edinburgh University Press.

Ferguson, C. (1959) 'Diglossia'. *Word*, 15: 325–40.

Ferrar, M. (1993) *The Logic of the Ludicrous*. PhD thesis, University College London.

Flavell, J.H., F.L. Green and E.R. Flavell (1986) 'Development of knowledge about the appearance–reality distinction'. *Monographs of the Society for Research in Child Development*, 51, serial no. 212.

Flores d'Arcais, G.B. (1988) 'Language perception'. In F. Newmeyer (ed.), *Linguistics: The Cambridge Survey*, Cambridge: Cambridge University Press, vol. 3, pp. 97–123.

Fodor, J. (1975) *The Language of Thought*. New York: Crowell.

Fodor, J. (1983) *The Modularity of Mind*. MIT Press.

Fodor, J. (1992) 'A theory of the child's theory of mind'. *Cognition*, 44: 283–96.

Forguson, L. and A. Gopnik (1988) 'The ontogeny of common sense'. In J.W. Astington, P.L. Harris and D.R. Olson (eds), *Developing Theories of Mind*, Cambridge: Cambridge University Press, pp. 226–43.

Frazier, L. and K. Rayner (1982) 'Making and correcting errors during sentence comprehension: eye movements in the analysis of structurally ambiguous sentences'. *Cognitive Psychology*, 14: 178–210.

Frith, U. (1989) *Autism: Explaining the Enigma*. Oxford: Basil Blackwell.

Frith, U. (1991) 'Asperger and his syndrome'. In U. Frith (ed.), *Autism and Asperger Syndrome*. Cambridge: Cambridge University Press, pp. 1–36.

Fromkin, V.A. (1987) 'The lexicon: evidence from acquired dyslexia'. *Language*, 63: 1–19.

Gopnik, M. (1990) 'Feature-blindness: a case study'. *Language Acquisition*, 1: 139–64.

Gopnik, M. (in press) 'Impairments of syntactic tense in a familial language disorder'. *Journal of Neurolinguistics*.

Gopnik, M. and M.B. Crago (1991) 'Familial aggregation of a developmental language disorder'. *Cognition*, 39: 1–50.

Gordon, P. (1989) 'Levels of affixation in the acquisition of English morphology'. *Journal of Memory and Language*, 28: 519–30.

Gorrell, P. (1995) *Syntax and Parsing*. Cambridge: Cambridge University Press.

Gould, S.J. (1981) *The Mismeasure of Man*. Harmondsworth, Middx: Penguin.

Greenberg, J. (1963) 'Some universals of grammar with particular reference to the order of meaningful elements'. In J. Greenberg (ed.), *Universals of Language*, Cambridge, Mass.: MIT Press, pp. 73–113.

Grice, H.P. (1967) 'Logic and conversation'. William James Lecture. In H.P. Grice, *Studies in the Way of Words*, Cambridge, Mass.: Harvard University Press, 1989.

Guilford, J.P. (1966) 'Intelligence: 1965 model'. *American Psychologist*, 21: 20–6.

Guilfoyle, E. and M. Noonan (1988) 'Functional categories and language acquisition', paper presented at the Thirteenth Annual Boston University Conference on Language Development.

Gutt, E.-A. (1991) *Translation and Relevance*. Oxford: Basil Blackwell.

Haegeman, L. (1995) *The Syntax of Negation*. Cambridge: Cambridge University Press.

Happé, F. (1995) 'The role of age and verbal ability in the theory of mind task performance in autistic subjects with autism'. *Child Development* 66: 843–55.

Hermelin, B. and N. O'Connor (1986) 'Idiot savant calendrical calculators: rules and regularities'. *Psychological Medicine*, 16: 885–93.

Hermelin, B. and N. O'Connor (1987) 'Musical inventiveness of five idiot-savants'. *Psychological Medicine*, 17: 685–94.

Hermelin, B. and N. O'Connor (1990) 'Art and accuracy: the drawing ability of idiot-savants'. *Journal of Child Psychology and Psychiatry*, 31: 217–28.

Horn, L. (1989) *A Natural History of Negation*. Chicago, Ill.: Chicago University Press.

Hornstein, N. (1990) *As Time Goes By*. Cambridge, Mass.: MIT Press.

Howard, D. and K. Patterson (n.d.) 'Pyramids and palm trees'. Unpublished.

Howe, M.J.A. (1989) *Fragments of Genius*. London: Routledge.

Huang, J. (1984) 'On the distribution and reference of empty pronouns'. *Linguistic Inquiry*, 15: 531–74.

'Hugo' (1980) *Greek in Three Months: Simplified Language Course*. Woodbridge, Suffolk: Hugo Language Books.

Hurford, J. (1991) 'The evolution of the critical period for language acquisition' *Cognition*, 40: 159–201.

Hurst, J.A., M. Baraitser, E. Auger, F. Graham and S. Norell (1990) 'An extended family with an inherited speech disorder'. *Developmental Medicine and Child Neurology*, 32: 347-55.

Hyams, N. (1986) *Language Acquisition and the Theory of Parameters*. Dordrecht: Reidel.

Hyams, N. (1987) 'The theory of parameters and syntactic development'. In T. Roeper and E. Williams (eds), *Parameter Setting*, Dordrecht: Reidel.

Jaeggli, O. (1982) *Topics in Romance Syntax*. Dordrecht: Foris.

Jaeggli, O. and N. Hyams (1988) 'Morphological uniformity and the setting of the null subject parameter'. University of California, Los Angeles, MS.

Jodlowiecz, M. (1991) 'What makes jokes tick'. *UCL Working Papers in Linguistics*, 3: 241–53.

Johnson Laird, P. (1983) *Mental Models*. Cambridge: Cambridge University Press.

Karmiloff-Smith, A. (1992a) *Beyond Modularity: A Developmental Perspective on Cognitive Science*. Cambridge, Mass.: MIT Press.

Karmiloff-Smith, A. (1992b) 'Abnormal phenotypes and the challenges they pose to connectionist models of development'. Carnegie Mellon University, *Technical Report PDP.CNS.92.7*.

Kayne, R. (1989) 'Null subjects and clitic climbing'. In O. Jaeggli and K. Safir (eds), *The Null-subject Parameter*. Dordrecht: Kluwer, pp. 239–61.

Kiparsky, P. (1982) 'From cyclic phonology to lexical phonology'. In H. van der Hulst and N. Smith (eds), *The Structure of Phonological Representations*, Dordrecht: Foris.

Kiparsky, P. (1983) 'Word-formation and the lexicon'. In F. Ingemann (ed.), *Proceedings of the 1982 Mid-America Linguistics Conference*, Lawrence, Kansas: University of Kansas.

Kirk-Greene, C.W.E. (1990) *NTC's Dictionary of Faux Amis*. Lincolnwood, Ill.: National Textbook Company.

Koopman, H. and D. Sportiche (1991) 'The position of subjects'. *Lingua*, 85: 211–58.

Koot, J. van de (1990) *An Essay on Grammar–Parser Relations*. Dordrecht: Foris.

Laka, I. (1990) *Negation in Syntax: On the Nature of Functional Categories and Projections*. PhD thesis, Massachusetts Institute of Technology.

Lasnik, H. and M. Saito (1984) 'On the nature of proper government'. *Linguistic Inquiry*, 15: 235–89.

Lasnik, H. and T. Stowell (1991) 'Weakest crossover'. *Linguistic Inquiry*, 22: 687–720.

Leslie, A.M. (1987) 'Pretense and representation: the origins of "theory of mind" '. *Psychological Review*, 94: 412–26.

Leslie, A.M. (1988) 'Some implications of pretense for mechanisms underlying the child's theory of mind'. In J.W. Astington, P.L. Harris and D.R. Olson (eds), *Developing Theories of Mind*. Cambridge: Cambridge University Press, pp. 19–46.

Leslie, A.M. and U. Frith (1987) 'Metarepresentation and autism: how not to lose one's marbles'. *Cognition*, 27: 291–94.

Levelt, W.J.M. (1989) *Speaking: From Intention to Articulation*. Cambridge, Mass.: MIT Press.

Liceras, J. (1989) 'On some properties of the pro-drop parameter: looking for missing subjects in non-native Spanish'. In S. Gass and J. Schachter (eds), *Linguistic Perspectives on Second Language Acquisition*. Cambridge: Cambridge University Press.

Linebarger, M.C. (1989) 'Neuropsychological evidence for linguistic modularity'. In G. Carlson and K. Tanenhaus (eds), *Linguistic Structure in Language Processing*, Dordrecht: Kluwer, pp. 197–238.

Lukes, S. and I. Galnoor (1987) *No Laughing Matter: A Collection of Political Jokes*. Harmondsworth, Middx.: Penguin.

Manzini, R. and K. Wexler (1987) 'Parameters, binding theory and learnability'. *Linguistic Inquiry*, 18: 413–44.

Marcus, G.F., S. Pinker, M. Ullman, M. Hollander, T.J. Rosen and F. Xu (1992) 'Overregularization in language acquisition'. *Monographs of the Society for Research in Child Development*, 57.

Marslen-Wilson, W. (1987) 'Functional parallelism in spoken word recognition'. *Cognition*, 25: 71–102.

Marslen-Wilson, W. (1989) 'Access and integration: projecting sound onto meaning'. In W. Marslen-Wilson (ed.), *Lexical Representation and Process*, Cambridge, Mass.: MIT Press, pp. 3–24.

Marslen-Wilson, W. and L.K. Tyler (1980) 'The temporal structure of spoken language understanding'. *Cognition*, 8: 1–71.

Marslen-Wilson, W. and L.K. Tyler (1987) 'Against modularity'. In J. Garfield (ed.), *Modularity in Knowledge Representation and Natural-Language Understanding*. Cambridge, Mass.: MIT Press.

McGregor, R.S. (1972) *Outline of Hindi Grammar*. Oxford: Clarendon Press.

Metzler, J. and R.N. Shepard (1982) 'Transformational studies of the internal representation of three-dimensional objects'. In R.N. Shepard and L.A. Cooper (eds), *Mental Images and their Transformations*, Cambridge, Mass.: MIT Press, pp. 25–71.

Miller, G. and N. Chomsky (1963) 'Finitary models of language users'. In R. Luce, R. Bush and E. Galanter (eds), *Handbook of Mathematical Psychology*, New York: John Wiley, vol. 2, pp. 419–91.

Miller, L.K. (1988) *Musical Savants: Exceptional Skill in the Mentally Retarded*. Hove, Sussex: Lawrence Erlbaum.

O'Connor, N. (1989) 'The performance of the "idiot-savant": implicit and explicit'. *British Journal of Disorders of Communication*, 24: 1–20.

O'Connor, N. and B. Hermelin (1978) *Seeing and Hearing and Space and Time*. London: Academic Press.

O'Connor, N. and B. Hermelin (1984) 'Idiot savant calendrical calculators: maths or 'memory?' *Psychological Medicine*, 14: 801–6.

O'Connor, N. and B. Hermelin (1987) 'Visual memory and motor programmes: Their use by idiot-savant artists and controls'. *British Journal of Psychology*, 78: 307–23.

O'Connor, N. and B. Hermelin (1989) 'The memory structure of autistic idiot-savant mnemonists'. *British Journal of Psychology*, 80: 97–111.

O'Connor, N. and B. Hermelin (1991) 'A specific linguistic ability'. *American Journal on Mental Retardation*, 95: 673–80.

O'Connor, N., N.V. Smith, C. Frith and I.-M. Tsimpli (1994) 'Neuropsychology and linguistic talent'. *Journal of Neurolinguistics*, 8: 95–107.

Ouhalla, J. (1988) *The Syntax of Head Movement*. PhD thesis, University College London.

Ouhalla, J. (1991) *Functional Categories and Parametric Variation*. London: Routledge.

Perner, J. (1991) *Understanding the Representational Mind*. Cambridge, Mass.: MIT Press.

Perner, J. (1993) 'The many faces of belief: reflections on Fodor's and the child's theory of mind'. Sussex University, MS.

Perner, J., S. Leekam and H. Wimmer (1987) 'Three-year-olds' difficulty with false belief: The case for a conceptual deficit'. *British Journal of Developmental Psychology*, 5: 125–37.

Perner, J., U. Frith, A. Leslie and S. Leekam (1989) 'Exploration of the autistic child's theory of mind: knowledge, belief and communication'. *Child Development*, 60: 689–700.

Pesetsky, D. (1989) *Language Particular Processes and the Earliness Principle*. Massachusetts Institute of Technology, MS.

Pesetsky, D. (1991) *Zero Syntax*. Massachusetts Institute of Technology, MS.

Philippaki-Warburton, I. (1985) 'Word-order in Modern Greek'. *Transactions of the Philological Society*, 113–43.

Piaget, J. (1970) *Genetic Epistemology*. New York: Columbia University Press.

Piattelli-Palmarini, M. (1989) 'Evolution, selection and cognition: from "learning" to parameter setting in biology and in the study of language'. *Cognition*, 31: 1–44.

Pierce, A. (1989) 'On the emergence of syntax: a cross-linguistic study'. Unpublished PhD thesis.

Pina, F.H. (1984) *Teorías Psicosociolingüísticas y su Aplicación a la Adquisición del Español como Lengua Materna*. Madrid: Siglo XXI.

Pinker, S. (1984) *Language Learnability and Language Development*. Cambridge, Mass.: Harvard University Press.

Pinker, S. (1989) *Learnability and Cognition*. Cambridge, Mass.: MIT Press.

Pollock, J.-Y. (1989) 'Verb movement, UG, and the structure of IP'. *Linguistic Inquiry*, 20: 325–424.

Progovac, L. (1994) *Negative and Positive Polarity: A Binding Approach.* Cambridge: Cambridge University Press.

Radford, A. (1990) *Syntactic Theory and the Acquisition of English Syntax: The Nature of Early Child Grammars of English.* Oxford: Basil Blackwell.

Randall, J. (1990) 'Catapults and pendulums: the mechanics of language acquisition'. *Linguistics*, 28: 1381–1406.

Reichenbach, H. (1947) *Elements of Symbolic Logic.* New York: Free Press.

Reinhart, T. (1983) *Anaphora and Semantic Interpretation.* London: Croom Helm.

Rizzi, L. (1982) *Issues in Italian Syntax.* Dordrecht: Foris.

Rizzi, L. (1986) 'Null objects in Italian and the theory of pro'. *Linguistic Inquiry*, 17: 501–55.

Rizzi, L. (1990) *Relativised Minimality.* Cambridge, Mass.: MIT Press.

Roeper, T. and E. Williams (eds), (1987) *Parameter Setting.* Dordrecht: Reidel.

Ross, J.R. (1967) *Constraints on Variable in Syntax.* PhD thesis, Massachusetts Institute of Technology; published (1986) as *Infinite Syntax.* Norwood, N.J.: Ablex Press.

Roussou, A. and I.-M. Tsimpli (1993) 'Definiteness and the expletive determiner in Modern Greek'. Paper presented at the GB Workshop, Salzburg.

Sampson, G. (1989) 'Language acquisition: growth or learning?' *Philosophical Papers XVIII*, 3: 203–40.

Schwartz, B. (1993) 'An alternative account of apparent inaccessibility of UG in L2A'. *Newcastle and Durham Working Papers in Linguistics*, 1: 240–50.

Schwartz, B. and R. Sprouse (1993) 'Word order and nominative case in nonnative language acquisition: a longitudinal study of (L1 Turkish) German Interlanguage'. In T. Hoekstra and B. Schwartz (eds), *Language Acquisition Studies in Generative Grammar: Papers in Honor of Ken Wexler from the GLOW 1991 Workshop.* Amsterdam: John Benjamins.

Seidenberg, M.S. (1989) 'Reading complex words'. In G. Carlson and K. Tanenhaus (eds), *Linguistic Structure in Language Processing*, Dordrecht: Kluwer, pp. 53–105.

Selfe, L. (1977) *Nadia: A Case of Extraordinary Drawing Ability in an Autistic Child.* London: Academic Press.

Shallice, T. (1988) *From Neuropsychology to Mental Structure.* Cambridge: Cambridge University Press.

Siegel, M. (1977) *Topics in English Morphology.* PhD thesis, Massachusetts Institute of Technology.

Slobin, D.I. (1973) 'Cognitive prerequisites for the development of grammar'. In C.A. Ferguson and D.I. Slobin (eds), *Studies of Child Language Development*, San Diego, Cal.: Holt, Rinehart and Winston.

Smith, A. (1988) 'Language acquisition: learnability, maturation, and the fixing of parameters'. *Cognitive Neuropsychology* 5: 235–65.

Smith, N.V. (1983a) 'On interpreting conditionals'. *Australian Journal of Linguistics*, 3: 1-23.

Smith, N.V. (1983b) *Speculative Linguistics*, Inaugural Lecture, University College London.

Smith, N.V. (1989) *The Twitter Machine: Reflections on Language.* Oxford: Basil Blackwell.

Smith, N.V. (1990) 'Observations on the pragmatics of tense'. *UCL Working Papers in Linguistics*, 2: 82–94; French translation in J. Moeschler (ed.), *Langages*, 112: 26–38.

Smith, N.V. (1991) Review of Yamada (1990) *Mind and Language*, 6: 390–6.

Smith, N.V. (1994) Review of Karmiloff-Smith (1992). *European Journal of Disorders of Communication*, 29: 95–105.

Smith, N.V. and A. Smith (1988) 'A relevance-theoretic account of conditionals'. In L. Hyman and C. Li (eds), *Language, Speech and Mind: Studies in Honour of Victoria A. Fromkin.*, London: Routledge and Kegan Paul, pp. 322–52.

Smith, N.V. and I.-M. Tsimpli (1991) 'Linguistic modularity? A case-study of a "savant" linguist'. *Lingua*, 84: 315–51.

Smith, N.V. and I.-M. Tsimpli, (1993) 'A specialist intelligence: the case of a polyglot *savant*'. *UCL Working Papers in Linguistics*, 5: 413–50.

Smith, N.V. and D. Wilson (1992) 'Introduction'. In D. Wilson and N.V. Smith (eds), *Relevance Theory*, special issue of *Lingua*, 87: 1–10.

Smith, N.V., I.-M. Tsimpli, and J. Ouhalla (1993) 'Learning the Impossible: The acquisition of possible and impossible languages by a polyglot *savant*'. *Lingua*, 91: 279–347.

Sorace, A. (1992) 'Lexical conditions on syntactic knowledge: auxiliary selection in native and non-native grammars of Italian', PhD thesis, University of Edinburgh.

Sperber, D. (1994a) 'Understanding verbal understanding'. In J. Khalfa (ed.), *What is Intelligence?*, Cambridge: Cambridge University Press, pp. 179–98.

Sperber, D. (1994b) 'The modularity of thought and the epidemiology of representations'. In L. Hirschfeld and S. Gelman (eds), *Mapping the Mind: Domain-specificity in Cognition and Culture*, Cambridge: Cambridge University Press, pp. 39–67.

Sperber, D. and D. Wilson (1986) *Relevance: Communication and Cognition*. Oxford: Basil Blackwell.

Sternberg, R.J. (1988) 'Intelligence'. In R.J. Sternberg, and E. Smith (eds), *The Psychology of Human Thought*, Cambridge: Cambridge University Press, pp. 267–308.

Suñer, M. (1987) '*Haber* + past participle'. *Linguistic Inquiry*, 18: 683–90.

Swinney, D. (1979) 'Lexical access during sentence comprehension: (re)consideration of context effects'. *Journal of Verbal Learning and Verbal Behavior*, 18: 645–59.

Taft, M. and K. Forster (1975) 'Lexical storage and retrieval of prefixed words'. *Journal of Verbal Learning and Verbal Behavior*, 14: 638–47.

Teuber, H.L. (1955) 'Physiological psychology'. *Annual Review of Psychology*, 9: 267–96.

Thal, D., E. Bates and U. Bellugi (1989) 'Language and cognition in two children with Williams Syndrome'. *Journal of Speech and Hearing Research*, 32: 489–500.

Theophanopoulou-Kontou, D. (1986) 'Dhomes estiaseos kai i apalisi tou amesai antikimenou sta nea ellinika'. *Studies in Greek Linguistics*, 7: 87–108.

Torrego, E. (1984) 'On inversion in Spanish and some of its effects'. *Linguistic Inquiry*, 15: 103–29.

Treffert, D.A. (1988) 'The idiot savant: a review of the syndrome'. *American Journal of Psychiatry*, 145: 563–72.

Treffert, D.A. (1989) *Extraordinary People*. London: Black Swan.

Tsimpli, I.-M. (1989) 'On the properties of the passive affix in Modern Greek'. *UCL Working Papers in Linguistics*, 1: 235–60.

Tsimpli, I.-M. (1990) 'The clause structure and word order of Modern Greek'. *UCL Working Papers in Linguistics*, 2: 226–55.

Tsimpli, I.-M. (1992) *Functional Categories and Maturation: The Prefunctional Stage of Language Acquisition*. PhD thesis, University College London.

Tsimpli, I.-M. (1995) 'Focussing in Modern Greek'. In K. Kiss (ed.), *Discourse Configurational Languages*. Oxford University Press, pp. 176–206.

Tsimpli, I.-M. and J. Ouhalla (1990) 'Functional categories, UG and modularity'. University College and Queen Mary and Westfield College, London, MS.

Tsimpli, I.-M. and A. Roussou (1991) 'Parameter-resetting in L2?'. *UCL Working Papers in Linguistics*, 3: 149–69.

Tsimpli, I.-M. and A. Roussou (1992) 'Negation and tense in Modern Greek: inner islands and polarity'. Newcastle University and University College London/ University College of North Wales, MS.

Tsimpli, I.-M. and A. Roussou (1993) 'Polarity items in Modern Greek: their distribution and interpretation'. *UCL Working Papers in Linguistics*, 5: 129–59.

Tsimpli, I.-M. and N.V. Smith (1991) 'Second-language learning: evidence from a polyglot *savant*'. *UCL Working Papers in Linguistics*, 3: 171–83.

Tsimpli, I.-M. and N.V. Smith (1993) 'LF and post-LF in a polyglot *savant*'s grammars'. *Newcastle and Durham Working Papers in Linguistics*, 1: 276–91.

Tsimpli, I.-M. and N.V. Smith (1994) 'The lexicon in a polyglot savant's L1, L2, Ln: evidence from cognates'. Paper presented at the Eighth International Symposium on English and Greek, Thessalonica.

Van der Lely, H. (1994) 'Canonical linking rules: forward vs. reverse linking in normally developing and specifically language impaired children'. *Cognition*, 51: 29–72.

Van der Lely, H. and L. Stollwerck (in prep. (a)) 'Language modularity, binding theory and specifically language impaired children'.

Van der Lely, H. and L. Stollwerck (in prep. (b)) 'A grammatical specific language-impairment in children: an autosomal dominant inheritance?'.

Weissenborn, J. (1990) 'Functional categories and verb movement: the acquisition of German syntax reconsidered'. In M. Rothweiler (ed.), *Spracherwerb und Grammatik. Linguistische Untersuchungen zum Erwerb von Syntax und Morphologie*, *Linguistische Berichte* (special issue) 3: 190–224.

Wellman, H.M. (1990) *The Child's Theory of Mind*. Cambridge, Mass.: MIT Press.

Wexler, K. (1993) 'Optional infinitives, head movement and the economy of derivations in child grammar'. MIT Occasional Paper no. 45.

Wexler, K. and R. Manzini (1987) 'Parameters and learnability in binding theory'. In T. Roeper and E. Williams (eds), *Parameter Setting*. Dordrecht: Reidel.

White, L. (1985a) 'The pro-drop parameter in adult second language acquisition'. *Language Learning*, 35: 47–62.

White, L. (1985b) 'The acquisition of parametrised grammar: subjacency in second language acquisition'. *Second Language Research*, 1: 1–17.

White, L. (1989) *Universal Grammar and Second Language Acquisition*. Amsterdam, Benjamins.

Wilson, D. and D. Sperber (1986) 'Pragmatics and modularity'. In A. Farley, P. Farley and K.-E. McCullough (eds), *Chicago Linguistic Society 22, Parasession on Pragmatics and Grammatical Theory*, pp. 67–84; reprinted in S. Davis (ed.), *Pragmatics: A Reader*, London: Oxford University Press, pp. 583–95.

Wilson, D. and D. Sperber (1993) 'Linguistic form and relevance'. *Lingua*, 90: 1–25.

Wiltshire, S. (1987) *Drawings*. London: J.M. Dent.

Wing, L. (1991) 'The relationship between Asperger's syndrome and Kanner's autism'. In U. Frith (ed.), *Autism and Asperger Syndrome*, Cambridge: Cambridge University Press, pp. 93–121.

Witkin, H.A. (1969) *Embedded Figures Test*. Palo Alto, Cal.: Consulting Psychologists Press.

Yamada, J. (1990) *Laura: A Case for the Modularity of Language*. Cambridge, Mass.: MIT Press.

Zaitchik, D. (1990) 'When representation conflicts with reality: the preschooler's problem with false beliefs and "false" photographs'. *Cognition*, 35: 41–68.

Index

Brandi, L., 92, 132
Brody, M., 49, 117, 118
Brown, R., 83
Browne, R., 216
Browning, M., 48, 50, 118
Burgess, P. W., 171, 221
Burton-Roberts, N., 60, 62

calendrical calculators, 2
Camphill, 2
Caplan, D., 221
Carlile, J., 212
Carroll, S. E., 85, 86, 90, 216
Carston, R., 28, 60, 62, 175, 213
case, 24, 55, 84
Catalan, 213
central system, 27, 29–31, 33–5,
    37–9, 40–1, 43, 58, 67, 79, 81, 86,
    91, 120–2, 138, 149, 152, 165,
    169, 171–2, 175, 188, 214, 221–2
centre-embedding, 57–8
Chao, W., 92, 132
Chapman, S., 60
chatterbox children, 3, 40
Chinese, 18, 137, 213
chocolate biscuit test, *see*
    appearance-reality test
Choe, H. S., 49
Chomsky, N., 23, 24, 26, 27, 28,
    29, 48, 49, 50, 118, 123, 125, 131,
    137, 140, 165, 188, 213, 215, 216
Cinque, G., 50, 107
Clahsen, H., 35, 219
clefts, 44, 48, 49, 51, 53, 56, 60,
    117, 215
clitic-doubling, 91, 92, 106–12, 121,
    218
clitic-left dislocation, *see* dislocation
cognates, 85–91, 163, 174, 203–5,
    216, 217
cognitive prerequisites, 3
cohort model, 85
Columbia Greystone Mental
    Maturity Scale, 4
communication, 81, 184, 188
competence, 22, 37–9, 40, 41, 43,

78–9, 106, 121, 129, 131, 137,
    164, 173, 178–87, 189
complementizers, 24, 26, 96, 98–9,
    103
computer languages, 32
concepts, 27, 28, 34, 188
conditionals, 112
connectives, 28, 72, 167
conservation of number, 5, 39
context, 28, 37–8, 54, 69
continuity hypothesis, 23–5
contradiction, 62–3, 71
conversation, 67–9, 122, 163, 164–9,
    171, 175–6
Cook, V. J., 217
Corbett, G., 143–5, 219
Cordin, P., 92, 132
coreference, 48–57, 104, 107–8, 110,
    217
Cormack, J., 213
Cossu, G., 3, 40
Courchesne, E., 4
Crago, M. B., 3, 41
Cristoffanini, P., 85, 90
critical period, 23, 24, 36
Cromer, R., 3, 40
crosswords, 20
Culicover, P., 49
Curtiss, S., 23
Cyrillic, *see* scripts
Czech, 18, 213

Danish, 12, 160, 213
deafness, 3
Denya, 132
determiners, 24, 25, 84
Devanagari, *see* scripts
diglossia, 81
discourse, 52, 72–4
dislocation, 48–54, 56–7, 91,
    106–12, 131–2, 173, 215, 217, 218
double dissociation, 2–3, 40–2, 183,
    221
Draw a Man test, 5
dual, 220
Dutch, 12–13, 18, 19, 158–9, 213